Exotic Nation

Exotic Nation

Maurophilia and the Construction of Early Modern Spain

Barbara Fuchs

PENN

UNIVERSITY OF PENNSYLVANIA PRESS

Philadelphia

Publication of this volume was assisted by a subvention from the Program for Cultural Cooperation Between Spain's Ministry of Culture and United States Universities.

Published by
University of Pennsylvania Press
Philadelphia, Pennsylvania 19104-4112

Printed in the United States of America on acid-free paper
10 9 8 7 6 5 4 3 2 1

Library of Congress Cataloging-in-Publication Data

Fuchs, Barbara, 1970–
    Maurophilia and the construction of early modern Spain / Barbara Fuchs.
        p.   cm.
    ISBN: 978-0-8122-4135-8 (alk. paper)
    Includes bibliographical references and index.
    1. Muslims—Spain—History.   2. National characteristics, Spanish.
3. Spain—History—711–1516.   4. Spain—Civilization—Islamic influences.
5. Spain—Ethnic relations.
DP102.F783   2009
946′.02—dc22   2008040619

Para Luly y Javier, indispensables interlocutores

Contents

Introduction

Africa begins at the Pyrenees.
　　　—attr. Alexander Dumas, père

IN THE WESTERN IMAGINARY, Spain often evokes the romantic, colorful culture of "Moorish" al-Andalus. This is the Spain of Washington Irving's *Tales of the Alhambra*, of courtyards lined with *azulejos*, and of recent tourism campaigns that tout sunny Andalucía as the essence of Iberia. Despite the fall of Granada to the Catholic Kings in 1492 and the subsequent repression of Islam in Spain, Moorish culture—dress, art, architecture—plays an enduring role in our perception of the nation that emerged in place of al-Andalus.[1]

This book explores how Moorish culture complicates the construction of Spain in the early modern period, both by Spaniards themselves and by other Europeans. During the eventful century between the fall of Granada and the expulsion of the Moriscos (Muslim subjects forcibly converted to Christianity) in 1609, an emerging Spain repeatedly attempted to come to terms with its own Moorishness, both by repressing Muslim and Morisco subjects and by negotiating the rich cultural heritage of al-Andalus. The paradoxes in the construction of Spain in this period are striking: we are used to thinking of Spain's self-definition as a process whereby both Jewish and Moorish elements were excised from its culture; the conquest of Granada in 1492 and the concurrent expulsion of the Jews are taken as signal events in the emergence of Spain as a nation. Yet after 1492 Spanish culture retained and even celebrated the culture of al-Andalus; in many cases, it was impossible to separate what had become by that point hybridized and local forms. As the historiography of medieval and early modern Spain puts pressure on older notions of *convivencia* and *mudejarismo*, the field has moved to more nuanced accounts of Iberian identities and cultural production. This new work has superseded the by now arch-canonical debates between the philosemitic school of Américo Castro and the *casticista*, ultranationalist camp that stretches from the his-

torian Claudio Sánchez Albornoz to the Arabist Serafín Fanjul. Critics of
Castro have long maintained that in his efforts to link Spanish identity to
the contributions of Jews and Moors as well as Christians he unwittingly
replicated the essentialism, and even the racism, of those whose timeless,
Gothic Spain he denounced.[2] Castro's groundbreaking work was hugely
important in contesting the promotion of an ultra-Catholic Spain by a
Franco regime that identified with the Catholic Monarchs' supposed restoration of religious and cultural purity.[3] Yet its oversimplifications have
sat uneasily with poststructuralist critics more suspicious of unchanging
national identities, however multiple. With an eye to these critiques, my
own project historicizes the construction of Spanish identity for a specific
period, as it is variously expressed in material culture, on the one hand,
and in maurophile versus maurophobe discourses, on the other.

There is a growing recognition that hybridity—a concept developed
in postcolonial studies but eminently suited to a wide range of frontier
societies—may best describe much of Iberian culture in the late medieval
and early modern period.[4] The new emphasis on hybridity in the work of
such pathbreaking art historians as Cynthia Robinson and María Judith
Feliciano takes the question of the *Mudéjar* or "hispano-Moorish" style,
from architectural history, where it has always been most at home, to a
much broader swath of cultural productions. Costume, language, furnishings—all these evince the lasting, if varied, effects of al-Andalus on the new
Christian polity.[5] Although the role of the Andalusi heritage is obviously
stronger for some parts of Spain than for others, much of the transcultura-
tion involves aristocratic practices that quickly transcend local tradition.
This book is less concerned with the historical particularities of hybridization, which necessarily differed from region to region according to the
length and mode of coexistence with Moors than with the imaginative
construction of Spain, in which Moorishness plays a large role, becoming,
at times, a synecdoche for Spain itself.

If we reconstruct Spain's affinity with Moorish culture in the period
without adopting a post-facto, teleological perspective, we find a far more
nuanced situation than the shriller contemporary denunciations of the
Moors' presence in Spain would suggest. Spanish attitudes toward Moors
and the Moorish heritage underlie key cruxes in Spain's development as a
nation, touching not only on the obvious question of religious assimilation
vs. the racialization of minorities, but also on local vs. national cultures,
the tension between a centralizing monarchy and regional aristocracies,
and the struggles between political exigency and religious policy. The

project of imagining a unified nation involved regularizing and regulating Moorishness itself, through both a repressive legal apparatus and the Inquisition. The *place* of the Moors within Spain after 1492 is more than a figure of speech; it gets at the very heart of debates pitting the accommodation of local practices against assimilation into a Christian polity that was becoming a centralized nation. Although the so-called "Reconquista" was fought protractedly over a porous frontier, with all the resulting cultural mixture, the fictive nation that it led to was imagined as a pure, contained space from which even Christian Moors ultimately had to be excluded. Yet accounts of the Spanish nation that emerged reveal the varying extent to which its many cultures were irreducibly marked by the Andalusi past.

In assessing Spain's relation to this heritage, *Exotic Nation* also challenges powerful but often ahistorical contemporary models for the interaction between Christendom and the world of Islam. The most influential of these models is doubtless Edward Said's *Orientalism*—a Foucauldian account of Europe's construction of its Eastern Other based primarily on the eighteenth- and nineteenth-century English and French experience—which, while rich in theoretical insights, clearly needs to be revised for Spain. Said himself recognized, in the preface to the Spanish translation of his text, that he had "said very little" about Spain.[6] Spain complicates the generalizations of *Orientalism* on two fronts. First, Spain's hybridity makes Moorishness a habitual presence in Iberian culture, so that Andalusi elements are intimately known and experienced. Second, Spain itself, though the westernmost part of Europe, is orientalized by its European rivals in a deliberate attempt to undermine its triumphant self-construction as a Catholic nation from 1492 on. These discrepancies between the Spanish case and the Saïdian model have been noted by scholars, although the early modern dynamics that I address here are often ignored. Thus critics working on post-Enlightenment Spain have been quick to point out how the Romantic orientalization of Iberia itself trumps Said's distinction between "Europe" and its others, rendering Spain an exotic object of desire. Yet they have not delved into the complex history of this orientalization in a much earlier period. In a recent response to Said, Miguel Angel de Bunes Ibarra focuses on the forgotten Spanish roots of modern orientalism in accounts of North Africa or the Ottomans, yet often minimizes the importance of Spain's own experience of al-Andalus. Thus while he recognizes the importance of the Orient in the Spanish early modern imaginary, he theorizes a "preorientalism" whose terms are nonetheless dictated by nineteenth-century orientalism, that is, by the fascination, or lack thereof, with the difference of the Ottomans and their North African territories.[7] José Antonio González Alcantud offers as an alternative to orientalism the notion of Andalucía as an intermediate space, both colonizer and colonized, in which an entire compensatory imaginary emerges to supplement the nostalgia for a lost al-Andalus.[8] Yet his rich conceptual model also relegates Spain's Moorishness to a contained past, focusing primarily on its reverberations after the Morisco expulsions. *Exotic Nation* explores the complexities posed by Spain's proximity to and even intimacy with Moorishness to argue that conceptual models based on the distance between West and East miss the more interesting and paradoxical connections of the Spanish case, and, moreover, that from the fall of Granada, if not earlier, Spain itself is often orientalized in the European imagination.

My aim is thus to provide the early modern background for the famous gesture of exclusion that I take as my epigraph, by showing how Spain, as a space marked by Moorishness, has long been considered somehow beyond Europe. Efforts to render Spain African, I argue, reinforced and were reinforced by the Black Legend, with profound consequences for the marginalization of Spain within Europe. The early modern construction of Spain in this vein underlies the much later vision of an exotic nation in a high imperialist mode, as a colorful Andalucía of Moors and gypsies comes synecdochically to represent the nation for Europe.[9] It also ensured the disciplinary marginalization of Spanish, as somehow less European, in historical and literary studies, particularly in the Anglo-American academy. Meanwhile, the French and broader European reception of Spanish maurophile texts contributed to the sense of an exotic Spain: while the material culture that the genre invoked was habitual within Spain, in its broader European circulation the colorful accounts of Moorish knights in full exotic panoply confirmed Spain's "oriental" difference.

Critics have long explored the complex literary representation of Moors in the sixteenth century, yet they have been less concerned with material culture. Accounts of literary maurophilia—the corpus of sixteenth-century texts that portray Moors in a positive fashion—have typically dismissed it as idealizing and remote from the realities of early modern Spain or the marginalized Moriscos. The enormously influential philologist Marcelino Menéndez Pelayo argued that maurophile literature included recognizably Spanish customs such as bullfighting and games on horseback, as well as an atmosphere of gallantry, because Nasrid Granada had been penetrated by "Castilian culture," without stopping to consider the reverse phenomenon. Even more problematically, he established the idea that maurophilia was a "generosa idealización que el pueblo vencedor hacía de sus antiguos dominadores, precisamente cuando iban a desaparecer del suelo español las últimas reliquias de aquella raza" ["generous idealization on the part of the conquering people of its old masters, precisely when the last relics of that race were about to disappear from Spanish soil"].[10] Menéndez Pelayo's account empties out the present moment: maurophilia looks back to idealize a defeated enemy, and proleptically memorializes the absence of that vanquished "race" from Spain, but nowhere, in his formulation, does the corpus reflect on the pressing concerns about the place of the Moriscos in Spain in the sixteenth century, or the ways in which the massive cultural legacy of al-Andalus was to be managed.

Maurophilia as a literary genre was codified in a series of articles published in the *Bulletin Hispanique* in 1938–44 by the French Hispanist Georges Cirot.[11] Although Cirot usefully catalogued the corpus against the backdrop of historical events in sixteenth-century Spain, he effectively divorced the texts from their broader cultural setting, focusing instead on the contradictions between their idealizations and the increasing repression of the Moriscos. While critics such as María Soledad Carrasco Urgoiti and Francisco Márquez Villanueva have insistently argued for contextualizing such literary production within the ideological struggles over the fate of the newly converted, the general perception of the texts remains marked by casual accounts of their exoticism and conventionality. *Exotic Nation* is an attempt to challenge the notion of a literary maurophilia that can somehow be understood independently from Spain's cultural indebtedness to al-Andalus in the sixteenth century. I thus juxtapose textual and material representations of "Moorishness" to demonstrate that the canon of maurophilia invokes the lived practices, the costume, and the architecture in which the hybridity of Spain emerges most fully. Far from idealizing fantasies, the texts participate fully in the urgent negotiation of a Moorishness that is not only a historiographical relic but a vivid presence in quotidian Spanish culture. To further contextualize the literary texts, this book reveals both maurophile and maurophobe discourses as the self-conscious tip of the iceberg. These calculated rhetorics give voice and agency to the full-bodied imaginary of a culture marked everywhere by unwitting Moorishness—what I call the Moorish *habitus*.

Material culture tells a very different story from that of the pronounced historiographical break at 1492. Foreigners visiting Spain constantly noted that "Moorish" ways were often, unremarkably, the local vernacular or habitus for a wide range of practices, from building to gardening to fashion. Spaniards often did not even notice what foreigners found most striking—to them, these were merely local ways of doing things. Hence the basic tension between the Iberian quotidian and the traveler's exotic, which I analyze in Chapter 1. As the foreigners oscillate between fascination and contempt for the Moorishness of Spain, Spaniards, to the extent that they can recognize their own difference, attempt to come to terms with their Moorish inheritance.

This is not a book about what Spain takes from al-Andalus; that project would be impossibly large, and it has been addressed piecemeal by historians, art historians, and historians of science and medicine, as well as by some literary critics. Instead, after a brief survey of the prevalence of Andalusi-derived forms, I focus largely on the subset thematized in the maurophile literary canon: architecture, costume, horsemanship. I show, for example, how the idealizing chivalry depicted in maurophile texts invokes specific forms of horsemanship and how jousting games recall the extent to which Spanish *caballería* is based on Moorish forms. The texts thus call into question any distinction between what is Moorish and what is Spanish or simply local. Admittedly, many of these shared forms, in their most basic iterations, ultimately hark back to common Roman or Mediterranean origins. Yet in sixteenth-century Spain they were generally recognized as being of Moorish origin but nonetheless embraced, even as Moriscos themselves suffered increasing political repression. The prevalence of these forms adumbrates not only the internal construction of a national past and a national identity, but also the external perception of early modern Spain as distinct from its Moorish origins.

Although the negotiation of Moorishness is thus a key element in the construction of early modern Spain, it is important to acknowledge that my project deals largely with lay culture, mirroring the lay genres of maurophilia: ballad, chivalric romance, historical novel. I privilege the domains of culture for which Moorishness—as distinct from Islam and its attendant practices—is most prevalent, because they skirt the more blatant exclusion of Islam by a militant Christianity.[12] (One might nonetheless argue that the whole affair of the counterfeit gospels of the Sacromonte, which I have discussed elsewhere, is an effort to expand maurophilia into the religious arena by imagining a syncretic past for the two religions.[13]) While the history I trace is thus a partial one, I offer it as a corrective to influential historiographical accounts of a triumphant Christian nation that in every way managed to leave Moorishness behind, fictions that have shaped Spain's self-understanding from 1492 onward.

For the sake of clarity, I have organized chapters around a central set of practices: after an introductory survey of how the Spanish quotidian is perceived as Europe's exotic, I consider architecture in Chapter 2, costume in Chapter 3, and horsemanship in Chapter 4. Yet these practices obviously interpenetrate and overlap beyond what such a structure might suggest. More important, these chapters present different modes of trying on, preserving, or engaging with Moorishness: memorialization, fashion, impersonation, role-playing, denial, fetishization or eroticization, and assimilation. The fetishistic or erotic fascination often ascribed to maurophilia is only one such mode; it implies a distance between the Christian or European self and the oriental other that is not always a given in the Spanish case. For, as Chapter 5 shows, even as the official discourse in Spain emphasized the essential, ancestral Christianity of the nation, rival European states busily constructed it as the racial other of Europe. Most often, the European orientalist gaze seems to have taken Spain itself as one more instance of the East, or of Africa. Itself the target of this broader European discourse of Spanish "blackness" and "Moorishness," early modern Spain rarely espoused the models of orientalism that critics have developed for northern Europe. Much Spanish interaction with things Moorish was actually too proximate or intimate to fall under this mode of objectifying, distant fascination, which thus remains only one of the possible forms of engagement that I chart here.

By considering the enduring Moorishness of Spain through a multiple lens of diverse cultural negotiations, I offer a historicized account of literary maurophilia's ideological investments. After the fall of Granada, the cultural and literary fascination with Moorishness becomes, if anything, more acute. Given that the genre of maurophilia is defined by its sympathetic preoccupation with Moors, rather than by a single literary form, its sixteenth-century canon appears in a number of guises. Poetic representations become markedly more sophisticated, as authors rework the *romancero viejo*—the popular ballads of the preceding centuries—into more complex Renaissance versions featuring, for example, Moorish heroes endowed with mottos and shields from classical mythology. Beyond the new *romancero morisco*, the most significant literary treatment of Moors appears in three widely read texts largely in prose: the anonymous novella *El Abencerraje* (1561/1562/1565), which also circulated broadly as an interpolated tale within Jorge de Montemayor's pastoral best-seller

Diana (from its second edition, in 1561); Ginés Pérez de Hita's two-volume historical-novel-cum-history *Las Guerras Civiles de Granada* (1595, 1619); and Mateo Alemán's story of Ozmín and Daraja, interpolated in the picaresque *Guzmán de Alfarache* (1599). All were popular in their own right, though *El Abencerraje* and "Ozmín y Daraja" circulated even more broadly within their respective best-sellers.

While critics from Menéndez Pelayo on often dismiss the fascination with Moors as the culturally innocuous idealization of a defeated enemy, these texts reveal the issue to be significantly more complex. Far from being politically inert, literary maurophilia harnesses the larger fascination with exoticized Moors in a highly self-conscious fashion, to intervene in urgent debates about national identity. The Moorish question was hardly a dead letter in sixteenth-century Spain, as the new nation struggled to reconcile its loud rhetoric of exclusivist and homogeneous Christianity with the presence of large numbers of variously assimilated Moors in its territory. As the Crown considered ever more repressive measures against the Moriscos, questions of their essential difference, their possible acculturation, and their ultimate place within a Spanish polity became paramount. Through their sympathetic portrayal of Moorish characters, the texts I discuss here make an explicit argument for the Moors within Spain.

My inquiry thus reclaims literary maurophilia from the more trivializing sense of fad or amusement for a more profound notion of advocacy for the Moors in the construction of a national imaginary. Although it is difficult to chart the reception of the maurophile novellas, given their inclusion in texts that were hugely popular in their own right, there is invaluable textual evidence for the reception of the new *romancero morisco*—the ballads on Moorish topics that were all the rage in the latter decades of the sixteenth century. As I argue in Chapter 3, the rabid poetic response to the Moorish personae of the *romancero* points to an acute struggle over the valence of maurophilia as a cultural and political phenomenon. Even as the repression of the Moriscos becomes more severe over the course of the century, maurophilia continues to propose a vision of Spain that includes what came before. Its sympathetic portraits of Moors and Moriscos, I argue, should be read not as a counternationalist discourse but rather as an alternative vision of the Spanish nation, predicated on a particular version of Spain's Moorish past, and on the privileging of often aristocratic cultural compatibility over the suspicion of religious difference.

Throughout this study, I expand my reading of Spanish texts, artifacts, and practices by charting the broader European construction of Spain, deliberately othered as "Moorish," "Jewish," or "African" in the period by travelers and Protestant propagandists alike. Because one potential pitfall in a project that sets out to examine the construction of difference is that it may reify and confirm that difference for readers, my crucial goal is to demonstrate the *constructedness* of Spain's exoticism. It is far from my intention to reinscribe cultural or genealogical prejudices about Spain's otherness, or its difference from Europe, even as I recognize the many ways in which early modern Spanish culture was idiosyncratic in its distinctive hybridization. Instead, I want to show how that distinction was only the baseline for the thematization and exaggeration of Spain's exoticism in so many early modern accounts by foreigners. The difference of this exotic nation was not just a given, but instead a set of distinctions constructed and used, as in the anti-Spanish propaganda of the Black Legend.

In the case of literary maurophilia, familiar Spanish practices that would not have been particularly foreign for their first readers became exotic or "oriental" only as the texts were translated and savored by readers in France and elsewhere in Europe. Consider the telling account of Spanish literature by the Swiss critic Simonde de Sismondi, in 1813:

Tandis que son essence est tirée de la chevalerie, ses ornemens et son langage sont empruntés des Asiatiques. Dans la contrée la plus occidentale de notre Europe, elle nous fait entendre le langage fleuri, elle étale l'imagination fantastique de l'Orient. . . . Si nous considérons la littérature espagnole, comme nous révélant en quelque sorte la littérature orientale, comme nous acheminant à concevoir un esprit et un goût si différens de nôtres, elle en aura à nos yeux bien plus d'intérêt; alors nous nous trouverons heureux de pouvoir respirer, dans une langue apparentée à la nôtre, les parfums de l'Orient et l'encens de l'Arabie.

[While its essence is chivalric, its ornaments and language are borrowed from the Asiatics. In the westernmost country of our Europe, it allows us to hear the flowery language, it spreads the fantastic imagination of the Orient. . . . If we consider Spanish literature as in some sense revealing to us the literature of the Orient, leading us to conceive of a spirit and a taste so different from our own, it will take on a new interest in our eyes; thus we will find ourselves happy to breathe, in a language related to our own, the perfumes of the East and the incense of Arabia.][14]

Sismondi's fascination with Spanish literature is matched only by his confident assertion of its otherness. And while his assessment is obviously colored by the new Romantic vogue for Spain, it essentially echoes the French reception of Spanish texts from the early seventeenth century onward. Over this long period, literary maurophilia's tremendous European popularity paradoxically contributed to the marginalization of Spain. In excavating Spain's cultural history, it thus behooves us constantly to remember the political and cultural uses to which the nation's difference was put, both during the conflictive sixteenth century and in subsequent accounts thereof.

Some of the historical sources also suggest, intriguingly, that Spain's hardening attitude toward Moors or Moriscos over the course of the sixteenth century may stem in part from the force of European constructions of a Moorish Spain. This circularity seems logical: to the extent that Spaniards—or their Habsburg rulers—could recognize Spanish difference and its utility for anti-Spanish propaganda, the official stance toward Moorishness would harden. Some of the ambivalence toward the memorialization or erasure of Moors is apparent, to take one noted example, in Charles V's incongruous Renaissance palace imposed on the Alhambra, which I discuss in Chapter 2. Yet at the same time it is clear that the performance of Moorishness also provided a sense of a distinct national culture, deliberately rehearsed in princely entertainments at home and abroad. Insofar as Moorishness could be enlisted in the construction of a national identity, therefore, its role was not purely negative.

The problem of reconstructing the valence of Moorish culture in this sixteenth-century context is thus (at least) twofold. How does Spain, in its development as a nation-state, negotiate its often contradictory identifications with Moorishness, and how does this relationship change over the course of the sixteenth century, as the vestiges of al-Andalus recede and the Counter-Reformation puts pressure on all forms of heterodoxy? Conversely, how does the rest of Europe represent Spain's connection to the Moors, and how is this connection exploited for particular political goals? Rather than a binary opposition between "Europe" and "Islam" (if we could ever imagine such simplified actors), the real interest lies in the strategic characterizations of Spain as Moorish, by Spaniards themselves and by other Europeans, at a time of striking political and religious upheaval. Maurophilia is an unstable and often risky proclivity, which makes its embrace all the more intriguing for a cultural history of the encounters between East and West, and of Spain's development as a (quasi-)European nation. Yet that history cannot be separated from intra-European pressures, and from the discourses that enlist Moorishness to construct legends of national distinction. The story of maurophilia must be told dialectically, from within and from without Iberia, and across the cultural spectrum, reading its sophisticated textual productions alongside the habitus of Moorishness that so profoundly marked Spain.

I

The Quotidian and the Exotic

Sang, moeurs, langage, manière de vivre et de combattre, en Espagne tout est africain. Si l'Espagnol était maho-métan il serait un Africain complet.
—Stendhal

CULTURAL TRANSFORMATIONS do not align themselves neatly even with such major events as the end of the Christian conquest of Granada. The gradual nature of Christian military advances meant that Christian and Moorish practices coexisted more or less uneasily for centuries in Iberia, even in areas where the Christians had triumphed. In terms of everyday life, the fall of Granada was far from decisive: the treaty known as Capitula-ciones de Santa Fe, which detailed the terms of the Moors' surrender, included significant protections for Moorish culture and religious prac-tices.[1] Although these terms were not respected for long, and Muslims were increasingly persecuted, Andalusi cultural forms nonetheless survived for decades in a variety of guises. The neat model of supersession that appears so frequently in official historiographies is thus primarily a rhetori-cal fiction designed to consolidate an emerging sense of national identity. And yet, for all that, it has been extraordinarily powerful: for centuries Spain's self-fashioning has been predicated on the strict boundary between then and now, mapped onto Moors versus Christians. Even from our own more sophisticated historiographical purview, we tend to assume that ev-erything changed in 1492. Yet a culture profoundly marked by Andalusi forms survived in sixteenth-century Spain, long after the fall of Granada, and stood as an often unacknowledged challenge to the official narrative of supersession. Its various quotidian practices, often linked to Moorish-ness by Spaniards and especially by travelers to Spain, usefully complicate our understanding of historical rupture and the construction of national identity, by showing how daily life confutes or modifies ideological stric-tures.

The effort to recover these practices poses significant methodological challenges. First, there are several distinct geographical spaces in which Andalusi-derived cultural practices appear: the valence of Moorish costume, for example, is very different in Granada—a border zone only gradually incorporated into the new nation—and elsewhere in Castile. In Granada, the Moorish survivals not only counter the supersessionist narrative, but also exemplify the larger problem of center versus periphery, or regional versus national culture. As the Morisco advocate Francisco Núñez Muley, whom I discuss in Chapter 2, powerfully argued, "Moorish" practices were also the local, Granadan culture. Similarly vexed is the issue of how to read the Christians' continued embrace of many self-consciously Moorish practices, such as the *juegos de cañas*, or jousting games, which I discuss in Chapter 4. Should this be read as a nostalgic revival of a culture safely defeated, or as a ceremonial, symbolic enactment of the other that helps to solidify the self? These explanations, while plausible in some cases, fail to account for the complex self-identification of Spain with Moorishness in certain situations, or for Arab-derived domestic practices, such as sitting on cushions among braziers, so commonplace that they are not even recognized as such by Spaniards themselves. One solution is to turn to travelers' accounts of Spain, which describe its self-presentation to foreigners as well as the everyday practices that, while invisible to Spaniards, are strikingly unfamiliar to other Europeans of the time. These narratives, at the intersection of the quotidian and the exotic, provide the most significant evidence of Spain's continuity with its Moorish past.

But of course the methodological challenge does not end here. Travel narratives—a heterogeneous category in their own right—are themselves invested in constructing a particular version of Spain. Courtiers, merchants, and ambassadors all come to Spain with specific agendas and preconceptions. As I note in Chapter 5, over the course of the sixteenth century the difference and specificity of Spain often become part of hostile accounts of its exceptional cruelty or greed—the war of words we refer to as the "Black Legend." Thus the appearance of Spanish difference in the travel accounts, and particularly in any discussion of Moorishness, must always be handled with great care, for the travel literature often reflects primarily what foreigners wish to find in an exoticized, racialized Spain.[2] Nonetheless, and despite all these caveats, the travel narratives remain a key source for recovering the persistent hybridity of everyday culture in early modern Spain, however occluded it might be by the opposed prejudices of Spaniards and of foreigners.

The *Convivencia* of Objects, Spaces, and Practices

For the medieval period, there is clear evidence of the widespread use of Andalusi goods among Christians and of their influence on quotidian practices. In high aristocratic culture, this was a long-standing phenomenon, especially as the Christians conquered the sophisticated cities of Toledo (1085) and Seville (1248). Colin Smith, whose felicitous phrase I borrow for my heading to this section, argues that the Christian élite "enjoyed . . . a daily *convivencia* with Moorish objects in their homes and places of work."[3] As Smith notes, and as more recent work has explored in greater detail, Christian monarchs, like their Muslim counterparts, regarded Andalusi goods as the gold standard of luxury. Although, as Smith carefully points out, the use of such objects does not indicate Islamicization, it does bespeak a pronounced taste for Moorish cultural production. Moreover, beyond the choices that taste makes consciously, Andalusi forms are often reproduced without an explicit or conscious aim, in what I propose to call a Moorish habitus, widespread throughout Iberia.[4]

Perhaps the most famous example of Christian taste for Moorish goods is the trove of Andalusi textiles found in the royal pantheon at the monastery of Las Huelgas, in Burgos. Here, in a part of Spain that had largely escaped Moorish domination, thirteenth-century Christian monarchs nonetheless chose to be buried in fine Andalusi silks. As María Judith Feliciano points out, this practice seems paradoxical primarily because such luxury textiles have typically been read both as manifestations of a particular religion—Islam—in isolation from the dense network of social relations that would account for such a choice on the part of a Christian elite.[5] Moreover, as Feliciano and others have argued, the presence of such Moorish objects is surprising only when we abstract them from the larger dynamics of cultural borrowing and interpenetration that characterize Iberia in the period. The shrouds, Feliciano posits, reflect a "pan-Iberian aesthetic vocabulary" (105) in that "the consistent use of Andalusi materials to fashion Castilian clothes was a well-established cultural practice that amounted to a clear, unambiguous, and easily intelligible sign of respectability and propriety" (109).

The last Christian conquests, which gradually led to the fall of Granada, did not significantly change the dynamic of cultural interpenetration, which continued apace in the late medieval period. Conquest also brought new forms of forced intimacy, as Christian immigrants to Andalucía occupied the very houses abandoned by Muslims who had fled the invasion, as the law intended and their own impoverished circumstances demanded.[6] In the time that most concerns me here, from the late fifteenth to the early seventeenth century, travelers to Spain constantly noted the Moorishness of Iberia, in everything from its built landscape to its domestic practices to its costume. While fascinating to the foreigners who experienced it, the Spain that emerges from these accounts is also suspect for its exoticism.[7] Nonetheless, while the travelers are hardly objective, they notice aspects of Iberia that often go unremarked by Spaniards themselves.

One of the Spanish peculiarities most often remarked upon in this light was the *estrado*. This often luxurious household space, primarily for the use of women, was furnished with a low platform covered in carpets, as well as tapestries and wall-hangings, cushions, and braziers. Derived from Arab practices that may or may not have been gender-specific, the *estrado*, which can be viewed in sixteenth-century houses preserved in Spain (Casa de Lope de Vega, Madrid; Casa Natal de Cervantes, Alcalá de Henares), continued to be used throughout the sixteenth and seventeenth centuries, even as the Renaissance fashion for furniture gradually penetrated Iberia.[8] The *estrado* was "the leisure space par excellence" of the house, in which ladies entertained each other or the occasional male visitor, for whose benefit low stools were provided.[9] It was also the space in which they performed hand labor such as needlework. The actual and imagined presence of "Turkish" rugs in the *estrado* contributes to its reception as an exotic or Oriental space, as in the Burgundian courtier Jean de Vandenesse's description of the *estrado* in the Madrid Alcázar, in 1560. For Vandenesse, the finery of the Queen's apartments is apparent in the proliferation of sumptuous cloth, with every surface covered in richly embroidered hangings or "Turkish tapestries."[10]

What struck visitors as much as the space itself was the custom of women sitting on the floor. Antoine de Lalaing, the Flemish courtier who accompanied Philip the Fair to Spain in 1501, notes: 'Monsigneur se assist sur une chayère de velour et Madame par terre sur coussins de draps d'or"[11] ["My lord sat on a velvet chair and the princess on the floor on cushions of cloth of gold"]. The practice persisted through the early modern period, in the most exalted Spanish households. In the palace of the Infantado, in Guadalajara, home to the powerful Mendoza family, Helen Nader writes: "Until late in the seventeenth century, Christian women sat on the floor Muslim style; to accommodate this custom, in the women's salon, a low platform (*estrado*) covered with carpets and cushions occupied most of the floor space."[12] The practice is clearly not controversial in Iberia, yet it marks both Spain's difference vis-à-vis Europe and the undeniable hybridity of early modern Spanish culture.

In the much later narrative of the French almoner Barthélemy Joly (1603–4), the *estrado* and its practices are explicitly conflated with the oriental seraglio and, for good measure, the convent. Joly describes the female attendants to the Queen:

Les principales sont celles dictes de l'*estrado*, qui assistent partout sa personne et s'assient sur des oreillés pres d'elle . . . [La Royne] disne en public trois ou quatre fois l'année, et ces jours là comme ceux du bal, sont fort attendus et desirez des gentilzhommes seruiteurs de ces dames, qui ont le priuilege durant le disner de la Royne d'entretenir chacun la sienne et, me disoit-on, le chapeau en teste, sans estre interrompus ny qu'on oye ce qu'ilz disent, moyennant que la Royne les voye. Apres cela, plus de moyen de parler à elles, estant guardees comme au serrail par gens appellés *guardadamas*, mesme leurs parens ne leur pouuans parler sans permission de la Royne et encor par des tournois ou grilles comme à des religieuses.[13]

[The principal ones are those called of the *estrado*, who assist with her person everywhere and sit on cushions near her . . . [The Queen] dines in public three or four times a year, and those days, like those of the ball, are anxiously awaited and hoped for by the gentlemen who serve those ladies, who have the privilege during the Queen's dinner of addressing each his own and, I was told, with their hats on their heads, without being interrupted or anyone hearing what they say, as long as the Queen can see them. Beyond this, there is no way to talk to them, as they are guarded as in a *seraglio* by those called *guardadamas*; even their relatives cannot speak to them without the Queen's permission, and then through a turnstile or bars like nuns.]

Beyond the explicit orientalization of the *estrado* and its practices in Vandenesse and Joly, however, there was a widespread perception that Iberian architecture and architectural practices were primarily inward-looking, with buildings offering a deceptively simple exterior that disguised secluded private spaces.[14] The Italian ambassador Andrea Navagero notes in his 1523 account of Toledo:

[Toledo] Ha gran numero di bone case, e palazzi commodi quanti forsi nessun'altro loco di Spagna: ma son senza vista alcuna ne demostration di fora: son tutti fabricati con i cantoni, & alcune parti solo de pietra viva o di pietra cotta, & tutto il resto di terra al costume di Spagna. Fanno pochisimi balconi, & picoli, & questo dicono che è per il caldo e freddo: & il più delle lor sale non ha altro lume che quel de la porta: lor fabricar è far il patio in mezzo, et poi i quattro quarti, come che a lor pare divisi.[15]

[It has many good houses and comfortable palaces, more perhaps than any other city in Spain, but from the outside they look like nothing at all; they are all made with only the corners and some part of stone and of brick and the rest of stucco as is the custom in Spain; they have few balconies and those are small, which they say is because of the heat and the cold, and most of their rooms have no other light than what comes through the door: their way is to build the courtyard in the middle, and then four rooms, so that they seem divided.]

The sense of delightful, secluded spaces away from public view was reinforced by the prevalence of the *patio*, or inner courtyard, in Iberian architecture. While courtyards obviously existed elsewhere in Europe, the organization and circulation of domestic life around the *patio* was perceived as particularly Iberian.[16] Laurent Vital, one of Charles V's courtiers, describes its centrality:

Il monta une montée, pour venir sur une belle large gallerie, qui circuoit les quatre sens de la maison, comme en ce pays; et là c'est assés bien la coustume, et principallement aux logis des seigneurs et grants maistres, lesquelz sont carrés et à jour par le milieu de la maison de quelque terre ou pavement, à manière d'une courch: et alentour, hault et bas, ce sont larges galleries pour y pourmener à secq et hors du soleil. Alentour de cesdictes galleries de tous sens il y a des huys, pour aller de chambre en aultre.[17]

[He climbed some stairs to reach a beautiful wide gallery that went around all four directions of the house, as in that country; and there it is very much the custom, and principally in the houses of lords and great masters, which have a square, open-air space in the middle of the house, earthen or paved, like a courtyard, and all around, above and below, there are wide galleries for strolling while keeping dry or away from the sun. Around these galleries in all directions there are doors for going from one room to the other.]

The *patio* is literally and conceptually at the center of the building, intimately connected both to its functionality and to the leisure its inhabitants take in it.

The *patio* as garden was also novel to these travelers—Lalaing makes special mention of a "jardin tout pavé" ["fully paved garden"] in the Alcázar in Seville.[18] Gardens themselves were especially praised, and their Moorish provenance recognized.[19] In 1585, the Flemish courtier Henri Cock still notes that the well-tended orchards he finds everywhere are "the work of Moors": "Confirman también ser edificio de moros los huertos cultivados que tiene, porque en muchas partes de España he visto que esta gente es más inclinada a cultivar y plantar que otra alguna"[20] ["They confirm that its cultivated gardens are also the work of Moors, for in many parts of Spain I have seen that these people are more inclined to cultivate and plant than any other"]. Gardens planted centuries earlier and preserved by the Christians reflect the continued Moorish influence on the Spanish landscape, as do new gardens built in the older tradition. Renaissance gardens made abundant use of the same techniques and elements: irrigation, bricks and tiles, plaster-work, and carved ceilings.[21] While Renaissance fashion might have changed its ornamentation, the garden vernacular remained overwhelmingly Andalusi.[22]

Thus the built environment, the cultivated landscape, and their associated practices all signaled the enduring place of the culture of al-Andalus in Spain. The continuities were apparent to travelers, and, in some cases, such as the accounts of the Castilian language that I discuss below, to Spaniards themselves. Despite the evident hybridization of Iberian culture, however, Spanish historiography—both at the time and subsequently—would loudly announce the break with all things Moorish in 1492, to the glory of a pure, Gothic Spain. Yet if, as Smith, Feliciano, and others have argued, Andalusi-derived forms and practices were not a sign of Islamicization, it is not obvious that any stigma would have attached to them. If these traits were so fully incorporated into Spanish culture that in many cases they were only visible to foreigners, how and why were they identified and disparaged? Could unmarked (and unremarked) cultural practices be attacked as maurophilia? How, to put it most simply, did Spaniards come to construe what was Moorish about their own culture as foreign or exotic? I want to propose here two intricately linked accounts of how Moorishness becomes suspect in the late fifteenth and early sixteenth centuries, one internal and dynastic, the other pan-European and more broadly political.

Rehearsing Maurophobia

My first hypothesis for the stigmatization of Moorishness is the conflation of maurophilia with deviance in the propagandistic construction of Enrique IV of Castile (r. 1454–74) by the chroniclers of his successor, Isabel, in the last decades of the fifteenth century. In the version of Spanish history advanced by such key figures as Alonso de Palencia and Fernando del Pulgar, part of what Isabel is rectifying, as she takes the throne that should have passed to Enrique's daughter Juana and undertakes the conquest of

Granada, is her predecessor's maurophile tendencies. As William Phillips
and Barbara Weissberger have argued, Isabel's historians successfully imposed a vision of Enrique as both sexually and culturally corrupt, the better to disguise the illegality of Isabel's own rule.[23] Weissberger shows how
the attacks on Enrique's masculinity, which impugn the legitimacy of his
daughter and heir, participate in a larger discourse of sodomy that stigma-
tizes "Jews, Moors, Portuguese, conversos, parvenus, and women."[24] Enrique's maurophilia becomes another key component in his indictment by
the Queen's chroniclers, a confirmation of his general debauchery.

In this vein, Palencia emphasizes Enrique's supposedly Moorish tastes
and hints at even worse proclivities: "uerum etiam ueste, incessu uictuque
quotidiano et recubatione ad mensam atque torpioribus seorsum abusibus
habitus omnes Machumetistarum preferret Christianae religioni"[25] ["even
in his dress and in his gait, in his food and in his habit of reclining at the
table, and in other secret and more indecent excesses, he had preferred the
customs of the Moors to those of the Christian religion"]. Critics pointed
also to Enrique's Moorish guard—which was in fact composed of converted Moors, and largely inherited from his father—as a clear sign of his
excessive regard for Moors.[26] More damningly, they held he had not pursued the wars against the Moors with sufficient zeal: Palencia claims that
Enrique went to a siege of Granada "ciutatem illam potius contemplaturus
quam oppognaturus" (3.8.85–86) ["more to behold that city than to combat it"]. He also refused to conduct the war by destroying Granadan crops
and orchards, claiming, in order to disguise his "evil," Palencia writes in
disgust, that the destruction ultimately harmed him, as future owner of
these lands (3.8.62–65). When the lands in question did not immediately
surrender, Palencia observes:

nam potius expugnabatur honor et gloria gentis, dum obsequebatur regi seorsum
colloquia Maurorum maxima cum iocunditate uel acceptanti uel requirenti, atque
impudenter auideque degustanti quaeque deferrentur ex cibis Arabicis secundum
Machumetistarum sectam acceptis. Itaque iam Ismaelite persuasi moribus Henrici
eius uitam non ueneficio terminari sed beneficio dilatari cupiebant; et proficiscenti
Henrico preuia interpretatione praefatorum equitum Maurorum qui eum prose-
quebantur obuiam procedebant caricas atque uuas passas, butirum, lac, mel affer-
entes, quae rex accubans humi more Ismaelitico placide degustabat, omniaque
actitabat consentanea illis. (3.8. 157–65)

[what surrendered instead was the honor and the glory of our people, at obeying a
king who accepted or requested secret interviews with the Moors with the greatest
pleasure, and who with insolence and avidity savored whatever Arab delicacies in

the fashion of Mohammed's sect were offered to him. Once the Moors thus knew of his habits, far from wanting to shorten his life with poison, they wished to dilate it with all kinds of attentions;[27] on the marches, by previous arrangement with his guard of Moorish horsemen mentioned before, they would come out to meet him with figs, raisins, butter, milk, and honey, which the King savored with delight, sitting on the floor in the Moorish fashion, adapting himself in everything to their tastes.]

Yet, as Phillips points out, in most respects Enrique was merely continuing the policies that had characterized many medieval Christian monarchs before him.[28] Palencia is in fact creating the differences he claims to find—there is no evidence that Enrique was unique in his cultural choices. The rhetorical traces of this deliberate construction of otherness are patent in the chronicler's innuendo—"other secret and more indecent excesses"—and in the false opposition between "the customs of the Moors" and "those of the Christian religion." While the Moorish habitus embraced by Enrique extended to many areas of his experience, it did not conflict with Christian religious practices. Palencia's asymmetrical construction of culture versus religion is a blatant attempt to produce maurophobia, for, as my extensive catalog above demonstrates, there was no contradiction between the Moorish-derived practices that characterized much of Spain in the period and an allegiance to Christian dogma.[29]

Beyond Isabel's chroniclers, the evidence of travelers' accounts helped solidify Enrique's reputation as a maurophile king. Gabriel Tetzel, traveling in the retinue of the Bohemian nobleman Leo of Rozmital, passed through Castile in 1466 or 1467, and left a marked impression of the king's "heathenness" in a likeminded Spain: "The inhabitants are for the most part heathens. The old King has many at his court and has driven out many Christians and given their land to the heathen. Also he eats and drinks and is clothed in the heathen manner and is an enemy of Christians."[30] Phillips usefully contextualizes Tetzel's account, however, to show how he was influenced by the raging dynastic conflict, and how others in his party had a different view of Enrique's court. As in Palencia, maurophilia is mobilized as an accusation: it has less to do with actual cultural practices than with the significance of the person accused of such proclivities.

In discussing Enrique's purported sodomitic tendencies, Weissberger recalls Alan Bray's useful characterization of sodomy as a practice that "only became visible when those who performed those acts, or even were accused of performing them, were persons who threatened the established

social order: heretics, traitors, spies, and so on."[31] Maurophilia here seems
to function in a similar fashion: a long-standing cultural hybridity, common to Spanish kings before and after Enrique (and presumably also to
their "heathen" subjects), is anathemized in the case of Isabel's rival. Although the historiographical maurophobia of Palencia and others was only
one discourse among many, and coexisted with a widespread Moorish
habitus in Spain, it effectively expanded the religious fervor against Muslims that animated the final campaigns in Granada into the realm of culture, problematizing what had long been standard Iberian practices.

My second, broader explanation for the exacerbation of maurophobia
in the period follows historian Alain Milhou's thesis on the "desemitization" of Spain in the sixteenth century. I should clarify at the outset that
this account of European agency does not attempt to exculpate Spain for
its attitude toward the Moors; clearly Palencia and his fellow historiogra-
phers found enough to work with in domestic anti-Muslim feeling in the
late fifteenth century that they could take on the project of making Moorish culture suspect. But I do want to complicate the story of an inherent,
timeless Iberian opposition to the Moors by pointing out how Spain's very
success in its consolidation as a nation was accompanied by a pronounced
European denunciation of its Moorishness, particularly as northern Europeans came to rule and administer Spain. In a brilliant article that has not
received enough critical attention, Milhou argues that in order for Spain
to become part of Europe in this period, it must loudly renounce its identification with all things Semitic—both Jewish and Moorish.[32] In this light,
Milhou stresses, desemitization corresponds not only to "Old Christian"
priorities, but rather to a vision of Europe in contradistinction to a Semitic
Spain, expounded by writers both within and outside Iberia.

Milhou identifies a first stage of the Black Legend, in which Spain is
stigmatized for its "biological and cultural *mestizaje*," as a border nation
of bad Christians who are "half Jewish and half Moors."[33] This early characterization of Spain has been abundantly established, particularly for
Italy, first by the great early twentieth-century philologists Benedetto
Croce and Arturo Farinelli, and more recently, with an account also of the
German Protestant context, by Sverker Arnoldsson.[34] As these authors
note, the repudiation of the Spanish as a race of *marranos* or secret Jews
goes hand in hand with the stigmatization of its "Moorish" culture. Croce
and Arnoldsson both highlight the figure of the Neapolitan humanist
Antonio di Ferrariis, known as Il Galateo, who in his 1504/5 treatise *De
Educatione* blames the Spaniards for introducing a whole range of emascu-

lating behaviors to Italy, including excessively refined food, a wan and
tearful mode of singing, soft beds, the use of ointments and perfumes, and
so forth. If the Orient corrupted Italy in the past, Il Galateo avers, the far
west corrupts Italians now.[35]

Viewed in this context, Tetzel becomes just one more voice in the
orientalization of an earlier Spain. The process is aided from within by the
apologists for Isabel, who propound, Milhou avers, the "de-Africanizing,
de-judaizing, and cultural Europeanization that would become radical
under the Catholic Kings."[36] Maurophobia thus stems not just from Isa-
belline policy, but also, dialectically, from travelers' and other Europeans'
vision of a Moorish Spain. Consider in this light the courtier Antoine de
Lalaing's account of Philip the Fair's surprise at the multitude of "white
Moors" he finds on his visit to Spain in 1501:

En ce tampz mil V c et ung, en may, Monsigneur, estant à Toulette avoecq le roy
et la royne, fu adverti de la multitude des blans Mores habitant ès Espaignes. Es-
bahy du cas, enquist pourquoy on le souffroit, et on luy respondit que les grands
deniers des tribus qu'ilz payoient estoit la cause: car chescune teste grande et petite
payoit par an ung ducat d'or. Et Monsigneur respondit que quelque jour ils pour-
roient faire plus de domage au royaume que leur tribut ne vault, comme ils ont
aultrefois faict et cuidet faire encoire plus. Tant continua Monsigneur ses paroles
qu'elles entrèrent ens oreilles de la royne. Par quoy, pour complaire à Monsigneur,
cognoissant aussy qu'il disoit chose vraye, comanda que, dedens quatre mois ou
chincq ensiévans, widassent de ses pays ou se feissent baptisier et tenir nostre foy:
ce que pluseurs firent, plustost, ce tien-ge, aulcuns pour garder leurs biens que
pour l'amour de Dieu. Les aultres retournèrent en leurs pays: dont les pluseurs
furent destroussés et pilliés aux passages.[37]

[In this time, in May 1501, my Lord, while in Toledo with the King and the Queen,
was advised of the multitude of white Moors who lived in the Spanish kingdoms.
Surprised at this case, he inquired why it was suffered, and was told that the great
sum of tribute that they paid was the cause: because each head great and small
paid a gold ducat a year. And my Lord replied that someday they might do more
damage to the realm than their tribute was worth, as they had once done and
could do again. My Lord so prolonged his words that they made their way into
the Queen's ears. For this reason, to please my Lord, and knowing also that he
spoke the truth, the Queen ordered that within the four or five months that followed, [the Moors] should leave their lands or should have themselves baptized
and hold our faith; which many of them did, some of them more, I believe, to
preserve their property than for the love of God. The others went back to their
lands, and many were robbed and looted on the way.]

With his apocryphal anecdote, Lalaing gives the foreign prince credit for
the forced baptisms of the Moors of Castile.[38] In this telling, Isabel follows

Philip's advice not only because she recognizes he is right, but primarily to please the foreigner. The foreign chronicler also introduces the paradox of the place of the Moors within Spain—they are compelled to leave their *pays* unless they convert, but the ones who choose not to convert go back to their *pays*, by which Lalaing presumably means North Africa. Yet these Moors are not foreigners but long-term inhabitants of Iberia, however shocking that might prove to Northern Europeans.

A similar dynamic of externally imposed maurophobia is at work in the story recounted by Henry Charles Lea of Charles V's decision to compel the conversion of the Moors of Aragon. When Francis I of France, taken prisoner at the battle of Pavia, was held in the castle of Benisan in Valencia, he was reportedly scandalized at seeing Moors working the fields on a religious holiday. Lea conjectures that while "Charles had long been preparing for [the forced conversions], there may be partial truth in the story that he was stirred to immediate action by the gibes of his captive."[39] As in the Lalaing passage above, the point is less the historical truth of the matter than the account of shared responsibility for the repression of Moors—a foreigner pointing out to the Spanish sovereign (in this case, also a foreigner) that Muslims should not be tolerated. The price of Europeanization seems to be not only the excision of Islam but Spain's submission to European opinions on the matter.

Milhou's account of a dialectical relation between Spanish and European maurophobia suggests that Spain's refusal of its Moorish heritage was born not solely of some essential Spanish and anti-Moorish spirit but also as a response to *European* attitudes. The Spanish repression of Muslims in fact represents an attempt to approximate European—particularly French—stances toward religious or cultural others. Milhou stresses: "It must be put in strong terms: all of Christian Europe shares responsibility for the adoption of religious exclusivism that put an end to the Spain of the three cultures."[40] As is clear from the first Lalaing passage above, Christian Europe was only too happy to claim that responsibility.

Strikingly, however, the animus against Muslims that is evident in such exchanges only partially extends to Moorish-derived practices. While Lalaing reports Philip's suspicion of the "white Moors," he also notes with pleasure, and in great detail, the Moorish dress of the Castilian nobles, and of Philip himself, at chivalric games, including the *juego de cañas* (185–86). He recognizes, too, the excellence of the Moorish silk still for sale in Granada, which is bought for the Italian market. These silks, he writes, "ouvrés à la morisque . . . sont moult beaus pour la multitude des

coleurs et la diversité des ouvrages" (205) ["worked in the Moorish fashion, are very beautiful for their multitude of colors and the variety of their
work"]. The desemitization Milhou describes thus operates more in the
religious than in the cultural arena, particularly during the first half of
the sixteenth century. The cultural practices that come under the greatest
scrutiny—baths, refusal of wine or pork products—are those that reflect
religious strictures.[41] As I discuss in Chapter 3, there were later attempts
to forbid Moorish dress, but the regulations were often repeated and thus
presumably ineffective.

Certainly, when legislation targeting Moorish cultural practices was
enforced it had a huge impact on the Morisco community. Laws forbidding everything from Moorish names to contracts in Arabic were first
passed by Charles V in 1526, although their enforcement was very limited.
When more stringent and repressive legislation was passed by Philip II in
1566, its enforcement led directly to the Morisco uprising in the Alpujarras,
the bloody and protracted struggle that convulsed Spain in 1568–71. Yet,
without in any way minimizing the persecution suffered by Moriscos, it is
important to note that at any point the prohibitions targeted only a small
fraction of Andalusi-derived practices. In some cases, this is explicitly acknowledged in the legislation: a 1532 law stated specifically that the "music,
songs, and dances" of the newly converted—that is, the Moriscos—were
to be allowed, as long as they did not mention Mohammed.[42] Other laws,
which I discuss in more detail in Chapter 3, attempted to prevent the
Christian adoption of Moorish costume. Certainly, by the 1560s the range
of practices targeted as signs of the Morisco failure to accept Christianity
fully had increased, but never contemplated most of the quotidian, wholly
Iberian practices that I have described here. The legislation may have re-
pressed circumcision or the use of Arabic, but building in what Europeans
would consider a Moorish style, sitting Moorish-style in the *estrado*, and
a whole host of other practices continued intact. In some cases, these persisted because they were not even identified as Moorish by Spaniards—
they were simply Spanish ways. In other cases, such as the *juego de cañas*,
they continued even when their Moorish origins were abundantly recognized.

As this complex situation suggests, the repressive legislation and
forced conversions coexisted with a widely shared, enduring habitus of
Moorishness that was more difficult to change than the externalized religious practice of the Muslim minority, itself driven underground. As
Milhou notes, in many realms Moorishness never registered as problem-

atic, despite the strenuous efforts of Isabel's chroniclers, noted above, and European observers' exoticization of Spain.[43] Even for foreigners, who constantly dwelled on Spain's difference, the construction of an exotic, Moorish nation in the early sixteenth century involved moments of maurophilia as well as the crassest maurophobia. While the cultural script of maurophobia—animated by both internal and external prejudice—became available in the last decades of the fifteenth century, it did not take uniformly, perhaps because so many of its potential targets were by this time quotidian Iberian practices, fully incorporated into Spanish subjects' dispositions. Maurophobia attempted to label the Moorish habitus of Iberia as culpable maurophilia, but with mixed success at best.

Fighting Words

Nosotros pronunciamos la x como los árabes, de cuya vezindad nos la dejaron en casa con otros trastos cuando se mudaron. (Mateo Alemán, *Ortografía castellana*, 1609)

[We pronounce the *x* as do the Arabs, our neighbors, who left it in our home with some other bits and pieces when they moved.]

I turn now to a rich corpus on the place of Moorishness in Iberia: the various accounts of the role of Arabic in the Spanish vernacular. These discussions are particularly revealing because, unlike many of the practices I have described, they are self-conscious, and also because they index a more generalized anxiety about the many domains of culture touched by Arabic-derived words. What was the role of Arabic in the Castilian vernacular, the language that, as the famous humanist Antonio de Nebrija claimed in his 1492 *Gramática de la lengua castellana*, had an important role to play in the establishment of sovereignty? And what did that role suggest about Spanish culture more broadly? The preoccupation evinced by Nebrija, the Erasmian Juan de Valdés, and others is in this sense synecdochal: the Moorishness of the language suggests the Moorishness of the many quotidian objects and practices it describes.

Toward the end of Part II of *Don Quijote*, when the defeated knight and his squire imagine a pastoral alternative to their chivalric adventures, Don Quijote gives Sancho a curious lesson in etymology. Carried away while invoking the pastoral instruments that will provide the sound-track for their new fantasy, he mentions one that Sancho does not recognize:

"'¡Qué de churumbelas han de llegar a nuestros oídos, qué de gaitas zamoranas, qué tamborines, y qué de sonajas, y qué de rabeles! Pues ¡qué si destas diferencias de músicas resuena la de los albogues! Allí se verán casi todos los instrumentos pastorales."

"'¿Qué son albogues?" preguntó Sancho, "que ni los he oído nombrar, ni los he visto en toda mi vida."

"Albogues son," respondió don Quijote, "unas chapas a modo de candeleros de azófar, que dando una con otra por lo vacío y hueco, hace un son, si no muy agradable ni armónico, no descontenta, y viene bien con la rusticidad de la gaita y del tamborín; y este nombre *albogues* es morisco, como lo son todos aquellos que en nuestra lengua castellana comienzan en *al*, conviene a saber: *almohaza, almorzar, alhombra, alguacil, alhucema, almacén, alcancía*, y otros semejantes, que deben ser pocos más, y solos tres tiene nuestra lengua que son moriscos y acaban en *i*, y son *borceguí, zaquizamí* y *maravedí*. *Alhelí* y *alfaquí*, tanto por el *al* primero como por el *i* en que acaban, son conocidos por arábigos. Esto te he dicho, de paso, por habérmelo reducido a la memoria la ocasión de haber nombrado *albogues*." (1056)

["What flageolets will reach our ears, what Zamoran pipes, what timbrels, what tambourines, and what rebecs! Well, and what if among these different musics *albogues* should resound! Then we shall have almost all the pastoral instruments."

"What are *albogues*?" asked Sancho. "I've never heard of them or seen them in my life."

"*Albogues*," responded Don Quixote, "are something like brass candlesticks, and when you hit one with the other along the empty or hollow side, it makes a sound that is not unpleasant, though it may not be very beautiful or harmonious, and it goes well with the rustic nature of pipes and timbrels; this word *albogues* is Moorish, as are all those in our Castilian tongue that begin with *al*, for example: *almohaza, almorzar, alhombra, alguacil, alhucema, almacén, alcancía*, and other similar words; our language has only three that are Moorish and end in the letter *i*, and they are *borceguí, zaquizamí*, and *maravedí*. *Alhelí* and *alfaquí*, as much for their initial *al* as for the final *i*, are known to be Arabic. I have told you this in passing because it came to mind when I happened to mention *albogues*."] (Grossman, 901, with emendations)

At such moments, conjuring the multiple fictional narrators of Cervantes's text leads to an epistemological and ontological impasse. After all, what would it mean for Cide Hamete Benengeli to point out Arabic etymologies, or for the Morisco translator to do so? Why does this information come not from the *bachiller* Sansón Carrasco, or even the comical humanist of the Cueva de Montesinos episode, but from the knight himself?

Peculiar though it might seem in this context—as Don Quijote himself recognizes—the passage references in fascinating ways many of the debates about Spanish culture and its relation to Moorishness after the fall of Granada. First and foremost, it reminds us that maurophile literature typically conflated Moors and knights, and—as in *El Abencerraje* or Pérez de Hita's *Guerras civiles de Granada*—imagined no contradiction between the individual Christian knight's fondness for Moors or things Moorish and the larger project of Christian conquest. Thus it is significant that Don Quijote is the expert here. The actual content of Don Quijote's lesson is also striking. For decades, humanists had debated the undeniable place of Arabic in Spanish. While Arabic itself had been forbidden in the 1560s as part of the wholesale repression of Moriscos, Arabic-derived Spanish could not be purged. Yet, strikingly, the definition he gives is wrong, suggesting a certain avoidance of the common reed instrument that was fully adopted throughout Spain by this time, and that marked an incorporation of the Moorish heritage beyond language.[44] Moreover, Don Quijote's bad faith—there are many more words derived from Arabic than he suggests—is undone by his very categories, whereby words that are doubly marked as Moorish—by *al* and *i*—somehow do not count for the earlier lists. More important, Don Quijote invokes the larger problem of differentiation: how are Moors and their ostensible otherness to be identified?

The role of the pastoral in this exchange is also intriguing.[45] Critics of the inordinately popular *romancero morisco*, the ventriloquizing Moorish ballads that had mesmerized readers in the 1580s and '90s, and which I discuss in Chapter 3, had begged the poets to find personae that did not contradict their Spanishness, particularly recommending shepherds as an alternative to such renegade poetry. But here it is the pastoral that specifically leads Don Quijote to his lecture on Arabic etymologies. More generally, official policy leading to the Morisco expulsions of 1609–14 had attempted to quarantine Moorishness as something fundamentally other and polluting—a move that Don Quijote deftly counters with his simple catalog. Strikingly, our knight never calls the objects he describes Moorish: all that is Moorish is the *nombre*—the word. Although Sancho may never have heard an *albogue*, he exists in a culture fully permeated by Moorish objects and practices, so fully assimilated that they—unlike the rustic instrument—produce no dissonance. From his boots (*borceguíes*) to the lunch (*almuerzo*) he can only long for, to the rugs (*alhombras*) on which the Dukes no doubt received him, Sancho is surrounded.

As the pastoral-etymological reverie winds down, Don Quijote and Sancho try to sleep in the fields, only to be mowed down by a stampede of pigs on their way to market (1060). Though Don Quijote here takes the pigs quite literally—in marked contrast to the sheep taken for Asian and African armies in Part I—the reader cannot help but think that this unsubtle porcine irruption rather drowns out the sonorous mingling of the earlier moment. The *marrano*—both the insult hurled at Jews and Moors and the dietary test of their difference—tramples on the pastoral fantasy and on Don Quijote's admittedly partial account of a culturally hybridized Spain.

Unlike practices that were primarily visible to foreigners, the presence of Arabic within the Spanish language had long been remarked on by Spanish humanists, as part of the same dynamic of Europeanization and desemitization identified by Milhou. Reconciling Castilian with classical and European models became, for Spanish humanists, a task of the utmost importance. At the same time, recognizing the place of Arabic in Spanish was a necessary part of mastering the particularities of the vernacular. In his groundbreaking *Gramática*, the first study of a European vernacular, Nebrija ascribes to Arabic several letter sounds in Castilian—x, c, h, g—as he catalogs Spanish difference from its classical antecedents. Any elements disowned by Greek and Latin, occasionally even Hebrew, are by default marks of Arabic.[46]

Valdés, in his *Diálogo de la lengua* (c. 1535), also ascribes to Arabic what fails to conform to Latin or Greek, while recognizing that use has made "pronunciaciones del arávigo" ["pronunciations from the Arabic"] so habitual that they are preferred to Latin: "son tan recibidas en el caste-llano que . . . se tiene por mejor la pronunciación y escritura aráviga que la latina" ["they are so accepted in Castilian that . . . Arabic pronunciation and spelling are considered better than the Latin"].[47] Yet although Nebrija charts Spanish peculiarities as a falling away from Latin, and Valdés empha-sizes the development of the vernacular brought about by new linguistic elements, the latter's focus on usage betrays a striking discomfort.[48] Valdés deplores the Arabic elements of the Castilian vernacular, imagining the effects of the centuries of Moorish presence in Spain as a kind of conta-gion:

En este medio tiempo no pudieron tanto conservar los españoles la pureza de su lengua que no se mezclasse con ella mucho de la aráviga, porque, aunque reco-bravan los reinos, las cibdades, villas y lugares, como todavía quedaban en ellos muchos moros por moradores, quedávanse con su lengua, y aviendo durado en ella hasta que pocos años ha, el emperador les mandó se tornassen cristianos o se saliessen de España, conversando entre nosotros annos pegado muchos de sus vo-cablos. (58)

[During this interval, the Spaniards were unable to preserve the purity of their
language from having much of the Arabic mix with it. For although they recovered
the kingdoms, cities, towns and villages, the many Moors who remained living
within them kept their language so that it lasted until a few years ago, when the
emperor ordered them to become Christians or leave Spain, and speaking among
us they have stuck us with many of their words.]

The language of the *moros-moradores* exceeds the temporal and geographical limits of the Christian conquest, just as the etymologically false echo
in Valdés's prose unwittingly supplements his meaning.

Despite what Eric Beaumatin describes as Valdés's paradoxical embrace of the vernacular's "bastardy" as the mark of its identity,[49] Arabic-
derived usage troubles the Erasmian's equanimity. Valdés tries to contain
the Arabic influence, noting that the romance language offers perfectly
good alternatives for the Arabic words:

Y avéis de saber que, aunque para muchas cosas de las que nombramos con vocablos arávigos tenemos vocablos latinos, el uso nos ha hecho tener por mejores
los arávigos que los latinos; y de aquí es que dezimos antes alhombra que tapete,
y tenemos por mejor vocablo alcrevite que piedra sufre, y azeite que olio; y, si mal
no m'engaño, hallaréis que para solas aquellas cosas que avemos tomado de los
moros, no tenemos otros vocablos con qué nombrarlas sino los arávigos que ellos
mesmos con las mesmas cosas nos introduxeron. (58)

[You should know that for many of the things that we name with Arabic words we
have Latin words; custom has made us prefer the Arabic to the Latin, and thus we
say *alfombra* rather than *tapete* [for carpet], and consider *alcrevite* a better term
than *piedra sufre* [for sulfur stone], and *azeite* than *olio* [for oil]; and, if I am not
mistaken, you will find that it is only for those things that we have taken from the
Moors that we do not have any other words to name them than the Arabic ones
with which they introduced those things to us.]

Yet Valdés's attempts to re-exoticize Arabic are undermined by his admission that, despite having a choice, Spanish-speakers privilege Arabic terms,
and by the lack of examples for the hypothetical second category.

He returns to the issue more forcefully in another attempt to circumscribe the role of Arabic:

hallo que por la mayor parte los vocablos que la lengua castellana tiene de la latina,
son de las cosas más usadas entre los hombres y más anexas a la vida humana; y
que los que tiene de la lengua aráviga, son de cosas estraordinarias o, a lo menos,
no tan necessarias, y de cosas viles y plebeyas, los quales vocablos tomamos de los
moros con las mesmas cosas que nombramos con ellos. (117)

[I find that for the most part the words that Castilian has from Latin are for things most used by people and most connected to human life; and that those it has from Arabic are for extraordinary things, or at least, ones not so necessary, and for vile and plebeian things, which words we took from the Moors along with the very things we name with them.]

Tellingly, Valdés gives no examples for these highly dubious categories. What of the overlap between the "plebeian" and the useful or common? The central problem in Valdés's quest for linguistic purification is that it is not actually possible, in the sixteenth century, to circumscribe large parts of Spanish culture as a foreign, Moorish import. Both the omnipresence of the words from the Arabic and their quotidian, unremarkable referents suggest that impossibility, regardless of the humanist's fantasies of purity.[50]

Even at the lexical level, it is not clear that early modern philology can fully distinguish between actual Arabic imports and Latin look-alikes. In fact, Valdés warns against the over-assiduous search for Arabic, which leads to a kind of misrecognition of what is actually "ours": "Y si queréis ir avisados, hallaréis que un *al*, que los moros tienen por artículo, el qual ellos ponen al principio de los más nombres que tienen, nosotros lo tenemos mezclado en algunos vocablos latinos, el cual es causa que no los conozcamos por nuestros" (58–59) ["And if you care to know, you will find that the *al*, which the Moors use as an article and place before most of their nouns, we have mixed into some Latin words, which is why we do not recognize them as ours"]. Even in his effort to reclaim unduly suspect words with *al*, Valdés ruefully acknowledges the extent to which "our" Latin terms are occluded by Arabic influence. More important, his inventory recalls how many things are designated by Arabic terms because they represent Andalusi contributions to Iberia. As the lexicographer Sebastián de Covarrubias more broadly claims in his 1611 definition of *romance* [the vernacular], "lo turbaron todo los árabes" [the Arabs altered everything].[51]

By the early seventeenth century, when Cervantes imagined Don Quijote instructing Sancho on the origins of his language, the discomfort with imports from the Arabic had become widespread. The humanist cleric Bernardo Aldrete is generally regarded as the heir of Nebrija, elaborating on the role of linguistic domination in empire.[52] In his 1606 history of the Spanish language, *Del origen y principio de la lengua castellana*, Aldrete focuses above all on the Latin origins of the language, arguing that the Roman conquest had marked Spain linguistically. Yet although he acknowledges also the Moorish conquest of Iberia, he seems far more reluctant to spell out the influence of Arabic on Spanish. Instead, Aldrete recognizes that, despite the Nebrija tradition of language as instrument of empire, linguistic borrowing operates in multiple directions. Ideologically, the best Aldrete can hope for, given the undeniable mark of Arabic on Spanish, is some kind of reciprocity: thus, he announces, he will first list "algunos de los vocablos, que entiendo que tomaron de nosotros, i luego otros de los que tomamos nosotros dellos"[53] ["some of the words that I understand they took from us, and then others that we took from them"]. He argues that many words shared by the two languages in fact derive from Latin, and then proceeds to list his scant evidence.

After this partial rebuttal, he comes to the influence of Arabic on Spanish. When he dutifully proceeds to examples, however, he is over-whelmed by the sheer number of words to list. He gives over forty words beginning with *a*, by *f* he limits himself to two, and the rest of the alphabet is dispatched with six more examples: "Para exemplo bastan estos, pues no a sido mi intento traer los todos" ["These are enough examples, for it was not my intention to give them all," 367].[54] Aldrete's exhaustion sug-gests how futile is any attempt to avoid "Moorishness" within a Spanish culture that proclaims its distinctiveness, post 1492—it is so fully inte-grated as to be, if not indistinguishable, then inseparable. More striking even than the actual proportion of Arabic words is the discomfort that they produce in the humanist stewards of a Castilian imagined as the enabler of a discriminating empire.

The reluctant accounts of Castilian's indebtedness to Arabic are only one, particularly self-conscious part of the story of Spain's quotidian exoti-cism. The broader range of practices that I have described in this chapter are even more complicated to disentangle than language, as everyday life in sixteenth-century Spain continued to be profoundly influenced by the culture of al-Andalus and, indeed, in many cases incorporated it seam-lessly. Rhetorical efforts to stigmatize the Moorish influence, on the one hand, or to reduce Spain to an exotic culture, on the other, corresponded to complex domestic and international pressures that targeted the Spanish disposition. If anything, they succeeded in underscoring "Moorishness" and making (self)conscious what had been habitual, particularly when Spain was compared to Europe. Precisely because so-called Moorishness was quotidian, it became for foreigners an obligatory—and, for Spaniards, unavoidable—element in the construction of Spain.

2

In Memory of Moors: History, Maurophilia, and the Built Vernacular

de todos cuantos vençimientos hicieron los grandes reyes
y señores pasados, ni aún de los edeficios que fundaron
ni fazañas que ficieron no queda otra cosa sino esto que
dellos leemos; y aun los edifiçios que facen, por grandes
que sean, caen e callan, y la escriptura de sus fechos que
leemos ni cae ni calla en ningún tiempo.

> —Fernando del Pulgar, "Letra al Conde de Cabra"

[of all the many achievements of great kings and lords in
the past, nothing remains, not even of the buildings they
erected, nor of the deeds they did—except what we read
of them. However great they may be, their buildings fall
and are silent, but what is written of their deeds does not
fall, and is never silent.]

OVER THE COURSE OF THE SIXTEENTH CENTURY, humanist historiography came of age in Spain, in a process that culminated in the Jesuit Juan de Mariana's great *Historiae de rebus Hispaniae* (1592), an account of Spain from its first mythical settlement to Mariana's own time. The Latin history was so well received that Mariana translated it into Spanish as the *Historia general de España* to make it available to a broader audience.[1] Mariana's prologue to the translation, dedicated to Philip III, links the endurance of his history to the excellence of Spain: "Confío que si bien hay faltas, y yo lo confieso, la grandeza de España conservará esta obra" ("I trust that though there are errors, and I confess it, the greatness of Spain shall preserve this work," LII). In a tradition inherited from the earliest humanist historians (as in the epigraph from Isabel's chronicler Fernando del Pulgar, above), Mariana emphasizes the power of the written record above all other forms of memorialization:

La historia en particular suele triunfar del tiempo, que acaba todas las demás memorias y grandezas. De los edificios soberbios, de las estatuas y trofeos de Ciro, de
Alejandro, de César, de sus riquezas y poder, ¿qué ha quedado? ¿Qué rastro del
templo de Salomon, de Jerusalem, de sus torres y baluartes? La vejez lo consumió,
y el que hace las cosas las deshace. El sol que produce a la mañana las flores del
campo, el mismo las marchita a la tarde. Las historias solas se conservan, y por ellas
la memoria de personajes y de cosas tan grandes. (LII)

[History in particular often triumphs over time, which destroys all other memories
and grandeur. What is left of the magnificent buildings, of the statues and trophies
of Cyrus, of Alexander, of Caesar, of their riches and power? What trace of Solomon's temple, of Jerusalem, of its towers and bastions? Age consumed it all, and
he who makes things unmakes them. The very sun that creates the wildflowers in
the morning withers them in the afternoon. Only histories are preserved, and
through them the memory of such great figures and events.]

In lay as in biblical history, great men and their deeds succumb to the
effects of time, to be preserved only by the written account that the historian provides. As Roger Chartier puts it, "the mission of the written was
to dispel the obsession with loss."[2]

In his own text, Mariana establishes the conquest of Granada as the
heroic endpoint to which all of Spanish history has tended. Book 25, which
covers this period, is bracketed by a highly self-conscious reflection on the
place of the conquest in the larger course of events. The war in Granada
is the "fin deseado de toda esta obra" (211) ["desired end of this whole
work"], by which Mariana means not just his text but the nation-building
project whose teleology the history reinforces. The book ends by celebrat-
ing the Christian triumph in similarly conclusive—and circular—terms:
"toda España con esta victoria quedaba por Cristo nuestro Señor, cuya era
antes" (240) ["with this victory, all Spain was now for Christ our lord,
whose it had been before"].

Yet Mariana's conviction that only written history could enduringly
tell the story of the fall of Granada and of the Spain that ensued is abundantly challenged by a range of cultural productions over the course of
the sixteenth century. Explicit rewritings of the war on Granada engage
directly with the problem of what and how to remember, pinpointing collective memory as the conceptual ground on which conflicts over Spanish
identity must be fought.[3] A different challenge comes from the built landscape itself, where, despite Mariana's doubts, countless structures solidly
recall the presence of the Moors. In assessing the force of these alternative
remembrances, this chapter recasts the relation between maurophilia and

national memory in terms both of the textual record and of the broader *lieux de mémoire*, those spaces or monuments in which collective memory is embedded.[4] While Mariana's magisterial history makes the case that only texts will endure to ensure the nation's greatness, the artifacts I consider tell a very different story, both of the contested workings of memory and of the collectivity to which those memories correspond.

Chivalric Objects

A range of imaginative texts challenged official versions of the events in Granada, such as Mariana's historiography, and the central place they assigned the war in the history of the nation, by reanimating the codes of chivalry already present in most accounts. With its emphasis on the nobility of the individual knight, whatever his faith, chivalry proved an essential vehicle for maurophilia. Yet chivalry also brings out some of the central tensions in the representation of the "Reconquista," as the friendship between a single Moor and a Christian knight, to take one significant example, complicates the essentialism and othering on which the exclusionary versions of Spain depend. Such friendship is at the heart of one of the most influential texts in the maurophile literary canon, the anonymous novella *El Abencerraje*, published in several versions in the 1560s, which famously imagines the bond between a magnanimous Christian knight, Rodrigo de Narváez, and Abindarráez, the noble Moor whom he captures. Beyond the general usefulness of chivalry as a way to challenge anti-Moorish prejudice, however, the novella rehearses the particular role of chivalry in accounts of the fall of Granada, deliberately rewriting the idealization of that struggle for its own ideological purposes.

Although in many ways the war on Granada was a modern enterprise, with artillery attacks and carefully planned campaigns, influential accounts nonetheless represented it in a highly stylized and archaizing fashion. In particular, chroniclers attributed the heroic feats of the Spaniards to their chivalrous devotion to Queen Isabel. While Isabel does not seem to have deliberately mobilized the discourse of chivalry to the same extent as Elizabeth I of England would famously do, several accounts of the war on Granada claim that personal devotion to her, as an idealized lady, helped win the day.[5] The Venetian ambassador to Spain in the 1520s, Andrea Navagero, recreates the war in terms that emphasize Isabel's role and romanticize the entire enterprise:

Fu gentil guerra, non vi erano anchor tante artigliarie come sono venute dopoi, & molto più se potevano cognoscere i valent'huomini, che non si ponno hora i ogni dì erano alle mani, & ogni dì si faceva qualche bel fatto. Tutta la nobiltà di Spagna vi si trovava, & tra tutti era concorrentia di portarsi meglio, & acquistarsi più fama. . . . La Regina con la corte sua dava grande animo a ogn'uno. Non vi era Signor che non fusse innamorato in qualch'una delle Dame della Regina, le quali essendo presente, & certi testimoni du quanto si faceva da ciascaduno; & dando spesso le arme di sue mani a quelli che andavano a combattere, & spesso alcun suo favore, & forsi alle volte dicendoli parole che li facesse rocuore, & pregandoli che ne i portamenti loro, facessero cognoscere quanto le amavano, qual è quel huomo si vile, si di poco animo, si di poca forza, che non avesse vinto ogni potente & animoso adversario: & che non havesse osato perder mille volte la vita, più presto che ritornar alla sua Signora con vergogna; per il che si puo dir che questa guerra fusse principalmente vinta per Amore.[6]

[It was a beautiful war, with less artillery than what came later, and it was easier to recognize brave men. Every day there were encounters, and every day they carried out some fine feat of arms. All the nobility of Spain was there, and all were competing for the finest performance, and to gain the most fame . . . The Queen and her court gave great courage to one and all. There was not a lord present who was not in love with one of the Queen's ladies, and these being present and not only witnesses to what each accomplished, but also with their very hands giving their weapons to the sallying warriors, and granting them at the same time their favor, and perhaps saying to them some words that would make them blush, & begging them to show by their deeds how much they loved them, what man would be so vile, so lacking in courage, so weak, that he would not have overcome every powerful and courageous foe? Who would not have risked his life one thousand times rather than return to his lady in shame? Because of this it may be said that this war was won principally by Love.]

Strikingly, the same type of description occurs in the papal ambassador Baldassarre Castiglione's best-selling dialogue on the perfect courtier, *Il Cortigiano* (1528), quickly translated into Spanish by the poet Joan Boscán (1534):

Dicen también muchos que las damas fueron en parte gran causa de las vitorias del rey don Hernando y reina doña Isabel contra el rey de Granada; porque las más veces, cuando el exército de los españoles iba a buscar los enemigos, la Reina iba allí con todas sus damas, y los galanes con ellas, hablándoles en sus amores hasta que llegaban a vista de los moros; después, despidiéndose cada uno de su dama, en presencia dellas iban a las escaramuzas, con aquella lozanía y ferocidad que les daba el amor y el deseo de hacer conocer a sus señoras que eran amadas y servidas de hombres valerosos y esforzados; y así muchas veces hubo caballeros españoles que con muy poco número de gente desbarataron y mataron gran multitud de moros.[7]

[Many say also that the ladies were to a large extent responsible for the victories of King Fernando and Queen Isabel against the king of Granada, for on most occasions when the Spanish army set out in search of the enemy the Queen and all her ladies went with them, and their suitors too, speaking to them of their love until they came within sight of the Moors; then, each saying farewell to his lady, they went into the skirmishes in their presence, with the vigor and ferocity that came of love and of the desire to let their ladies know that they were loved and served by brave and strong men; and so on many occasions there were Spanish knights who with but a few men routed and killed a great multitude of Moors.]

For Italians, a Granada won for love became the antithesis to more proximate Spanish violence in their own lands, which would culminate in the infamous 1527 sack of Rome by the troops of Charles V.[8] The Italian ambassadors' versions of the war on Granada suggest how chivalry could adapt this key historical event to specific ideological purposes, in this case to rehabilitate an earlier Spain in contradistinction to the violence of the imperial troops in Italy.

Native chroniclers also viewed Granada through the lens of chivalry, in their case to emphasize the heroism of those involved and the general excellence of the enterprise. Although the popular history of the Catholic monarchs by the curate Andrés de Bernáldez (written c. 1500) emphasizes the providential nature of the war, the author dwells on the panoply and chivalry of the conflict. Fernando's army is "muy grande e muy maravillosa e muy fermosa"[9] ["very large and very marvelous and very beautiful"], as they make their "hermosa entrada" (155) ["beautiful incursion"] into Moorish territory.[10] When Isabel arrives in Illora after a Christian victory, she is received with tremendous panoply, "recebimiento . . . muy singular" (169) ["a most singular welcome"] as the troops parade before her. The monarchs' costumes feature various Andalusi-derived garments.[11] Bernáldez describes in great detail the mount and dress of the sovereigns and of their daughter the Infanta, then asks the reader to imagine the rest: "Los atavíos de los grandes que ay estavan eran muy maravillosos e muy ricos e de diversas maneras, assí de guerra como de fiesta, que sería muy luengo de escrevir" (170) ["The attire of the great ones who were there was very marvelous and very rich and of diverse sorts, for war and for festivities, so that it would take too long to describe"].

The presence of the queen makes the troops "muy alegres y esforzados" (209) ["very glad and brave"]. As in the Italian accounts, she inspires them and looks on as they fight, so that she is credited with their victory (227–28). Besides Isabel's almost miraculous role, however, Bernáldez emphasizes the chivalry of the enemy, as in the case of the Moor who spares young Christian lads "porque no vide barbas" (187) ["because I saw no beards"]. When the queen comes to Málaga, "todos los del real pensavan que por la venida de la reina se avían de dar los moros; e ellos, como personas de España e segundos zamoranos en su tema, esforçadamente salían a pelear" (182) ["All those in the camp thought that the Moors would surrender because of the Queen's arrival; yet they, as persons from Spain and second Zamorans in their concern, bravely came out to fight"]. Although the passage may seem confusing to readers accustomed to the excision of Moors from Spain in later historiography, here it is the besieged Moors who are characterized as Spaniards and "segundos Zamoranos." The analogy is particularly striking: as Bernáldez's modern editors note, at the time Zamora was identified with ancient Numantia, the famous Celtiberian town besieged by the Romans whose inhabitants chose mass suicide over surrender to the conqueror. Given the association of Numantia with a heroic, transcendental Spain (as in Cervantes's famous 1582 play of that name), the equation here of the besieged Moors with Numantine resistance suggests how chivalric idealization destabilizes the exclusionary thrust of anti-Moorish rhetoric.

The complex *Novela del Abencerraje y Jarifa*, whose anonymous authorship has long signaled to critics a questioning of dominant ideology, is centrally concerned with both the logic of chivalry between different faiths and the memorialization of chivalric feats. The text plays constantly with the tension between itself and other forms of commemoration, rehearsing the tenor of the descriptions of the war on Granada to imagine chivalry as the conduit for a generous relationship to Moors. The novella tells the story of a historical hero of the Reconquista, Rodrigo de Narváez, who captures the noble Moor Abindarráez—a member of the powerful Abencerraje clan of Nasrid Granada—in a border skirmish. Abindarráez relates to Narváez the tragic story of his lineage, falsely accused of treason and destroyed or exiled by the king of Granada. Given the text's sympathetic depiction of cross-cultural contacts, critics have read Abindarráez's lament as an oblique reference to the suffering of Spanish Jews and Moors, exiled or persecuted as New Christians.[12] The Moor then relates his love for his lady, Jarifa, whom he was traveling to meet when he was captured. Narváez releases him on his word so that he can rejoin Jarifa and marry her secretly. When Abindarráez, to Jarifa's dismay, insists on returning to Narváez to fulfill his promise, she decides to accompany him. Narváez befriends them and even intercedes in their favor with the king of Granada, leading to a lifelong friendship that persists, the text tells us, "aunque las leyes sean diferentes"[13] ["though their faiths/laws be different"]. The intense chivalric and homosocial ties between Christian and Moor adumbrate the novella's historical context of border conflict. They also contrast sharply with the situation of the Moriscos at the time of its publication, as the respite from legal persecution which they tenuously enjoyed began to seem increasingly fragile.[14]

Scholars have identified three main versions of the text, two of which appear in authored works, but have not reached any definite conclusions about its authorship. The anonymous edition of 1561 presents itself as a fragment of a historical narrative, under the title *Parte de la Corónica del ínclito Infante don Fernando, que ganó a Antequera*. The novella also appears as an interpolated tale in the 1562 edition of the wildly popular pastoral *Diana*, by Jorge de Montemayor, as well as in its many subsequent editions, and as one of the items in Antonio Villegas's literary miscellany, the *Inventario* of 1565. Both authors are generally presumed to have been *conversos*. In the *Corónica* edition, the only one in which the novella is presented as a stand-alone text, the anonymity is compounded by a striking dedication to Jerónimo Jiménez de Embún, lord of Bárboles and Oiture, an Aragonese nobleman who participated in the local resistance to the persecution of Morisco vassals by the Inquisition and other agents of the centralized state.[15] As scholars have noted, the novella's favorable portrayal of the Moors would have had particular relevance in the context of the defense of the Moriscos in Aragón.

Ironically, the *Corónica* edition ends not on a note of eternal amity, as do the other two, but instead with a return to the border raids that begin the narrative, highlighting the contrast between the intense bonds of private friendship and public enmity. After they return from a gift-laden embassy to the Moors with rich gifts in return, the *escuderos* "quedaron entendiendo en hazer correrías en tierra de moros: como antes solían prósperamente"[16] ["planned to conduct raids into Moorish lands, as they once did prosperously"]. Israel Burshatin argues that this narrative circularity, which critics have rejected for its incongruity, "reclaims the primacy of the adversary element in Christian-Muslim relations."[17] Yet the discordant ending may also be read as an ironic reflection on the border conflict: the great exchange of gifts far outdoes any spoils or ransom, rendering the *correrías* slightly ludicrous.

Burshatin's larger argument emphasizes the discursive primacy of Narváez as a metaphoric version of the Spanish conqueror's ascendancy.

He reads the novella as ultimately "a self-flattering depiction of Christian control over the Moor and his world."[18] His provocative reading attempts to correct what he deems an excessive critical emphasis on the amicable exchanges in the novella. Critics have in fact considered *El Abencerraje* everything from a literary divertissement on Moorish themes, as remotely idealizing as the pastoral or the chivalric romance,[19] to a serious intervention against prevailing orthodoxies.[20] Though it provides an important corrective, Burshatin's reading of the highly wrought and sophisticated text ultimately leads to a Foucauldian impasse, akin to what makes Said's account of orientalism so suffocating: any contestation in the text is completely contained by the conqueror's discursive framework. Yet surely, by foregrounding the chivalric equation of Moor and Christian, the novella turns Christian Spanish ideology upon itself.

In a balanced assessment, Claudio Guillén emphasizes that *El Aben-cerraje* succeeds "in offering, above all, a forceful contrast with the historical present."[21] But Guillén refuses any connection between the idealized portrait of the Moor in the text and the historical reality of the Moriscos: "the exaltation of the Moorish knight, always a nobleman, was far from being incompatible with a profound scorn for the *morisco*, who was always plebeian. The enthusiastic praise of the gallant Moorish knight—who in the final analysis was not different from a Christian nobleman—could only intensify everyone's impatience with the stubborn *moriscos*, who persisted in their faith, their ways, their otherness."[22] Guillén here repeats in an uncritical fashion the vision of the Moriscos propounded by the state: they are unassimilable and undesirable. A very different picture emerges from María Soledad Carrasco Urgoiti's reconstruction of the multi-cultural community in the town of Epila, center of the noble and humanist circle from which, she avers, *El Abencerraje* emerged, and which included prosperous families of both Moriscos and *conversos*.[23] Not all Moriscos were "plebeian," even if such a characterization made it easier to imagine expelling them.

While it may be impossible to recover the full force of *El Abencerraje*'s effect on contemporary readers, the text obviously engages pressing historical issues. Rather than neutralizing the novella's ideological force, the recourse to chivalry ironizes the relationship between the Spain of the mid-sixteenth century and its mythologized past. The homosocial bonds between the two knights both shape the text and point beyond it, to the larger problem of the collective ties and predilections that might follow from such individual allegiances. At the same time, the frame of *El Aben-*

cerraje insistently poses a set of metahistorical questions. How is Spain's past to be told and recorded? Beyond the pieties of the Reconquista myth, what place will the Moors have in the story? And what kind of relation does the text itself bear to the recording of that history, or to alternative forms of memorialization? Reflections on memory and national tradition eloquently frame the *Inventario* version of *El Abencerraje*. In this, its most sophisticated form, the novella counters the nationalist myth of the Reconquista and the construction of a Spanish national identity based on militant Christianity by underscoring the limitations of such a partial vision. In its introduction and conclusion—the latter in the *alcaide*'s own voice—the text links the individual incident that brings together Narváez and the Moor to larger historical preoccupations.

The introduction foregrounds the problem of commemoration with respect to the Christian hero of the narrative. The governor of Antequera and Alora is literally larger than life. The historical Rodrigo de Narváez participated in the conquest of Antequera in 1410 and was named *alcaide* of the town; he died in 1424. He could thus never have been the same Narváez as the *alcaide* of the second town, Alora, which was not taken by the Christians until 1482.[24] The conflation of at least two separate historical figures in one character, "notable en virtud y en hechos de armas" (131) ["famous for his virtue and feats of arms"], suggests that the narrative's engagement with history is allegorical rather than documentary. Despite the idealization of its hero, this is not a flattering literary version of Narváez's family history in the mode of Renaissance epic or humanist historiography—those genres could not very well accommodate such confusion vis-à-vis the protagonist.[25] The amalgamation suggests instead a preoccupation with a larger sense of the Reconquista rather than with any specific encounter, so that the plot takes on an almost metonymic quality.

Yet the text insists on the importance of fame and commemoration. No sooner is Narváez named than we are told:

Este, peleando contra moros, hizo cosas de mucho esfuerzo, y particularmente en aquella empresa y guerra de Antequera hizo hechos dignos de perpetua memoria, sino que esta nuestra España tiene en tan poco el esfuerzo, por serle tan natural y ordinario, que le paresce que cuanto se puede hacer es poco; no como aquellos romanos y griegos, que al hombre que se aventuraba a morir una vez en toda la vida le hacían en sus escriptos inmortal y le trasladaban en las estrellas. (131–32)

[Combating the Moors, this knight performed great feats, and particularly in that enterprise and war of Antequera wrought deeds worthy of perpetual memory, except that this our Spain dismisses such efforts, for they are so natural and ordinary to her that she considers all that may be done too little, unlike those Romans and Greeks who immortalized in their writing and in the stars the man who once risked his life.]

While the passage claims Spanish superiority, with modern warriors who routinely outperform the classical heroes of the past without their nation taking the least notice, it hints also at a grudging refusal to acknowledge heroism or, at the very least, a problem with memorialization.[26] *El Abencerraje* insists on the textual indifference despite a substantial tradition of praise for the Reconquista and the fame it confers, as in Juan de Mena's political allegory, the 1446 *Laberinto de Fortuna*: "¡Oh, virtüosa, magnífica guerra!, / en ti las querellas volverse debían, / en ti do los nuestros muriendo vivían/ por gloria en los cielos y fama en la tierra"[27] ["Oh, virtuous, magnificent war! All quarrels should be transformed into you, in which ours lived while dying, for glory in the heavens and fame on earth"]. López Estrada, in his edition of *El Abencerraje*, nonetheless identifies a topos of Spain's disregard for the efforts of its warriors, citing Fernán Pérez de Guzmán's presumably remedial *Loores de los claros varones de España* (*Praises of the Famous Men of Spain*):

España no caresció
de quien virtudes usase,
más menguó y fallesció
en ella quien las notase;
para que bien se igualase
debían ser los caballeros,
de España, y los Homeros
de Grecia, que los loase.[28]

[Spain did not lack for those who displayed virtues, but there were none within her to note them. To reach the same level, the knights should be from Spain, and the Homers from Greece, to praise them.]

With its mention of Greek and Roman "escriptos" that convey immortality, *El Abencerraje* echoes Guzmán's invocation of the epic and commendatory literature that Spain ostensibly lacks.[29] The reader might reasonably expect that this narrative, with its praise of Narváez's virtue, will fill the gap.[30] As Burshatin observes, "the Abencerraje presents itself as a sorely needed version of epic and asserts what is for Spain synonymous with the genre—praising the deeds of Christian heroes over Muslims."[31]

But the text's position vis-à-vis epic is rather more complex. Rather than supplementing the absence of epic, the narrative takes an alternative turn. The account of Spain's insouciance toward its heroes is immediately followed by the ironic admission that Narváez *is* rewarded, first with the command of one city, and then the other: "Hizo, pues, este caballero tanto en servicio de su ley y de su rey, que después de ganada la villa le hizo alcaide de ella" (132) ["Thus this knight did so much in the service of his law and of his king, that after the town was won the king made him its *alcaide*"].[32] And of course, as the modern editor has pointed out, the first Rodrigo de Narváez appears frequently in fifteenth-century *crónicas* and in Fernando del Pulgar's *Claros varones de Castilla* (*Famous Men of Castile*, c. 1485), where his bravery against the Moors is emphasized.[33] Narváez is abundantly recognized for his public actions against the Moors; it is the private amity with Abindarráez, one must assume, that is unacknowledged and insufficiently celebrated by Spain. (The *Diana* version never mentions Spain's disregard for its heroes, and states only that Narváez "alcançó nombre muy principal entre todos los de su tiempo"[34] ["achieved a great name among all those of his own time"]). Thus the narrative turns from the epic and historical mode of the introduction and the initial encounter between Christians and Moors, concerned with the large-scale history of the Reconquista and the fame of Spain's heroes, to chivalric romance, a more fitting mode for chronicling the encounter between the noble protagonists and the love story of Abindarráez and his bride.

One sign of the fractious transition between these traditions is the uneven *escaramuza* in which Abindarráez is defeated by the Christians. Romance enters the text with the marvelous description of Abindarráez, dressed in his best Moorish finery and singing with joy as he approaches the spot where the Christians have hidden themselves. "Transportados en verle" ["transported by the sight of him"], the narrator tells us, "erraron poco de dejarle pasar" (136) ["they almost let him pass"]. As Laura Bass notes, the narrator emphasizes Abindarráez's allure for the Christians. But whereas Bass, and Bollard after her, ascribe this attraction to the tale's "Orientalism," linking it to the emasculation of the Moor, the erotics of the episode are more complicated.[35] Although Narváez will, as Bass argues, eventually be able to restrain his desire and thus mark his difference from the Moor, the scene opens a window onto the complex erotics of maurophilia, in which male Christian desire must constantly negotiate the appeal of a proximate Moor.

Recovering from their delight in him, the Christian squires surprise Abindarráez in an ambush. After he overcomes the first Christian to take him on, the rest gang up on him. When they prove unable to subdue him, Narváez finally defeats Abindarráez in single combat, but only after the Moor has been badly wounded in the thigh during his encounter with five *escuderos*.[36] From the perspective of chivalric romance, this scene shows the Spaniards in a terrible light—they fight like villains. But from a historical perspective it reflects the nonheroic realities of the *escaramuza* (skirmish) and the *algazu* (border raid), the preferred—and rather small-scale— tactics for attacking Moorish possessions on the frontier.[37] The dissonance between the historical and the chivalric readings of this episode suggests that the discourse of chivalry can voice a critique of epic and national ideologies.

The delicacy of the exchanges between Narváez and his captive, and the magnanimity with which he treats the Moor, transform the world of the frontier into a space of amity rather than the frontline of an inexorable war. This romance refiguration is underscored by the intensity of the homosocial ties between the two, as Bass notes. The Petrarchan analogy between Abindarráez's erotic entrancement and his actual captivity becomes an organizing principle of the novella.[38] In this vein, Abindarráez sets the limits to Narváez's power over him by protesting that he has been defeated by another: "—Matarme bien podrás—dijo el moro—que en tu poder me tienes, mas no podrá vencerme sino quien una vez me venció" (137) ["You may well kill me," said the Moor, "for I am in your hands, but I cannot be conquered except by the one who once conquered me"]. Yet the remarkable closeness, even tenderness, that develops between the two men as Narváez binds the Moor's wounds and listens sympathetically to his story makes the metaphor reversible: love is like captivity, but captivity is a little bit like love. Abindarráez's vow to return when he takes his leave of Narváez both recalls the earlier promises exchanged by the lovers and anticipates their secret marriage. The performative—"¿Vos prometéisme, como caballero, de volver . . . ?" "Sí prometo" (150) ["Do you promise me, as a knight, to return . . . ? "Yes, I promise"]—binds the two knights as closely as Abindarráez is bound to Jarifa.

The force of this chivalric homosociality is most evident when, after his clandestine marriage, Abindarráez returns to keep his promise, accompanied by Jarifa. Narváez expresses his concern for Abindarráez's wounds, which Jarifa has somehow missed as she and her lover consummated their passion. The text underscores Jarifa's discomfiture: twice she is described as "alterada" by the realization that a greater intimacy—the symbolically laden wounds in the thigh and the arm—binds the two men, even as Abindarráez reiterates the Petrarchan conceit of the wounds her love has caused him. Here, the relationship between the two knights goes well beyond tolerance to an intimacy that Jarifa finds threatening. It is important to recover the intensity of this relationship—even within the parameters of the idealizing novella—in order to appreciate the full force of its reimagining of Moorish-Christian relations. Not only does the chivalric, homosocial relationship temporarily supplant the heterosexual bond between Abindarráez and Jarifa, it also replaces more common fiction of exogamous romance—the love of a Christian man for a Moorish woman—through which Moorish/Christian relations are often managed in cultural fantasy. (A trace of that fantasy persists, one might argue, in Narváez's exchanges with Jarifa at the end of the text, in which he directs himself to her to avoid addressing Abindarráez). Moreover, the intense feeling for Moors is never questioned within the novella. As I pointed out in Chapter 1, maurophilia, much like early modern sodomy, only calls attention to itself when practiced by a subject already stigmatized or marginal. Unlike the despised Enrique IV, whose Moorish proclivities become part and parcel of his broader condemnation, the heroic Narváez can cherish Moors without any problem.

As Bass has noted, homosociality also marks Narváez's relations to other Spanish men, not only at the beginning of the narrative, where much is made of the *escuderos'* loyalty to him, but in a curious interpolated tale of love and chivalry.[39] On their way to Narváez's castle, Abindarráez and Jarifa encounter an old man who tells them a story about the knight's virtue. This is a traditional tale of a knight who refuses the advances of a married lady won over by her own husband's praises for him. In this version, Narváez had actively wooed the lady beforehand, but when she explains why she suddenly wants to give herself to him, he cannot bring himself to betray the man who has spoken so well of him. Jarifa's commentary provides an alternative point of view on the chivalric conventions, one that the text cannot fully assimilate:

—Por Dios, señor, yo no quisiera servidor tan virtuoso, mas él debía estar poco enamorado, pues tan presto se salió afuera y pudo más con él la honra del marido que la hermosura de la mujer.

Y sobre esto dijo otras muy graciosas palabras. (158)

["By God, my lord, I would not wish for such a virtuous lover. But he must have been only a little in love, for he left so quickly and was moved more by the honor of the husband than by the wife's beauty."

And about this she said some other witty things.]

Jarifa's unspecified "graciosas palabras" are an oblique textual rem(a)inder of the effort required to present a seamless ideology in the novella. The interlude presents chivalry—the queerness of which Jarifa recognizes—as a formative template for relations between men, one that trumps more immediate appetites or antipathies. The story of Narváez's intense connection to Abindarráez that surrounds this embedded fragment, for its part, highlights the queer erotics of maurophilia, which leaves both Narváez and his *escuderos* at least temporarily in the thrall of the Moor.

Narváez's close male-male relations, whether to Christian or Moorish knights, tend to displace any heterosexual relation of his own, including, as I suggest above, the common trope of the Christian man's fascination with a Moorish woman. This seems particularly puzzling given Narváez's concern for his descendants ("mi posteridad y descendencia," 164) at the end of the narrative. For when the text restates the friendship that binds the protagonists, a striking imbalance is revealed: "De esta manera quedaron los unos de los otros muy satisfechos y contentos y trabados con tan estrecha amistad, que les duró toda la vida" (164) ["Thus they remained very satisfied and content with each other and bound in such close friendship that it lasted their whole life long"]. But there is no actual parallelism behind the construction *los unos de los otros* (literally, "the ones in the others"): on the one hand is the Moorish couple, on the other Narváez, either strikingly alone or, presumably, representing the exclusively male Christian community. The imbalance is clearer even in the epistolary exchange: Abindarráez writes to the *alcaide*, but Narváez writes to the now fully unavailable Jarifa. The text suggests a certain sterility within the Christian camp, as the homosocial bonds of chivalry supplant Narváez's own potential union and lineage. Thus while Bass may be right to point out that Narváez triumphs over his own desire, the outcome of this repression is a foreshortened Christian line.

The text's emphasis on posterity foregrounds these questions. Even though he emphasizes his own descendants, however, Narváez's concern with fame and commemoration privileges the national over the individual. In a letter to Jarifa thanking her for the rich gifts that she and Abindarráez have sent him, he reiterates how monumental his own actions seem to him :

Hermosa Jarifa: No ha querido Abindarráez dejarme gozar del verdadero tri-
umpho de su prisión, que consiste en perdonar y hacer bien; y como a mí en esta
tierra nunca se me ofresció empresa tan generosa ni tan digna de capitán español,
quisiera gozarla toda y labrar de ella una estatua para mi posteridad y descendencia.
(163–64)

[Fair Jarifa: Abindarráez has not allowed me to enjoy the real triumph of his
captivity, which consists in forgiving and doing good, and as I have never in this
land witnessed such a generous deed, or one as worthy of a Spanish captain, I
would like to enjoy in its entirety and to craft a statue of it for my posterity and
descendants.]

Narváez's feat of generosity to the Abencerraje here becomes exemplary,
unique "in this land" and unprecedented in "a Spanish captain."[40] By
presenting the *alcaide* as a model national subject, worthy—at least in
his own eyes—of a national monument and national fame, *El Abencerraje*
transforms the memory of Reconquista conquests into a counter-national-
ist monument to coexistence and amity, even if the actual audience for the
gesture seems lacking.[41] Where history might recall Narváez's role in the
conquest of Antequera, his imagined statue, as well as the literary monument that effectively commemorates him, both focus on his generosity to
a Moor.[42] Thus the chivalric strain in the narration of the war of Granada
becomes the occasion for imagining an entirely different relationship to
the Moors, commemorated by its own *lieu de mémoire*.

The preoccupation with posterity and memorialization in Narváez's
final letter rehearses the discussion about how Spain remembers its heroes
with which the text opens. These framing moments of concern for the
nation's self-representation transform the novella from a simple romance
refiguration of Moorish-Christian relations into a much larger intervention into contemporary debates about Spanish history and identity. For
they address an essential problem: how is the nation's history to be written
if all but the most violent interactions between Moors and Christians are
excised? How, especially is the region that was for so long the frontier, or
under Arab rule, to present its own past? *El Abencerraje* supplies a different
kind of history, both in its romance narrative and in its projection of an
artifact—the imagined statue—that would somehow represent materially
that which texts cannot sufficiently convey.

Monuments of Maurophilia

As historians of Granada have long recognized, the conceptual incorporation of the sometime frontier into the nation presented its own set of

problems.[43] Not only was the border riven by rebellion and imperfectly controlled by the centralized state, its past resisted the narrative of Christian heroism and exclusivist "Gothic" identity embraced by the Crown. For the Kingdom of Granada did not have a timeless past of heroic Christian exploits to offer up to the national project. Unlike other regions, aside from the final campaign, it had a Moorish history, one that became increasingly tragic as well as romanticized at the frontier. In some cases, this history was actually inscribed in the Andalucian landscape, as in the striking Peña de los Enamorados [Lover's Rock] encountered by Navagero on his travels. It is named, he recounts,

dal caso di dui inamorati, un Christian di Antechera, & una mora d'Archidona; liquali . . . ne sopportassero esser divisi, ne viver l'un senza l'altro, elessero morir insieme: & riduttisi nel più alto scoglio del monte, dopoi molte lacrime & lamenti de la loro adversa fortuna, vedendosi già vicini quelli che li seguitavano, abracciati insieme strettissimi & gionta faccia a faccia, se precipitorno di quel scoglio che è altissimo: & lasciono il nome al monte.[44]

[for what happened to two lovers, a Christian from Antequera and a Moorish woman from Archidona, who . . . rather than be separated or live without each other, decided to die together, and climbing to the highest peak of the mountain, after many tears and laments for their ill luck, seeing those who pursued them come close, in a close embrace and with their faces joined leaped from that highest peak and gave their name to that mountain.]

The mountain thus recalls both maurophilia and the obstacles it encounters. Beyond such individual tragedies, however representative, the landscape is also famously imbued with a collective, emotive charge, notably at the "Moor's Last Sigh," the spot where Boabdil [Abu Abdullah], the last Moorish king of Granada, is said to have looked back at the city he and his subjects had lost to the Christians.[45] Thus, although the Crown embarked on a building and institutional program designed to Christianize Granada, the negotiation of memory was more complicated than simply overwriting the old city with new avenues and imposing buildings.

The problem of Granada's irreducible difference and its implications for national history was taken up by Morisco writers in the mid- to late sixteenth century, who, in an effort to defend themselves from persecution, argued for the preservation of their culture as a living monument to the past. In his *memorial* or petition to Don Pedro de Deza, head of the Audiencia or provincial court of Granada, Morisco advocate Francisco Núñez Muley defended Morisco cultural practices, under attack by increasingly repressive legislation, by suggesting that they were *Granadan*, not Moorish, customs.[46] He thereby recast the persecution of the Moors as a struggle between local culture and the centralizing force of the monarchy. In a more specific discussion of cultural memory, Núñez Muley laments the proposed erasure of Moorish clan names and other cultural markers: "Perderse an las personas y los linajes moriscos; no sabrán con quién tratan ni compran ni casan, no conociendo el linaje"[47] ["All the Moorish persons and lineages will be lost; they will not know whom they deal with or buy from or marry, not knowing the lineage"]. But of course such confusion and forced acculturation were precisely the Crown's intention in forbidding the names.

Núñez Muley's argument takes a more interesting turn when he addresses the problems that the erasure of the Moorish past will pose for Christian Spain:

Pues, ¿qué se sirue querer perderse tales memorias, ansy los ávitos y traxes, como en los sobrenombres, como en todo lo susodicho? ¿No le paresçe a V.S.R. que [en] quedar estas memorias ay grandes ensalzamientos de los Reyes que ganaron estos rreynos, de ver las diuersas maneras que ganaron? Y ésta fue la yntinción de los Reyes Católicos en anparar este rreyno en la manera que lo anparon y los arçobispos pasados; y esta yntención e voluntad tuvieron los Enperadores e Reyes Católicos en anparar las memorias de las casas rreales del Alhambra y otras memorias, tales que quedasen en la mysma forma que heran en el tiempo de los rreyes moros, para que se manyfestase lo que ganaron sus Altezas y se paresçería más claro.[48]

[For what is the point of wanting to lose such remembrances, or the costume and dress, or the last names, or all that I have mentioned? Is there not in the preservation of these remembrances great honor done to the Kings who won these kingdoms, in seeing the diverse ways in which they won them? And this was the Catholic Monarchs' intention in protecting this kingdom in the way they did, as did earlier archbishops; and this was the intention and will of the Emperors and Catholic Kings in protecting the memory of the royal houses of the Alhambra and other memories, so that they would remain as they had been in the time of the Moorish kings, in order that what their Highnesses won should show and appear more clearly.]

The memory of Moors thus becomes a key component of Spain's own past and present. The preservation of Moorish culture underwrites the greatness of Spain; by implication, the nation's stature is diminished by that culture's disappearance. Núñez Muley's moving (though ultimately ineffective) argument for a capacious cultural memory, one that accommodates the *diuersas maneras* in which Granada became part of Spain, recalls Narváez's closing wish in *El Abencerraje* for a statue to commemorate that *empresa generosa*, the amicable exchange between Christian and Moor. The erasure of such *empresas*, or of Moorish culture entirely, these authors claim, only impoverishes Spain's own past.

In a sense, the monuments of national history proposed by Núñez Muley answer the question implicit in the *Abencerraje*: how to preserve a Moorish past that involved much more than the battles of the Reconquista. His maurophilia has less to do with idealizing chivalric depictions than with urgent questions of cultural survival—the failure of his *memorial* would lead directly to the Morisco uprising in the Alpujarras. And yet its rhetorical sophistication, as he creatively engages the writing of a history for the nation, links him with canonical idealizations such as *El Abencerraje*. Conversely, it also serves to recover the political import of the literary text, rescuing the latter from a critical vision that, at its most reductive, considered it a sentimental chivalric romance in Moorish guise. More important, the emphasis on the *lieux de mémoire* in these texts reminds us that the history of maurophilia in sixteenth-century Spain must necessarily go beyond the texts themselves to a consideration of physical monuments and, indeed, the general built environment. An alternative canon of maurophilia as a cultural rather than literary genre might thus profitably include everything from a high Renaissance novella to the Alhambra itself, limning the many ways in which Spaniards imagined the place of the Moors within.

Núñez Muley's focus on the "royal houses of the Alhambra" underscores the central importance of the Andalusi palace as perhaps the most representative of all Spanish *lieux de mémoire*. The memorialization of this particular place reveals much about the contradictory attempts over the course of the sixteenth century both to preserve and to overwrite the Moorish past. While, as Núñez Muley points out, the Catholic kings had endeavored to preserve the Alhambra, Charles V is perhaps best remembered for his decision to place within it an Italianate Renaissance palace. The symbolic importance of the Alhambra made it subject to competing appropriations, much as the discourse of chivalry that it gave rise to would suffer different textual uses.

In the very month that Granada fell, Ferdinand and Isabel charged an Aragonese architect with repairing the walls of the fortress.[49] The palaces of the Alhambra were designated a Casa Real, or royal residence, and placed under the separate jurisdiction of an *alcaide*, Pedro Iñigo López de Mendoza, Count of Tendilla. Expert artisans—Moors for the most part— were hired to conduct repairs.[50] When the German traveler Hieronymus

Münzer visited Granada in late 1494, he was shown around the immacu-
late palace by the Count, after taking some refreshment while sitting
"super tapetas de seta"[51] ["on silken cloths"]. Münzer's admiration is
patent: "Simile credo in tota Europa non esse. Omnia adeo magnifice,
adeo superbe, adeo exquisite erant facta de vario genere, ut paradisum
credere. Non est mihi possibile omnia recensere" (47) ["I cannot believe
there is anything like it in all of Europe, for everything is so magnificent,
so majestic, so exquisitely made, as to think it paradise. Nor can I relate
exactly what I saw"].

    This exquisite production was expensive to maintain. The preserva-
tion of the Alhambra was deliberately arranged by royal decree, with proceeds set aside from taxes, fines, and other sources of revenue.[52] In her 1515
decree on its maintenance, Queen Juana specified the importance of the
building as a site of collective memory:

el rey mi señor e padre e la reyna mi señora madre, que haya santa gloria, ganaron
la cibdad de Granada e Alhambra della, donde está la Casa Real, que es tan suntuoso y excelente edeficio, e la voluntad de los dichos reyes mis señores e mía siempre
ha sido e es que la dicha Alhambra e Casa esté muy bien reparada e se sostenga,
porque queda para siempre perpetua memoria, e porque e esto se puede façer, he
acordado de le dar e señalar algunas rentas, para que con ellas, e con lo que más
mandaremos librar, la dicha Alhambra e edefiçios della estén bien reparados e no
se consuma e pierda tan eçelente memoria e suntuoso edefiçio como es.[53]

[the king my father and the queen my mother, holy glory be to her, won the city
of Granada and its Alhambra, where the royal palace is, which is such a sumptuous
and excellent building, and the wishes of said kings my parents and mine has always
been, and is, that the said Alhambra and palace be well repaired and maintained,
so that the perpetual memory of it last forever, and so that this may be done, I
have agreed to endow it and specify certain sums, so that with them, and with
whatever else we will order to be furnished, the said Alhambra and buildings
thereof will be well repaired and so that such an excellent memorial and sumptuous
edifice as this not be consumed and lost.]

The question, then, was not whether the Alhambra was to be maintained—the Christian victors recognized its value and protected it. Rather,
it was how this place would signify—what kind of collectivity it would
represent, what kind of history it would memorialize. Does the Alhambra
stand for the Christian triumph, or for centuries of Andalusi cultural
achievement? Can it signal both? Núñez Muley clearly read it as a synecdoche for the value of Andalusi contributions to Spain, and as the occasion

Figure 1. Courtyard, Charles V's Renaissance palace at the Alhambra, photo by Pedro Machuca. University of Wisconsin Digital Collections/Casselman Archive.

for extending much broader protections to Morisco subjects and their culture. For the Christians, however, Granada had a more ambiguous meaning: it served to mark their own victory, but it reminded them also of the magnificent cultural achievements of those defeated. This recognition clearly animated Christian sovereigns who deliberately copied Nasrid buildings in conquered Moorish cities, as King Pedro I of Castile did in his famous "Mudéjar Palace" in the Alcázar of Seville (1364–66).[54] In fact, when foreigners visited the Alhambra, they evinced some confusion over whether it reflected a Moorish or Spanish design. Navagero observed in this palace "dei Re Mori" ["of the Moorish kings"] a courtyard "al modo Spagnolo" ["in the Spanish style"].[55]

The initial care for the preservation of the Alhambra is complicated by Charles V's attempt to juxtapose the Andalusi space with an Italianate Renaissance palace by Pedro Machuca (Figure 1). The palace, begun in 1526 and never finished, is "the most Italianizing building of those carried out in Spain during the first half of the sixteenth century."[56] Its simplicity, "wholly at odd with the Spanish tradition," has been much remarked upon.[57] What is striking about this austere structure is how out of place it seems, not just in the middle of the Alhambra, but when compared with

many of the great palaces built for Spanish noble families in the same period. The almost complete absence of local elements in Machuca's palace
is the exception in a period that saw the increasing importation of Italian
Renaissance elements as an overlay on a Spanish vernacular profoundly
marked by Andalusi forms. Such unusually sober, classicizing buildings in
sixteenth-century Granada, from Charles's palace to the enormous Renaissance cathedral, thus seem meant precisely to stage the Christian triumph
in an architectural context still characterized by Andalusi elements.[58] As
Cammy Brothers notes, "on the site of the Alhambra any style which reflected Islamic influence would have inevitably appeared derivative and
second-rate. Instead, Charles chose to build in the style that presented the
greatest formal contrast with, and cultural challenge to, the Alhambra:
that of the High Renaissance in Rome."[59] Yet even within its alien form,
deliberately chosen to mark an alternative to the Alhambra, there are striking moments of syncretism and adaptation. Nasrid mosaic tile dados from
the Alhambra were adapted for Machuca's patio, incorporating "heraldic
elements from the reign of Emperor Charles I, among them the Nasrid
coat of arms of the kingdom of Granada."[60] Charles's palace could not
simply contrast with the Alhambra, much less erase it; it necessarily participated in the complicated negotiation of memory through built monuments and the craftsmanship that completed them.

Built Memory

Algunas veces se toma memoria por lo que dexan instituído nuestros mayores, por
lo cual tenemos memoria dellos, como hospitales y obras pías. Y estas son las bue-
nas memorias. Otros las dejan en mayorazgos o en suntuosos edificios.[61]

[Sometimes memory means what our elders institute, for which we remember
them, such as hospitals and pious works. And these are good memories. Others
leave them in entailed estates or sumptuous buildings.]

The written arguments for the place of Moors in Spain, such as
Núñez Muley's eloquent plea or the idealized amity of *El Abencerraje*, are
abundantly echoed in the built environment of the sixteenth century.
While there might not be statues commemorating friendship, there is
widespread evidence of a stylistic melding and preservation of the Andalusi
heritage in buildings of all kinds. Buildings made out of brick, with geo-
metrical patterns in stucco, wood carving, and tilework to decorate planar

surfaces had in fact existed throughout the long centuries of Christian expansion, becoming, as many contemporary observers and modern critics have argued, the very essence of Spanish form.[62] The obvious persistence of this style after the fall of Granada suggests how futile were the attempts to erase the memory of al-Andalus's place in Spain. While these gestures were not in most cases an attempt to memorialize Moors, but instead simply the local vernacular, the built environment often reinforced the sense of an Andalusi inheritance as an important component of Spanish architecture.

The art-historical debates over the recognition and characterization of an Andalusi inheritance crystallize around the notion of the *Mudéjar*. In its early nineteenth-century uses, the Mudéjar (a term problematically derived from the medieval Arabic notion of the *mudayyan*, which in turn designated the legal status of those who "stayed behind" after the Christian conquest), referred to the artistic production of Muslims living under Christian rule, starting in the thirteenth century. Thus the widespread production of Mudéjar art and architecture was attributed to actual persons marked by their religion or (after the forced conversions of 1502 and 1526) ethnicity, even though it is so ubiquitous as to strongly beg the question of its makers' ostensible difference.[63] More recent scholarship has sought to focus on the "actual object of inquiry, rather than its supposed origins."[64]

The recognition and conceptualization of the Mudéjar served to contest schematic models of art-historical periodization as they were applied to Spain, in what Rafael López Guzmán calls "transpyrenneic historiographic colonization."[65] The Iberian experience of hybridization and acculturation over the long period of Christian expansion clearly differed radically from what occurred in Northern Europe, so that both its duration and its frequent eclecticism defy traditional periods and styles.[66] Moreover, many critics argue that the Mudéjar is not merely a style like any other, but a much broader and ahistorical *form*. Here the recognition of Spanish difference becomes fetishized into a kind of exceptionalism, with the Mudéjar as a privileged, timeless marker of Spanishness.[67]

Recent work on the Mudéjar has developed a more nuanced understanding of its Iberianness, rejecting both the narrower biographical understanding and the ahistorical "national character" of earlier definitions. Gonzalo Borrás Gualis describes it as a particularly Hispanic, "Reconquista" phenomenon yoked to late medieval tolerance: "In the birth and development of Mudéjar art the fundamental elements are the social ac-

ceptance of the pre-existing Islamic monumental heritage, of the perma-
nence of Moors as a religious minority and of a Hispano-Muslim building
system that will adapt itself to the new functions and needs of a predomi-
nantly Christian society."[68] Nonetheless, Borrás Gualis is careful to note
that the Mudéjar does not end abruptly with the "political process of liqui-
dating the medieval social structure" but instead becomes linked to the
"slow process of sociocultural transformation over the course of the sixteenth century."[69]

While Borrás Gualis's attention to sociocultural factors and his emphasis on gradual transitions are useful, his privileging of a specific political
context—the late medieval tolerance of Muslim minorities in Christian
polities—artificially delimits the Mudéjar. One might argue instead for a
much broader realm of cultural production, not only because, as he himself notes, the Mudéjar does not end with the disappearance of that context, but because much of what is identified as Mudéjar becomes, over the
long period of cultural exchange, fully integrated into local vernaculars, or
what one might call, to recall my discussion in Chapter 1, the architectural
habitus. This seems to be the conclusion of recent scholarship that notes
the prevalence of Mudéjar in a broader chronological and geographical
context, including the New World.[70] López Guzmán goes even farther,
to argue not only that Mudéjar art persists after its original sociopolitical
framework disappears, but that it is adopted by the Catholic kings and the
Hapsburgs as the "expressive medium for a monarchy that is visually uni-
fying its territory." In this view, the Mudéjar does function as an Iberian
style, but in a specific and motivated political context.[71]

Whether we take the narrower definition offered by Borrás Gualis, or
the broader one in López Guzmán, the notion of the Mudéjar usefully
complicates any break in Iberian visual culture at 1492. What art historians
recognize is that even as the Christians expand and consolidate their territories Iberia becomes hybridized, so that the victors at Granada inhabit a
culture profoundly marked by al-Andalus. The Christian advance is not
only a gradual process (and hardly a linear one), but one complicated also
by the converse movement of ideas, fashions, and Andalusi culture more
generally.[72]

The complexity of this process is evinced in buildings throughout
Spain, in a dynamic far more subtle than Charles' superimposition of his
palace on the Alhambra. I want to consider here two noble residences,
one in Seville, one in Guadalajara, to show how generalized was the ongoing use of Andalusi elements in the grandest, most imposing domestic

architecture. This building type presumably follows the height of fashion and is relatively unencumbered by budget constraints. It is also designed to both ensure the comfort of its noble inhabitants and demonstrate their wealth and importance. These palaces' incorporation of Andalusi elements, whether as the local vernacular or as fanciful embellishment, is thus not a matter of necessity but a stylistic preference.

The palace of the Ribera family in Seville, commonly known as the Casa de Pilatos, was built over the course of two centuries, from the late fifteenth to the seventeenth, long after the city had fallen into Christian hands. It presents a fascinating combination of the local vernacular and high Renaissance Italian imports. As López Guzmán describes it, "The closed nature of the building, with the exception of its façade, its organization around courtyards of various sizes, and such decorative elements as the stucco (with Arabic inscriptions) or tile revetments serve as an umbilical cord to its own urban tradition, one that can mix cleanly with the correctness of an imported Renaissance that the court aristocracy adopted as its own"[73] (Figures 2–4). The palace includes a number of meaningful syntheses: panels of typical *azulejos* bordering the family coat of arms, also in tile; a main patio with Andalusi arches above columns of imported Genoese marble, punctuated by Greek and Roman sculpture (most of it added in later periods) and surrounding an Italian fountain, all against a backdrop of more *azulejos* and stucco. Moreover, the various elements do not follow a simple progression of styles: while it is clear that increasing contact with Italy over the course of the sixteenth century led to more Renaissance elements, the local vernacular building continued apace, with thousands upon thousands of tiles, for example, commissioned to decorate the grand and novel staircase.[74] Certain architectural elements seem hybridized in their own right: Vicente Lleó Cañal argues that the curious smooth capitols on the courtyard columns, which were part of a Renaissance remodeling of the earlier space, recall "the simplified pseudo-Nasrid capitols that were so popular in the medieval city [of Seville]."[75] Clearly, for the noble family who built this palace, it was not necessary to leave behind local vernacular forms to signal their cosmopolitanism and familiarity with Italy, much less their Spanishness. Even though the palace was built shortly after the fall of Granada, the new Italian fashion was layered on the enduring backdrop of local style, with no attempt to excise or censor it. The local allegiance of the building was preserved in major design elements and in a multitude of details.[76]

The enduring presence of elements derived from the Andalusi tradi-

Figure 2. Casa de Pilatos, coat of arms among tiles. University of Wisconsin Digital Collections/Casselman Archive.

Figure 3. Casa de Pilatos, patio. University of Wisconsin Digital Collections/ Casselman Archive.

Figure 4. Casa de Pilatos, patio arcade. University of Wisconsin Digital Collections/ Casselman Archive.

Figure 5. Façade, Palacio del Infantado. University of Wisconsin Digital Collections/Casselman Archive.

tion in Spanish building is even more striking outside Andalucía or Valencia, in areas that had been under Christian rule for hundreds of years. Such is the case with the grandiose Palacio del Infantado in Guadalajara, built for a different branch of the same powerful Mendoza family that served as *adelantados* in Granada and as *alcaides* of the Alhambra. The palace, built over the last two decades of the fifteenth century, features a striking façade (Figure 5), with an Arab-derived geometric raised pattern known as *sebka*, a highly ornamented *patio*, extensive use of *muqarnas* ("honeycomb work" in wood or plaster), spectacular *artesonados* (wooden paneled ceilings, most now lost as a result of the bombing of the palace during the Spanish Civil War), and tilework.[77] The principal architects of the palace were the Flemish Juan Guas (Wast) and Egas Cueman. Alí Pullate, named in construction documents as "engeniero moro alarife" (Moorish engineer/master builder Moor) was charged with bringing water to the palace and designing its water features, and a number of Muslim and non-Muslim artisans all contributed their skills.[78]

Thus the "Moorishness" of the Infantado palace has little to do with the North European origins of its principal designers, or, conversely, with an exclusively Moorish population capable of building it. In fact, in Castile as in Andalucía, Spanish buildings included a multitude of Andalusi-derived elements, long after the Moors had lost political control of a particular area. As the sixteenth century progressed, this local vernacular was overlaid with an increasing range of Italianate, Renaissance elements, but the basic style—the use of brick, the intensive decoration of flat surfaces using relatively cheap materials, the organization around more or less elaborate courtyards—remained. Much like the linguistic vernacular, the architectural vernacular was full of Moorish elements.[79] The stylistic hybridization of the Casa de Pilatos and the Palacio del Infantado thus suggests that architecture and material culture more generally might help us rethink the place of Moors in Iberian culture. While grandiose Italianate architecture in Granada and other sites might have served as a way to mark the Christian triumph, the norm in much of Spain was to build in a local style that, however silently, abundantly recalled the presence of Moors in Spain, whatever Renaissance elements might complement it.

The crux of the matter, of course, lies in the question of the buildings' silence. The Christian owners of these buildings were not setting out to memorialize Moors, although carpenters and builders were well aware of the need to preserve traditional techniques.[80] Patrons and craftsmen alike would probably have argued that their buildings were purely Spanish. Yet when the built landscape so clearly reflects the Moorish inheritance that was loudly rejected by sixteenth-century officialdom, we seem to have something like an unwitting or paradoxical *lieu de mémoire*.[81] If anyone imbued it with meaning as "Moorish," it was foreign travelers, who saw in this architectural habitus another sign of Spain's difference, much like the quotidian practices I discussed in Chapter 1. Thus the buildings' implicit rebuke of histories that marginalized or erased the Moors would primarily be apparent to outsiders who constructed the Spain their ideology demanded. And yet beyond the Andalusi disposition manifested in these buildings, there is some degree of agency at work. The same discursive and political context, in Spain and abroad, that led to the use of classicizing Renaissance styles in Granada to signal the Christian triumph indicates a certain self-consciousness about the built environment, as does the explicit advocacy of Núñez Muley or the recuperative efforts of master builders who attempted to preserve traditional techniques. The work of such practical conservators as Diego López de Arenas, whose 1633 book on carpentry set out to document what he saw as local tradition in Seville in the form of a Renaissance treatise, gives a sense of the multiple investments here. Side by side with the deliberate appropriation of Greco-Roman cultures in Italy, and subsequently in Spain, the preservation and continuation of Andalusi-derived building was an important local priority.[82]

In assessing the meanings of the built environment, it is problematic,

I submit, to make too trenchant a distinction between texts and material culture. After all, the latter is often textualized and imbued with self-consciousness, agency, and those other qualities we ascribe to texts. The historian Mariana, with whom I began this chapter, includes in his account of the conquest of Granada a fascinating narrative, also present in Fernando del Pulgar's chronicle,[83] of the imbrication of the textual and the material. Mariana relates how the Count of Tendilla (later Münzer's host at Granada) uses a painted "lienzo" (cloth) to cover a gap in the walls of Alhama, buying the Christians time to repair it. He also produces scrip to pay the soldiers, circulating "moneda de cartones" (cardboard money) with his signature on one side and its value on the other.[84] In both cases, which Mariana himself connects, the textual supplements the material in the service of Christian goals. Thus to assume an absolute distinction between an ineffable or fragile material culture and significant, enduring texts—as Mariana's own preface would have us do—unduly privileges the latter at the expense of the former.

The official project of erasing the Moors from Spain is countered by a genre that includes both material artifacts—the monumental Alhambra, but also myriad Mudéjar buildings—and texts, such as the *Abencerraje* or Núñez Muley's plea, that participate in their memorialization. As the frame of *El Abencerraje* argues, the proper commemoration of a Spanish past that includes many *empresas generosas* between Moors and Christians must necessarily involve an acknowledgement of Moors and their culture. This maurophile genre in itself becomes a *lieu de mémoire*, writing the Moors all over Spain, from the continuing syncretism of the built environment to the cultural and military struggles of the sixteenth century.

3

The Moorish Fashion

. . . los castellanos, lejos de sentir repulsión hacia los
pocos musulmanes refugiados en su último reducto de
Granada, se sintieron atraídos hacia aquella exótica civili-
zación, aquel lujo oriental en el vestuario, aquella esplén-
dida ornamentación de los edificios, aquella extraña
manera de vida, aquel modo de cabalgar, de armarse y de
combatir, aquella esmerada agricultura en la vega granadina . . . la maurofilia, en fin, se hizo moda.

 —Ramón Menéndez Pidal, *España y su historia*

[the Castilians, far from feeling any repulsion toward the
few Muslims taking refuge in their last holdout of Granada, felt attracted toward that exotic civilization, that
oriental luxury of dress, that splendid ornament in the
buildings, that strange way of life, that mode of riding,
arming oneself, and fighting, that painstaking agriculture
in the plain of Granada . . . Maurophilia, in sum, became
fashionable.]

Tanta Zaida y Adalifa,
Tanta Draguta y Darafa,
Tanto Azarque y tanto Adulce,
Tanto Gazul y Abenámar;
Tanto alquicer y marlota
Tanto almaizar y almalafa,
Tantas empresas y plumas,
Tantas cifras y medallas;
Tanta ropería mora,
Y en banderillas y adargas
Tanto mote y tantas motas,
¡Muera yo si no me cansan!

[So much Zaida and Adalifa, so much Draguta and Darafa, so much Azarque and so much Adulce, so much
Gazul and Abenámar; so much *alquicer* and *marlota*, so

much *almaizar* and *almalafa*, so many devices and feath-
ers, so many ciphers and medals, so much trade in Moorish clothing; and, on *banderillas* and shields, so many
mottos and flecks, they'll be the death of me!]

THERE IS AN IMPLICIT TENSION in the philologist Ramón Menéndez
Pidal's well-known account of literary maurophilia. While the critic rightly
recognizes the profound hybridization of Iberian culture, he nonetheless
describes the relation between Christian and Moorish forms as an uncon-
summated "attraction" to a civilization cordoned off in Granada. By describing maurophilia as a fashion, moreover, he delimits its effects,
reinscribing the exoticism dislodged by his initial account of the Spanish
familiarity and fascination with all things Moorish, in much the same way
as does the satiric ballad that is my second epigraph. Moreover, Menéndez
Pidal's contradictory passage is itself part of a much longer discussion of
maurophilia in which he provides evidence of such a long-term engagement between Christians and Moors that the notion of a momentary fashion seems increasingly insufficient. From this vantage point, the loud
complaints of the ballad are most striking for their effort to circumscribe
Moorishness to a literary vogue.

This chapter explores the problem of the "Moorish fashion" in Spain
in two registers: first, I trace the long-term Christian fascination with
Moorish attire to counter the notion of temporary maurophile attach-
ments in Spanish dress. Clothing thus serves as a case study for analyzing
what is at stake in the various characterizations of Iberian culture as
marked by a Moorish *fashion* rather than a more profound *hybridization*.
Second, I demonstrate that the characterization of maurophile ballads that
thematize the shared sartorial culture as themselves a mere fashion obeys
a similar dynamic, serving to diminish the ideological import of the genre.
In both cases "fashion," in the sense of fad, indicates a temporary, chance
attachment in opposition to a longstanding familiarity or interaction. For
purposes of this chapter, then, I consider fashion not as the complex semiotic system of rapidly changing dress that it represents in our more recent
critical understanding, but as it has been used in evaluating maurophilia:
as a reductive alternative to a more sustained engagement with Moorish
costume and custom.[1] While it is clear that a cultural phenomenon such
as the *romancero morisco* resonates in a particular time and place, the assumption that its popularity has no deeper significance because it is a
vogue is deeply problematic. As I will argue, while the contemporary sa-

tiric responses to maurophile poetry attempt to write it off as a tiresome
fashion, their loud protestations have occluded the much more complex
relationship between that corpus and the contemporary debates on the
place of Moorishness, and Moriscos, within Spain.

Moorish Habits

Although there is no Spanish equivalent for the resonant term *fashion*,
connoting as it does in English the permanent making of subjects as well
as their temporary attire,[2] early modern Spain nonetheless obsessed over
how dress fashioned those who wore it and, particularly, how the luxury
and variety of Spanish costume conspired against a solid national identity.
Sartorial change seems to have accelerated in Spain in the sixteenth century, as it did elsewhere in Europe.[3] Historian Fernández de Oviedo noted
in his old age:

desde que ove treze años hasta estar en éste, que corren 1555 años, podría testificar
de muchas mudanzas e trajes, pues ha 77 años que he que vivo; y aunque algún
tiempo anduve por otros reynos fuera de España, entre ninguna nasçión vi tantas
ni tan espesas vezes mudar los trajes como entre nuestra nasçión.[4]

[from the time when I was thirteen to this year of 1555, I could attest to many
changes and costumes, for I have lived for 77 years; and although I traveled for
some time through kingdoms beyond Spain, among no other nation did I see
costume change so much or so often as among ours.]

While changeability seems to have been a widely shared European preoccupation, Spain in particular evinced a complex relation to Moorish fashions. Moorish costume was pervasive yet largely unremarked, in part
because of its quotidian nature. Conversely, when Andalusi-derived garments used for special occasions were recognized as such they were often
prized for their elegance and splendor. As I noted in Chapter 1, historians
of costume have found a marked preference for Andalusi textiles on the
part of Christian élites already in the thirteenth century, suggesting a long-
term pattern of use. The move from textiles to specific Moorish garments
widely adopted by Christians is charted in the descriptive accounts of Carmen Bernís Madrazo, Ruth Matilda Anderson, and Rachel Arié, and, more
recently, in the incisive reevaluation by María Judith Feliciano Chaves.[5]
These critics all find evidence of such transfers in royal and aristocratic

inventories as well as in artistic representations and travelers' accounts. Obviously, Christian attire also influenced what Moors wore, both in an earlier age, and, through forced acculturation, in the sixteenth century.[6]

The remarkable range of Moorish garments adopted by Christians in the late medieval and early modern periods includes everything from *chapines* (chopines, early modern women's high platform shoes) and *borceguíes* (buskins, laced half-boots) to *tocas de camino* (headdresses very similar to turbans). Bernís has traced the wide acceptance of Moorish fashions among Christians in Spain, both before and after 1492, noting the gradual dissemination of Moorish costume through a widening swath of society. Some garments may initially have been adopted as fashionable by the upper classes, who prized the quality of Moorish textiles and often wore them for ceremonial occasions, but items such as the *toca* were eventually worn by plain folk in the Castilian countryside.

In Spain, such a headdress was hardly exotic. The *toca de camino* was virtually, Bernís claims, "un tocado nacional"[7] ["a national headdress"]. Initially adopted in the mid-fifteenth century, by the early 1600s it had become widespread. The Flemish courtier Laurent Vital, in his chronicle of the future Charles V's first trip to Spain (1517–18), describes the *toca* of a peasant, perhaps resembling that depicted by Christopher Weiditz in his 1529 *Tractenbuch* (Figure 6).[8] The headwrap Vital describes is both old-fashioned and common:

Ce bon viellard, au moyen de son accoustrement, sembloit estre l'ung des trois roys qui vindrent adorer nostre sauveur Jésus, en tel arroy estoit triumphamment venu. Il estoit tocquiet par la teste à la mode turquoyse ou judayque que Turcqz et Sarrazins se coiffent: c'est un habillement de teste qui se torteille, tout de linge, entour de la teste, comme en Castille on souloit user: mais à présent il s'y délaisse fort, si ce ne sont les anchiens, qui envys délaissent leurs anchiennes costumes et manières de faire, comme j'ay vu par dechà aulcuns anchiens entretenir les souliers à poulaine, ainsy font les aulcuns ces tocques. . . . Je ay veu plusieurs gens campestres en porter.[9]

[This good old man, by his costume, seemed like one of the three kings who came to adore our savior Jesus, so triumphantly was he dressed. His head was covered in the Turkish or Jewish fashion that Turks and Saracens use: it is a headdress wound several times around the head, all made of cloth, such as they used to wear in Castile, but now it is largely abandoned, except for the old people, who regretfully leave their ancient customs and ways of doing things; just as I have seen [in our country] some old people wearing their *poulaine* shoes, so do some of these with this headdress. . . . I have seen many country people wearing it.]

Figure 6. Peasant with *toca*, Christopher Weiditz, *Tractenbuch von 1529*, f. 19. Germanisches Nationalmuseum Nürnberg.

Strikingly, Vital's primary frame of reference for the *toca morisca* is the conventional artistic representation of the exotic Three Kings.[10] Thus the Castilian custom, albeit on its way out, is conflated with all manner of "oriental" garb: Turkish, Jewish, and Saracen. Vital's observation is as telling for its temporal specificity as for its geographical imprecision: although he stresses that the custom is increasingly abandoned, it nonetheless serves to connect Spain with an exotic East. Moreover, despite his impression, the *toca* had not lost its aristocratic associations: in a contemporary Italian travel account it is worn not by an anonymous peasant but by the marquis of Villena.[11] The quotidian, old-fashioned headdress both marks the survival of Moorish culture within Spain well into the sixteenth century— Bernís finds evidence of its use into the 1540s—and feeds into the European construction of an exoticized Spain. Despite the analogy to the "anchiens" Vital has seen "par dechà," Spain remains suspended between alterity and the familiar.

The *toca* was also commonly worn in the New World, where its representation led to much confusion about the presence of actual Moriscos. Feliciano highlights the striking depiction in the 1550's *Codex Yanhuitlán*, from New Spain, of Don Gonzalo de las Casas, heir to his father's Mixteca *encomienda*, in an elaborate headwrap (Figure 7).[12] Because historians cannot easily account for this "exotic" garment on normative Spaniards in the Americas, Feliciano explains, they assume the proximity of religious others from what is actually fully Iberian wear, or, alternatively, a depiction mediated by exoticizing European images. Yet, as her abundant visual and archival evidence demonstrates, *tocas* and other Andalusi-derived garments, often luxuriously made, served in the New World to distinguish a colonialist Spanish élite from the mass of indigenous peoples.[13]

Bernís emphasizes also the long-term use of the *marlota*, the ceremonial cloak regularly worn for *juegos de cañas* and other entertainments, from the fifteenth into the seventeenth century,[14] suggesting a much broader span than mere "fashion" would imply. Moreover, if, as Feliciano argues, the *marlota* is essentially the same garment as the *jubón*, then its use far transcends ceremonial occasions to become absolutely quotidian for both men and women: "Sartorial items commonly called 'Morisco,' therefore, oscillated between the realms of Iberian clothing (daily wear) and costume (theatrical, performance-oriented), depending on the wearers, the circumstances and the intended audience."[15] Despite such long-term and widespread uses, there is a marked tension in both Bernís's and Anderson's accounts between the recognition of Moorish influence on

Figure 7. *Encomendero* Don Francisco de las Casas and his son Don Gonzalo. Plate 7 from 1550s *Codex Yanhuitlán*, New Spain. Biblioteca José María Lafragua, Benemérita Universidad Autónoma de Puebla, México.

costume and the desire to quarantine that influence.[16] Anderson has a short separate section on "Moorish garments" for each sex, even though it is clear that such items as *camisas* (chemises) or, more broadly, patterns of embroidery and silkwork far exceed such limited categories.[17] Bernís, for her part, is careful to insist that, whatever the Moorish influence, Spanish dress was nonetheless "essentially European"; Moorish garments were exceptional. Yet she, too, recognizes the broader influence on female drawers (*zaragüelles*, from the Arabic *sarawil*) and chemises.[18]

Clearly, the work of these historians identifies both continuity and change. Certain garments—*zaragüelles, camisa, marlota, chapines*—and techniques, such as embroidery and silkwork, have a long life beyond fashionable variations in use (Figures 8 and 9). More significant than the Moorish fashion—changing styles both in al-Andalus and in Christian appropriation—is the habitus that underlies such variation.[19] As I argued in Chapter 1, this habitual recourse to what were originally Andalusi forms is endemic to medieval and early modern Iberian culture. Whatever changes in dress fashion might entail, they occur against the larger backdrop of a sustained and profound cultural hybridization. Thus my goal here is to problematize the idea of fashion and taste as temporary or individual alternatives to hybridity.

Sociologists such as Pierre Bourdieu have analyzed taste for its role in social distinction, and demonstrated that it is both contextual and contingent on class.[20] This "cultural-functionalist" model of taste, as Marcy Norton terms it, fully recognizes its socially constructed nature, whereas opposing models tend to foreground a subjective ethos.[21] In standard accounts of Spanish dress, the taste for Moorish clothing appears precisely as this subjective choice, based on a temporary predilection. Thus understood, "fashion" assumes that Christians fully choose to take on Moorish ways, and can choose to stop. Dressing as a Moor becomes a kind of performative costume that is as easily and deliberately put on as taken off. Borrowing from both Bourdieu and Norton, I propose instead a Moorish sartorial habitus that is both "autonomous and contingent," made up of "embodied habits and aesthetic dispositions" that transcend a particular moment and do not align themselves easily with ideological shifts.[22] Obviously, certain styles and garments are embraced at particular times, but other borrowings operate on a much longer, less fully conscious and more habitual continuum.[23] While fashion may be capricious and apparently unmotivated, that is, the sartorial habitus finds its explanation in the long-term historical and political circumstances of Iberia. As Bourdieu usefully

Figure 8. *Marlota*, Abraham van Bruyn. *Diversarum Gentium Armatura Equestris*, 1578. Anne S. K. Brown Military Collection, Brown University Library.

Figure 9. *Chapines*, Christopher Weiditz, *Tractenbuch von 1529*, f. 23. Germanisches Nationalmuseum Nürnberg.

notes in *The Logic of Practice*, "The habitus, a product of history, produces individual and collective practices—more history—in accordance with the schemes generated by history" (54). From this vantage point, the characterization of Moorishness as a mere fashion within Spanish dress appears as a post facto attempt to circumscribe its broader influence.

The reiterated legislation against Moorish dress in early modern Spain suggests how complex is the place of this sartorial habitus. The prohibitions return repeatedly to items that are worn by Castilian nobles and marginalized Moriscos alike. Items that were or would be forbidden appear in the royal inventories of Isabel and Charles V, as well as in those of many nobles, and, as I discuss in greater detail in Chapter 4, they are routinely sported by Spanish royals on ceremonial occasions.[24] Perhaps the clearest example of an oppositional stance to Moors that does not imply any refusal of Andalusi-derived wear is the chronicler Andrés de Bernáldez's detailed description of Isabel's arrival at Illora, during the war on Granada, which I discussed briefly in Chapter 2. The queen's appearance at the Christian camp is a momentous occasion, involving great ceremony. The dress of the royals is striking for the preponderance of Andalusi-derived garments and techniques. The queen wears "un capuz de grana vestido guarnecido, morisco" ["a Moorish embroidered red cloak"] and the Infanta's *capuz* echoes "la guarnición del de la reina" ["the Queen's embroidery"]. Fernando, for his part, "tenía vestido un jubón de clemesín de pelo, con quixote de seda rasa amarillo . . . e una espada morisca ceñida, muy rica, e una toca e un sonbrero" ["wore a fur and damask doublet, with a yellow silk jerkin . . . and a very rich Moorish sword, hung, and a headwrap and a hat"].[25] As Feliciano notes for a slightly later context, "when associated with or displayed by powerful members of society, the foremost symbols of orthodox Iberian Catholicism and imperial authority, Morisco clothing ceased to be "Islamic" and became "royal.""[26] Of course, as the scare quotes recognize, they were never "Islamic" in the first place, and bore no relation to religious practice.[27]

As the guarantees of religious and cultural protection offered the Moors at Granada were abandoned over the course of the sixteenth century, the repression of the Moriscos increasingly targeted their clothing.[28] Yet garments such as the *marlota* were proudly worn for aristocratic celebrations well into the seventeenth century. Moreover, the legislation did not target the pervasive presence of Andalusi-derived wear among Christians—those garments were too fully incorporated to signal any kind of difference or threat. *Chapines* and *tocas*, not to speak of "Moorish" embroidery, were essentially unmarked. What was targeted, in a clear sign of the continuing force of local acculturation, was the use of *almalafas* (Moorish cloaks) by Old Christian women in Granada. The law passed by Queen Juana, in 1513, specifically focuses on the bad example that this reverse acculturation sets for the newly converted, and on the immoral behavior that these women attempt to disguise behind their cloaks.[29] Strikingly, a whole series of laws passed in the city of Baza from 1524–25 forbids women from covering their faces with cloaks (*mantos*), but there is no sense that Moriscas are the particular target here, nor is the Moorish term *almalafa* used.[30]

In a later period, when partial veiling became fashionable for Spanish women, its Moorish origins were recognized, but the history of its repression for ethnic reasons seemed forgotten. Thus the jurist Antonio León Pinelo, in his well-known 1641 treatise on veils, compared the evident adoption of Andalusi face-covering to the incorporation of Arabic words into Spanish.[31] Spanish women, Pinelo notes, had fully appropriated the veil: "Y es que el tapado de medio ojo, como uso árabe, entró en España, o se introdujo más, con las árabes, y que de ellas ha quedado hasta hoy en las españolas, ya por tan propio suyo, que no hay mujeres con más afición, donaire y aseo, le usen"[32] ["Half-veiling, as an Arab usage, came to Spain, or was further introduced, by Arab women, and from them Spanish women have it to this day, now as so much their own, that no women wear it with greater liking, grace, and tidiness"]. When the fashionable *tapado* was censored, in a series of decrees between 1586 and 1639, it seems to have been targeted primarily for the cover it afforded women who used it to negotiate public spaces.

Overall, legislation in the period suggests both a stigmatization of Moorish dress and a striking lack of concern for many hybridized and incorporated items. Aristocratic practices also seem to have continued unabated, even though certain garments used in the *juegos de cañas* and other celebrations, such as the *marlota*, were specifically forbidden by law.[33] Perhaps the most interesting testament to the contradictory relationship Christians had to Moorish clothing, as alternately a sign of otherness and a coveted luxury item, is an account of the Christian looting of Morisco possessions as the latter were expelled from Valencia in 1609. Despite the radicalization of anti-Morisco feeling in the period immediately before the expulsion, and the frequent metaphors of filth and contagion applied to these marginalized subjects, their trappings retained their appeal. As the Moriscos were shipped out, their clothes and household goods were sold at bargain prices, which drew a massive crowd of Valencians to the port: "se hazia alli vna feria muy barata de vestidos riquissimos a la Morisca, de camas, pauellones, sauanas, toallas labradas de oro, camisas hechas a las mil marauillas, pieças de lienço finissimo, con otras muchas cosas, y quien tenia dinero, a poca costa boluia para su casa, rico destas alhajas"[34] ["they held there a very cheap fair of extremely rich clothes in the Moorish style, beds, tents, sheets, towels worked in gold, wonderfully made shirts, very fine pieces of linen, with many other things, and whoever had money, at small expense returned home rich with these jewels"]. As this admission makes clear, Moorish items remained objects of desire even when their owners, literally expelled from the body politic, were most abject.

What are the implications for literary history of the complex Christian relationship to Moorish dress? As I hope to have shown, the assumption that maurophilia—in any register—is a mere fashion fails to account for the long-term, habitual nature of a shared culture. It also fails to get at the intimacy, rather than exoticization, that characterizes such borrowings. The intricacy of Spain's relationship to "Moorishness" in the material realm suggests one avenue for reconsidering literary maurophilia, conventionally dismissed as a voguish genre largely devoid of any ideological import. As I demonstrate here, when the most "fashionable" of all maurophile productions, the late sixteenth-century ballads known as the *romancero morisco*, is reconceived as the fully political expression of a vexed yet shared culture, it yields new and revelatory meanings. Moreover, these poems' thematization of dress has often been understood as a trade in exoticism. Yet if we recognize within them the conflicted yet proximate relationship to Moorish dress that I have charted above, our sense of the cultural work they perform becomes very different.

Romances à clef

As I noted in the introduction to this study, the *maurophilie littéraire* proposed by Georges Cirot circumscribes the fascination with Moorish culture to a literary phenomenon, dismissing it as a fashion unrelated or frankly contrary to historical events.[35] This same impetus lies behind the diminutive *novelita morisca*, the term used by some critics to delimit as a *divertissement* or trifle the entire genre of pointedly political texts I discuss elsewhere in this study: *El Abencerraje, Guerras civiles de Granada,* and the story of Ozmín and Daraja. Yet a few scholars, most notably María

Soledad Carrasco Urgoiti, have recognized full well the larger significance of maurophilia.[36] As Ramón Menéndez Pidal pointed out more than fifty years ago in his *España y su historia*, the broad pervasiveness of the "Moorish fashion" and its larger implications for understanding early modern Spain cry out for further study.[37]

The *romancero morisco* was undeniably a fashionable genre: in the first part of the *Flor de varios romances nuevos*, a collection of "modern" ballads published in nine parts between 1589 and 1597, fully 40 percent of the poems dealt with Moorish topics, although the proportion gradually diminished after that.[38] Paradoxically, its meteoric success has obviated questions of its historical significance, as critics reiterate the claim of an inexplicable fascination. While there is a huge body of philological scholarship on this *romancero*, it is only in the work of such critics as Carrasco Urgoiti that its ideological filiations have begun to be explored.[39] When this particular corpus is relocated within a longer tradition of Spanish writing on the Moors, I submit, its connection to a *longue durée* of positive depictions, and its own political topicality—as opposed to unmotivated vogue—becomes visible. As more recent criticism recognizes, "the literary fashion of Moorishness was based on a social reality,"[40] even if its relationship to that reality was far more complex than simple mimesis.

In his own broad discussion of literary maurophilia, Menéndez Pidal notes that it by no means depends on the defeat of the Moors. The earliest medieval *cantares de gesta* and *romances* evince a sympathetic view of an enemy with whom Christians frequently allied, and with whom they lived. Yet Menéndez Pidal feels obliged to distinguish the earlier *romances*, whose historicity he accepts, from the newer ones, which he resolutely presents as mere vehicles for poetic expression by "los más señalados poetas de nuestros siglos de oro"[41] ["the most famous poets of our Golden Age"]. Thus these later ballads bear a complex relationship to their predecessors, the *romances fronterizos* of the late fifteenth century. The *fronterizos* are generally recognized as historical, topical, and epic; the *moriscos* are dismissed as lyrical trifles, showcases for Moorish regalia and chivalric pomp with no connection to the great national enterprise of the Reconquista. Yet as any survey of the *fronterizos* will reveal, they are abundantly concerned with love as well as war, and often idealize relations between Moors and Christians. More important, even if the critical commonplace is basically true—the Moors of the latter corpus are much more concerned with love and panoply than with war—this does not make the poems ideologically weightless, "lighter" fare. In fact, it is partly the somewhat arbitrary separation of the later corpus from its earlier avatars that threatens to render it meaningless, or significant only for its topical references to the lives of its authors. I will suggest that the *romancero morisco* need not deal explicitly with the Reconquista to make its political point; on the contrary, the very avoidance of the subject may be its most striking ideological feature, one abundantly noted by its contemporary critics.

As Menéndez Pidal's distinction suggests, the problem of the *romancero morisco*'s personae and that of its historicity are intricately connected. While these ballads were generally anonymous, it is well known that Lope de Vega in particular was responsible for several of the most famous examples, including "Mira, Zaide," and "Ensíllenme el potro ruzio," poems whose most immediate referents were his erotic misfortunes. Critics then assume that when Lope writes in the voice of a Moor in these *romances à clef*, he is simply in a kind of Moorish drag that has no ideological significance and functions in exactly the same way as the pastoral guise he adopts elsewhere. But the meaning of poetic texts that operate within such a long and rich popular tradition, and which are themselves transmitted at a furious pace both orally and through print circulation, cannot be limited to their most proximate referentiality.

The historicity of the *romancero morisco* is often dismissed by invoking the fanciful claims of Ginés Pérez de Hita, whose hugely influential account of the fall of Granada, *Guerras civiles de Granada* (1595) incorporates ballads both old and new, building a pseudohistorical narrative around them. In his text, the poems paradoxically underwrite the historical truth of a narrative they in fact inspire, with repeated claims that "Y por esto se dixo aquel sentido y antiguo romance, que dize . . ."[42] ["And because of this, this old and well-known ballad was recited, which goes . . ."]. Pérez de Hita's novel, which I discuss in more detail in Chapter 4, may be far from historical, and his use of the romances is highly fanciful, yet his recourse to them to construct a sympathetic Moorish culture is telling. For this author, the *romancero morisco* signifies something more than gossip on the love-lives of Lope et al. Although the ballads are not historical in their invocation of actual events, they necessarily reference the larger Spanish debates about the place of Moors and Moorish culture in Spain.

When this broader notion of historical referentiality is ignored, the question why Lope and other poets would so frequently choose a Moorish voice, a mere generation after the extraordinarily violent War of the Alpujarras (1568–71) against the Moriscos, goes begging. There are several possible explanations, all with political implications. First, as this chapter and the next argue, there is a particularly Spanish connection between Moorishness and aristocratic, chivalric culture—the culture of the *juegos de cañas*, riding *a la jineta*, and all the practices Christians learned from the Moors. To speak of the idealization of Moors in these poems as post facto praise of a defeated foe, aimed primarily at glorifying the Christian Spanish conquerors by association, evades the very real and ongoing Spanish indebtedness to Moorish culture.

Second, and perhaps more important, there seems to be, for authors as for readers, a real *jouissance* in consuming Moorish bodies. Rather than emphasizing bodily difference, these ballads foreground the pleasure to be found in the Moors. The genre suggests the possibility of a highly enjoyable, idealizing identification that is very different from the staging of otherness in European representations of an Islamic East outside the Spanish context. Although often it is the *mora*, as love object, who is eroticized, the male lover is also depicted in a highly aestheticized fashion, so that the male reader's pleasure in such figures approximates the destabilizing erotic thralldom of Narváez and his squires that I noted in *El Abencerraje*. The intense enjoyment of these identifications is perhaps clearest in Luis de Góngora's three poems on "El Español de Orán," which feature a Spanish soldier in the *presidio* who is in love with an "African," and who, in the third poem, releases the Moor he captures because he so sympathizes with the Moor's love for his own Moorish lady. If the third poem essentially reprises the main plot of *El Abencerraje*, the backstory is fascinating: in this version, the Spaniard can imagine the other's love only too well because he, too, loves an African lady.[43] Although, as Israel Burshatin has argued for the earlier novella, the Spaniard here also retains the upper hand, the erotic identification is striking. The multiple encounters and subject-positions in such ballads suggest that there is no easy distinction to be made across the corpus between a "European" self and an "Oriental" other, as in the theories of forsaken *jouissance* proposed by Mladen Dolar and Alain Grosrichard.[44] Instead, this *romancero* forces us to recognize how different the situation is for Spain from that of the rest of Europe, given the pervasiveness and familiarity of Moorish culture.

Neither the Saidian version of orientalism, in which the distance between self and other is crucial for the construction of European superiority, nor the Lacanian version of Dolar and Grosrichard fully accounts for the intimacy of these texts. While the *romances* may seem orientalizing in some respects, particularly in the heightened eroticism and luxury of the more conventional representations, they often undermine the Foucauldian ordering that seems so central to our usual understanding of orientalism. In part, this is because, although orientalism may well characterize the later reception of these depictions elsewhere in Europe, it is the wrong lens for considering the cultural proximity that characterized Spanish readers' relation to Moorish culture. It was instead a much more intimate exchange, predicated on a shared material culture. Thus, the ostensible other is not just given voice in a gesture of ventriloquism, he or she is fully *inhabited*. It would be naïve to assume that this identificatory *jouissance* has no political ramifications, in that so much of the anti-Morisco rhetoric of the period depends on the crassest othering, emphasizing the filth and contagious rot of the ostracized group. As is clear from the scene of the sale in Valencia that I cited above, the desire for clothing and other material artifacts whose worth was amply recognized by both Christians and Moors profoundly destabilized any rhetoric that attempted to ostracize the Moriscos.

I offer these rationales to suggest that Góngora or Lope's choice of subject, as that of their contemporaries, is not unmotivated. (Clearly, the tremendous popularity of the first poems immediately reinforces their maurophile tendencies.) Yet there are also political effects that do not necessarily depend on authorial motivation, and that have an impact regardless of the basic apolitical stance of the post-adolescent, lovelorn balladeer into which critics have made the maurophile Lope. In part, these ideological effects depend on the resonance of the Morisco problem in the period. Thus, in "Mira, Zaide que te aviso," Lope describes the hero's banishment from the presence of his beloved, with a highly conventional "que no pases por mi calle"[45] ["I warn you, Zaide, do not come by my street"]. The immediate autobiographical referent, as is well known, is Lope's exile from Castile in 1588 for his poison-pen attacks on Elena Osorio, the lover who had spurned him, and her family. As Menéndez Pidal noted long ago, Lope's judicial sentence specified "que de aquí adelante *no pase por la calle* donde viven las dichas mujeres"[46] ["that he no longer go by the street where the said women live"]. But in the satirical ballad "Háganme vuestras mercedes," a mordant response to Lope's inordinately popular poem, the lover's punishment is more clearly recognizable as exile, and thus echoes more closely the position of the historical Morisco subject, ostracized by maurophobia.

"Háganme vuestras mercedes" begins by listing all the trades who repeat Lope's verse: the apothecary, the tailor, the sailor all tell Zaide "que no pase por su calle."[47] Even the *buñoleros* [doughnut-sellers] "aunque son de su linaje" ["although they are of his own lineage"], that is, Moriscos like him, send him away. The *romance*'s very popularity, its geographical and social ubiquity, transform the beloved's interdiction into a more general banishment for the Moor. The poem then voices a plaintive complaint about his displacement:

¿Qué tiene este triste moro?
¿Está tocado de landre,
que así desterralle quieren
de todas las vecindades?

. . . .
¿Adónde ha de ir el cuitado
pues en el mundo no cabe?
Que tengo sospecha y miedo
no vaya a desesperarse.
Merezca el humilde moro
que su destierro se acabe,
que quien de humilde se venga,
humilde venganza hace.

[What is wrong with this sorry Moor?
Does he have a touch of plague,
That he is banished thus
From all neighborhoods?
. . . .
Where is this afflicted one to go,
Since he does not fit in the world?
I suspect and fear
He may take his own life.
May the humble Moor
Deserve an end to his banishment,
For he who takes revenge on the lowly
Takes a lowly revenge.]

In 1609, of course, exile would be Spain's violent solution to the problem of acculturating the Moriscos, leading to such paradoxical moments of cultural (be)longing as the scene in Valencia. Long before the general banishment, however, the Crown punished Morisco uprisings with forcible relocation within Spain. In 1570, as a result of the uprising in the Alpujarras, the Moriscos of Granada had been expelled from their homes and dispersed throughout Castile. Moreover, as L. P. Harvey notes, the decision to expel the Moors entirely from Spain had first been broached in the 1580s, although its execution was postponed while it continued to be debated.[48] In this apparently light-hearted ballad, Lope's metaphorics of exile thus reverberate with concurrent political debates about how to solve the Morisco question, and what claim, if any, these subjects had on a Spanish identity.

An even darker subtext appears in the exchange between the conventional *romances* that peddle Moorish trappings to their audiences and the satirical ballads that literalize the "trade" in Moors. The popular *romances* clearly capitalize on the Spanish fascination with Moorish wear, not only describing the *marlotas, tocas* and other garments of Andalusi provenance but also overlaying them with a complex apparatus of classicizing emblems and mottos. One of the best examples (and the ripest for parody) is "En la más terrible noche," in which the Moor Maniloro wears no less than eight "cansadas divisas" ["tired emblems"] on his arms, clothes, and jewelry. In the parodic version of this ballad, the humble protagonist gradually takes off and uses his adornments, eating the spears of wheat, riding the unicorn, and selling off everything else.[49] Because much of the appeal of the *romances* seems to depend on these trappings, satirists have a field day dismantling "tanta ropería mora"[50] ["so much Moorish wear"]: in "Colérico sale Muza," the Moor complains of how much his back aches from wearing what the poets put on him, as they pile on color after color till he resembles a "tapete de Levante"[51] ["Levantine rug"].

In the more biting "Quién compra diez y seis moros," the *madrileño* Gabriel Lasso de la Vega offers the fine Moors of the *romances* for sale as slaves, with the added advantage that their owner may also sell their ornate clothes, as depicted in the ballads, for a tidy sum:

—Yo quiero comprar dos dellos
que leña del monte traigan,
y escogeré dos Alcaydes
pues que tan baratos andan;
las marlotas venderé
de damasco azul y plata,
que me escusará, a lo menos,
el tomar una mohatra,
y a un hombre que alquila hatos
el Corpus para las danzas,
venderé toca, y turbante,
los datilados y manga;
dexarelos en pelota,
pues con unas alpargatas

y un zaragüelle de angeo
tendrán al fin lo que basta.[52]

[I want to buy two of them
To bring wood from the forest,
And I will choose two governors,
Since they are going so cheap.
I will sell the *marlotas*
Of blue and silver damask,
And I should be forgiven
For taking more than they're worth.
And the headwrap and turban,
The date-colored ones, and the embroidered sleeve,
I'll sell to a man who on Corpus
Rents out costumes for dances.
I'll leave them naked,
For with some sandals
And burlap drawers
They will have enough.]

Although the Moriscos imagined here are so abject that they are being sold off as slaves, their clothes still fetch a pretty price. Lasso de la Vega's attempt to satirize the appeal of the Morisco ballads unwittingly recalls the shared investment in an Andalusi-derived culture that, one might argue, is part of what makes the genre so appealing in the first place. The rhetorical effort to circumscribe Moorish wear to costume rented for Corpus Christi fails, given that other, unspecified buyers are invoked first, and also begs the question of the attraction of Moorish costume in the first place.[53] Moreover, despite the poem's odium, the Moriscos are hardly exotic here: deprived of their luxurious dress, they are reduced to the same *zaragüelles* and *alpargatas* that any dispossessed or rural Christian might wear. If the garments they once wore were desirable to a Christian audience who share a taste for them, the ones they are left with belong to a much more modest but nonetheless shared Moorish habitus.

To make the irony more acute, the new Morisco slaves will entertain their master with the *romancero* material:

Contaránme del Invierno
las noches prolijas, largas,
los asaltos de Jaén
y los combates de Baza,
la muerte de Reduán

y los amores de Audalla,
con el destierro de Muza,
porque el Rey quiso a su dama,
y tras esto dormirán
en el pajar con dos mantas.[54]

[They will narrate to me
On long, lingering winter nights,
The assault on Jaén
And the battles of Baza,
The death of Reduán,
And the loves of Audalla,
Along with the banishment of Muza,
Because the King loved his lady,
And after this they will sleep
In the hayloft with two blankets.]

Thus the literary value of the Moors as fashionable maurophile product is gradually transformed into the crassest economic good: their enslaved persons, telling fabulous stories by night but laboring by day, ultimately to be sold "a galera / cuando monedas no haya"[55] ["to the galleys, when I'm out of money"]. Again, the historical context makes the literary satire much more resonant: slavery was the fate of thousands of captured Moriscos in the Alpujarras, and the population of Morisco slaves in Spain rose considerably in the latter part of the century. Thus while it is certainly true, as critics suggest, that ballads such as "Quién compra diez y seis moros" point out the vast difference between the Moors of the *romancero* and the historical condition of the Moriscos, this distance itself becomes part of the debate about how to resolve the Morisco question. If the diminished Moriscos were once the heroic, beloved Moors of the *romancero*, does their decadence reflect well on Spain? And how is the stubborn popular attachment to both their past incarnation and a shared material culture to be negotiated?

Through poems on exile and on the traffic in Moors and their appurtenances, the literary phenomenon of the *romances moriscos*—and the sometimes virulent responses it elicited—became part of a broader cultural conversation on the Moriscos. From the "inconsequential" popular attachment to the ballads catalogued in "Háganme vuestras mercedes" to the satire on the fitting place of the Moors and their trappings in a hostile society, the poems constantly interrogate modes of relating to Moorishness. As a careful reading reveals, what might seem like a discrete literary vogue relied on the appeal of a shared material culture and sartorial habits developed over a very long period. As I will argue, it is precisely in the responses to the *romances* that the stakes of this appeal can be observed.

"Renegade" Poetry

The *romancero* is an especially rich corpus of maurophilia for the striking textual evidence of its contemporary reception, including what one might call maurophobic ripostes. Critics have long noted the subgenre of responses to the *romances moriscos*, which chart a variety of accusations against them.[56] Many of these dialogic poems register not only aesthetic ennui at the repetition of so much Moorish lore, but, more important, political outrage at the choice of topic. The responses also confirm the extraordinary popularity of the genre: as in the response to "Mira, Zaide," they provide evidence of an avid readership, poking fun at both the texts themselves and their popular reception. This well-documented readership (and subsequent oral reproduction) across social classes must be taken into account when assessing the contestatory force of the genre. While the poems' authors might not have set out to rehabilitate the Moors or mount them on a pedestal of national poetry, there is evidence that some readers thought they came dangerously close to doing just that. And while, as the satirical responses never cease to remind us, the idealizing corpus bears little relation to the experience of the average Morisco at the end of the century, its very popularity does lead us to wonder what kind of conceptual spaces, at least, the *romancero* offered a Morisco subject. If the ballads profoundly challenged exclusionary notions of national identity by invoking the shared materials of an aristocratic culture, the satirical responses attempted to delimit and mark Moorishness as problematic, adopting an orientalist stance strikingly absent from the original poems.

Many of the satirical ballads, such as Lasso de la Vega's, poke fun at the chasm of difference between the chivalric Moors of the texts and the Morisco muleteers, water-carriers, and agricultural laborers of contemporary Spain. Critics concur, arguing, as for *El Abencerraje*, that the representation of noble Moors, essentially Christian knights in disguise, bears little relation to the actual marginalized Morisco population of the sixteenth century.[57] Yet there are other possibilities for reading these idealizing representations. First, as Carrasco Urgoiti suggests, for Moriscos who were not quite as abject—and even those who were—this corpus may have

represented an alternative to everyday ostracism. As I noted above, the
satire rains particular scorn on the material trappings of chivalric fantasy:
liveries, costumes, arms, all abundantly described in the *romances*.[58] Yet
these descriptions are clearly an imperfect form of cultural survival: acci-
dental, ephemeral, and, more important, refracted through a Christian
sensibility that selected carefully for the more appealing elements of Moorishness. Nonetheless, insofar as they invoke a shared material culture, these
poems destabilize the othering of Moriscos that was so strident in other
cultural registers. Whereas these material survivals might not offer any so-
lace to Muslims who desperately held on to their own religion and culture,
their popularity would seem to suggest that there was nothing inherently
abhorrent about Moorishness—or about inhabiting such an identity—a
powerful point in the 1590s. Given the profound hybridization of material
culture that I trace throughout this study, moreover, the appeal of these
material trappings—and the resistance to them—evince a profoundly am-
bivalent relation to Moorish habits.

There is good evidence that the literary habit of maurophilia, which
constructs a sympathetic Moor, however fictive, was received with suspicion in some quarters. Critics responded with poems calling for Lope and
his imitators to give up their Moorish drag and write instead about Spanish
glories. One particularly striking example actually tags the maurophiles as
renegades—a loaded term of abuse in this historical context—who shower
glory on Mohammed while neglecting Spanish heroes of the Reconquista:

Renegaron de su ley
los romancistas de España
y ofrecieron a Mahoma
las primicias de sus gracias . . .
Los Ordoños, los Bermudos,
los Rasuras y Mudarras,
los Alfonsos, los Enricos,
los Sanchos y los de Lara,
¿qué es dellos y qué es del Cid?
¡Tanto olvido en glorias tantas![59]

[The balladeers of Spain
Reneged from their law
And offered to Mohammed
The first fruit of their talents . . .
The Ordóñez, Bermudos,
Resuras, Mudarras.

The Alfonsos, Enricos,
The Sanchos and the Laras—
What of them, and of the Cid?
So much forgetting of so many glories!]

In the eyes of these critics, the fascination with Moors implies a con-
comitant abandonment of a "proper" Spanish tradition, that is, of Spain
as a "Gothic" remnant that heroically triumphs over an encroaching
Islam. If the neglect of this ancestral Christian Spain is a central problem,
the poets' impersonation of Moors seems particularly threatening. One
response specifically attacks the Moorish habit, and suggests other forms
of literary artifice, such as the pastoral, as a more decorous disguise for
authorial identities:

¡Ah! Mis señores poetas,
descúbranse ya esas caras,
desnúdense aquesos moros
y acábense ya esas zambras;
váyase con Dios Gazul,
lleve el diablo a Celindaja,
y vuelvan esas marlotas
a quien se las dio prestadas.
Dejáis un fuerte Bernardo,
vivo honor de nuestra España;
dejáis un Cid Campeador,
un Diego Ordóñez de Lara.
¡Celebran chusmas moriscas
vuestros cantos de chicharra!
Si importa celar los nombres,
porque lo piden las causas,
¿por qué no vais a buscarlos
a las selvas y cabañas?[60]

[Oh, my poet lords,
Uncover your faces
Let those Moors disrobe
And those *zambras* [Moorish dances] end;
Let Gazul go with God,
And the devil take Celindaja,
Return those *marlotas*
To those who loaned them to you.
You leave behind a strong Bernardo,
Live glory of our Spain,
You leave a warring Cid,

A Diego Ordóñez de Lara.
Your cicada songs
Celebrate the Moorish rabble!
If names must be hidden,
Because the circumstances demand it,
Why do you not go seek them
In woods and huts?]

Presumably, a conventional shepherd or peasant would prove a far less discomfiting persona than a sympathetic Moor.[61] Yet the *romance morisco* was, for its authors, a more effective and powerful voice than the proposed alternatives, in part, because the identification was more proximate: as I have shown, the *marlota* singled out in the ballad as the mark of a borrowed Moorish identity had in fact been adopted not just by the poets of the *romancero* but by Christian Iberian aristocrats at large, as part of the hybridization of costume. The poets ostensibly dressed up as Moors, that is, wore perfectly recognizable Christian aristocratic costume. Thus the poetic fashion for Moorishness involves not just superficial Moorish drag on the part of the author but a more complex inhabiting of a shared material culture by writers and readers alike.

The unease with which this inhabiting is received suggests that, despite its frequent appearances, the figure of the *romance* Moor has not become inert through its conventionality, but instead challenges readers' notions of what is properly Spanish. Maurophilia coexists, however uneasily, with the maurophobic discourse of Spain's vulnerability to, and definition *against*, Moorish culture. This is perhaps clearest in a fascinating meta-ballad, "¿Por qué, señores poetas/ no volvéis por vuestra fama?"[62] itself a response to the satirical protests, and in particular to the question of whether Spanish and Moorish elements can be reconciled. The poem begins by decrying the poetic censure of other poets, by a "Judas" figure, thus summarily including one and all in the Christian "cuerpo":

Un miembro de vuestro cuerpo
quiere romper vuestras galas,
un Iudas de vuestro gremio,
que jamás un Iudas falta.

[A member of your body
Wants to ruin your fineries
A Judas of your trade,
For never is a Judas lacking.]

There follows a reflection on the tension between Renaissance and Moorish themes, which anticipates the more serious question of Moorish claims on Spain:

¿Qué le aprovecha a Gazul
tirar al otro la lança,
si hoy un ninfo de Leteo
quiere deshacer sus zambras?
Como si fuera don Pedro
más honrado que Amenábar,
y mejor doña María
que la hermosa Celindaxa.
Si es español don Rodrigo,
español el fuerte Audalla,
y sepa el señor Alcalde
que también lo es Guadalara.
Si una gallarda española
Quiere bailar doña Iuana,
las zambras también lo son,
pues es España Granada.

[What good is it for Gazul
To throw his lance at the other,
When today a nymph of Lethe
Wants to undo his *zambras*?
As though Don Pedro were
More honorable than Amenábar,
Or Doña María better
Than the beautiful Celindaxa.
If Don Rodrigo is Spanish,
Spanish is the strong Audalla,
And the lord Mayor should know
That so is Guadalara.
If Doña Juana wants to dance,
A Spanish *gallarda*,
The *zambras* are that too,
For Granada is Spain.]

In this context, the "ninfo de Leteo" suggests the willful forgetting of Spain's Moorish past, a deliberate erasure of anything but the high Gothic mode. Instead, as the poet suggests, the Moors are part of Spain—not an alternative, other history, but inherent in the nation's past.[63] Moreover, the historical problem here connects to the contemporary relation of the regional to the national: Granada and her *zambras* are not relics of a colorful past, but actual, present-day variations on a national theme. The ballad thus takes up the terms of the long-standing debate over the survival of Moorish—or is it Granadan?—culture, perhaps most eloquently defended by the Morisco notable Francisco Núñez Muley, discussed in Chapter 2.[64] In his petition to the Audiencia of Granada, against the repression of Morisco culture by the 1567 decrees, Núñez Muley had invoked precisely the same arguments as does the ballad: regional variations should be allowed to exist within the nation; what appears Moorish is actually Granadan, and finally, the greatness of the Reconquista can only be appreciated if the culture of the Christians' enemies is acknowledged and preserved. As "¿Por qué, señores poetas?" puts this last point,

No es culpa, si de los moros
los valientes hechos cantan,
pues cuanto más resplandecen
nuestras célebres hazañas.
Que el encarecer los hechos
del vencido en la batalla,
engrandece al vencedor,
aunque no hablen dél palabra.

[It is not a fault, if they sing
Valiant deeds of Moors,
For our famous feats
Thus shine all the more.
For praising the deeds
Of the loser in battle,
Ennobles the victor,
Even if not a word is said about him.]

The last line grudgingly acknowledges that it is hard to argue that the *romances moriscos* reflect glory on the Christians, when the latter often fail even to put in an appearance. The poet then moves to a less honorable justification: Moors should be the protagonists of all these love affairs and games, because true men—the Roman conquerors of Iberia, or its defenders—cannot be bothered with such trifles. Yet even at this apparently orientalist moment, the alternative to the Moor is not the Christian hero of the Reconquista, but a much earlier figure from before the Muslim invasion.

What stands between Núñez Muley and the anonymous balladeer, in historical terms, is nothing less than the failure of the Morisco advocate's last-minute petition, the subsequent uprising by the oppressed Moriscos in the Alpujarras, the bloody conflict, and the forced transport and relocation of Granadan Moriscos to Castile. The ballad alludes to this in its last lines, a surprisingly realistic and contemporary curse: "en conclusión te apedreen/los moros del Alpujarra" ["in the end may the Moors of the Alpujarra stone you"]. This huge historical distance is what makes the claims in the ballad—and the literary fashion of maurophilia—particularly striking. One would not imagine that this historical trajectory would leave such arguments, or proclivities, intact. And yet maurophilia endures, at this very late point in the century, suggesting an underlying phenomenon more profound than mere fashion. In fact, while critics have been quick to associate the disappearance of Moorish themes within the *romancero* with the increasingly hostile political climate of years leading to the expulsion, they offer no similar motivations for its original rise.

While the *romancero morisco* may well have become a fashionable and conventional corpus, it is nonetheless politically significant. Its central concern with a Moorish erotic confounds the maurophobe discourses of repudiation so common in the period leading up to the expulsions. Occasional poems obliquely address the problematics of exile and slavery, or of local versus national culture; others take on such meanings through their reception and parody. More important, because the poems so often invoke the shared sartorial culture of Iberia to construct their idealized, aristocratic subjects, they rehearse for readers a Moorish habitus that goes far beyond any narrow literary fashion. The resistance to this corpus thus seems motivated more by what the fashionable maurophilia reveals, as it "perform(s) in a conscious mode the operation that the habitus performs quite differently,"[65] than by its simple repetitiousness or conventionality. Although the Moriscos of the 1580s and 1590s may bear relatively little relation to the exalted protagonists of the ballads, the texts nonetheless call attention to the many ways in which "Moors" inhabit Spain, and to the many vectors of sympathy and pleasure that connect them to other Spaniards.

4

Playing the Moor

As I SUGGESTED IN CHAPTER 3, while the fashion for Moorish *romances* became a full-fledged craze in the 1580s and 1590s, other forms of mauro-philia and Moorish lore spanned a much longer period. This chapter fo-cuses on the ceremonial and chivalric uses of Moorishness, to show how it was paradoxically embraced by Spaniards as emblematic of national iden-tity long after the Christian victory in Granada. My title alludes to *Playing Indian*, the influential study of Indian impersonation by Philip Deloria.[1] Yet although Deloria describes the uses of impersonating the Other at the birth of a nation, and the cultural transactions that occur at the frontier, there are significant differences between the early U.S. instances he ana-lyzes and the Iberian dynamics that concern me here. Most important, Deloria argues for a deliberate agency behind the impersonation he re-counts. Even if it occurs in the "blur of half-consciousness that character-izes cultural rituals" (27–28), his U.S. colonists use impersonation for specific political ends, and, at least initially, remain in control of its signifi-cation. Indeed, they largely achieve their goals of differentiation from Brit-ain and development of a "native" U.S. identity, however unresolved. As I argue below, in the Iberian context a much less considered, more gener-alized hybridization of cultural forms underlies those deliberate, ceremo-nial occasions on which Spaniards play (like) Moors. This habitual, material connection, I suggest, destabilizes the significance of ceremonial occasions, particularly in the eyes of foreign observers, who often quite simply continue to equate Spaniards with Moors. It also gives the idealiz-ing literature of maurophilia a material resonance, as the textual imperson-ation of Moorish knights finds support in a wealth of shared practices recognizable to Iberian readers.

My focus here is not on the more famous ludic representations of the conflict between Moors and Christians—the various *moros y cristianos* festivals in Spain or the Mediterranean tradition of the *mauresque/morisca* dance—which have been widely studied.[2] Perhaps the single thread uniting those highly diversified performances is the staged opposition between the two camps. Instead, I examine those forms that presuppose an adoption of and identification with Moorish equestrian forms as Iberian chivalric practice. The close association of al-Andalus with the chivalric apparatus of early modern Spain, I suggest, takes the cultural phenomenon of maurophilia well beyond the literary to key aristocratic traditions of horsemanship and equestrian games. In what is perhaps the most famous literary account of such games, Ginés Pérez de Hita's hugely successful historical novel, *Guerras civiles de Granada* (1595), maurophilia operates in part by invoking these codes of aristocratic spectacle, which the text imagines as fully shared between Moorish and Christian knights. As a local writer and artisan abundantly familiar with hybridized practices, Pérez de Hita uses these traditions both to complicate the otherness of Moors— and, by implication, the distinctiveness of Christian identity—as he challenges the Crown's repression of Moriscos in his own time. While his Moors may well be virtual Christians, ripe for conversion, they also practice a chivalric Iberian culture that recalls Spain's indebtedness to the defeated Granadans. This shared culture of aristocratic spectacle thus serves as a crucial vehicle for the ideological force of Pérez de Hita's maurophilia.

Juegos and *jinetes*

Jineta y cañas son contagio moro;
restitúyanse justas y torneos,
y hagan paces las capas con el toro.[3]

[Jineta and cañas are a Moorish contagion; let them restore jousts and tourneys, and let the capes make up with the bull.]

Accounts of the *juego de cañas*, an equestrian game in which multiple quadrilles of horsemen throw light reeds at each other, suggest how complex was early modern Spain's relationship to its Andalusi heritage.[4] Modern scholars trace the *cañas* to the North African game of *djerid*,[5] and note also the Nasrid dynasty's long fascination with equestrian games in Granada. In the early fifteenth century, the *cañas* occasionally served as a diplomatic conduit between Moors and Christians, from the success of a Granadan embassy that played the sport for Juan II of Castile, to the gift of luxurious equipment for the game sent by Muhammad VIII to Alfonso V of Aragon in 1418.[6] For a later period, the *cañas* serve as a paradigmatic case of cultural maurophilia for three reasons. First, though the game was recognized as Moorish, it was embraced as an appropriate pursuit for Spanish nobles—a particularly Iberian version of the joust. Second, unlike the many versions of mock-combats between (mock)-Moors and Christians, for the *cañas* all participants dressed in "Moorish" style. Pedro de Aguilar indicated in his *Tractado de la cavalleria de la gineta* (1572), "Ha de lleuar cada una de las dichas quadrillas, vestida su librea, la qual ha de ser de marlotas o sayos moriscos, y caperuças, y capellares. Poniendo sobre las caperuças, para que mejor parezcan y esten mas firmes, en la cabeça algunas bueltas bien puestas, de una toca muy delgada"[7] ["Each of the said quadrilles must wear its own livery, of *marlotas* or Moorish cloaks, and hoods, and hooded cloaks. And so that the hoods look better and stay on more securely, they must wrap their heads well a few times around with a very thin headwrap"]. It thus seems difficult to dismiss this particular embrace of an Andalusi heritage as simply a reenactment of Christian superiority over Islam—the games are played exclusively by Spaniards in Andalusi-derived costume, in many cases to awe a foreign audience. Finally, and perhaps most important, the *cañas* were not only an exceptional performance; in their simpler form, they were instead a habitual practice or discipline, involving specific skills and the mastery of a particular style of horsemanship.

Riding *a la jineta* involved shortened stirrups and a much higher seat in the saddle, by contradistinction to the longer stirrups in the *brida* or Norman bridle.[8] The *Diccionario de Autoridades* emphasizes the North African provenance of the style: "Cierto modo de andar a caballo recogidas las piernas en los estribos, al modo de los Africanos. *Brevibus astrabis equitatio*"[9] ["A certain style of horseback riding with the legs gathered into the stirrups, in the style of the Africans. *Brevibus astrabis equitatio*"]. With shorter stirrups, the rider could use knees and heels to guide the horse through tighter maneuvers, including the complexities of the *cañas*.[10] The *jineta* was associated with the frontier, as a style that emulated the Moors' consummate horsemanship. The first mention of the term in Spanish occurs in the fourteenth-century *Crónica de Alfonso XI*, which describes the invasion of Spain by the Zenetes, a Berber tribe particularly good with horses, as the origin of a whole style of warfare: "dicen que estos fueron los primeros caballeros jinetes que pasaron aquen la mar"[11] ["they say these were the first *jinete* knights that crossed the sea"]. The lexical expansion of the term from the ethnic adjective *jinete* to a much broader modifier used for short arms (lance, sword) and the related

saddle to, finally, the general noun for horseman, suggests how profoundly North African and frontier horsemanship influenced Iberian martial and equestrian traditions.

Beyond the ceremonial displays of the *cañas*, the *jineta* style of riding
was viewed as essential for carrying out successful *escaramuzas* (skirmishes)
into enemy territory. In his 1572 *Tractado de la cavallería de la jineta*,
Pedro de Aguilar ascribes to it the success of the Christian conquest:
"aviendo consistido en ella, después de la voluntad divina, el principal
effecto de la restauración y recuperación de España del poder y subjectión
de los paganos"[12] ["it being the principal cause, after the divine will, of
the restoration and recuperation of Spain from the power and subjection
of the pagans"]. Ironically, then, for this knight of Antequera it is the
mimetic reproduction of Andalusi skills that enables the Spaniards to defeat their enemy; in the process, the *jineta* becomes the quintessentially
Spanish bridle.

The Flemish courtier Antoine de Lalaing, whom we have encountered earlier, ascribes frontier horsemanship to Queen Isabel's explicit
agency, obliquely recognizing the value of the *jineta*: "Et [Isabel] com-
manda que ceuls de la frontière des Franchois chevaulcheroient à nostre
mode, et les voisins à Mores chevaucheroient à la jennette"[13] ["And Isabel
commanded that those on the frontier with the French should ride in
our fashion, and those who neighbored Moors should ride *jineta* style"].
Lalaing's proprietary "our fashion" limns a European self, marked by the
longer stirrups of the *brida*, to which that other, frontier Spain is contrasted. Any properly Iberian bridle disappears—the larger passage ad-
dresses Isabel's supposed attempt to get Spaniards to ride horses in the
first place, instead of mules—as Spain becomes purely the imitation of
Europe or of Moors.[14]

In this light, one might be tempted to read the purported decay of
the *jineta*, lamented in Aguilar and other treatises, as part of the process
of Europeanization identified by Milhou, as well as of the general decay
of chivalry. Yet although the treatises present themselves as an attempt to
save an endangered practice, their sheer multiplication and popularity—at
least thirty in Spanish (some from the New World), and at least five for
Portugal, lasting well into the eighteenth century, argue for a vibrant regard for the *jineta*.[15] The most detailed account of the reasons for the
jineta's decline, in Luis de Bañuelos y de la Cerda's *Libro de la jineta y
descendencia de los caballos guzmanes* (Córdoba, 1605), laments the modern disregard for proper horsemanship of any style, across the board, and

blames the huge influx of New World gold, which turns the affections of Spanish ladies, for this as for many other social ills. Nowhere in this preface is there a rejection of the *jineta* for its Moorish origins.[16] Modern scholars argue that the exposure to Italian horsemanship paradoxically led to the gradual Spanish adoption of the *brida*, even though the *jineta* had proven its worth in the long Italian wars.[17] In any case, this was a slow and long-term transformation, and the *jineta* remained the popular style of riding in Andalucía.

The complexity of Spain's relation to the Andalusi equestrian tradition comes through in Covarrubias' lengthy and indecisive definition of *ginete* in the 1611 *Tesoro*, in which the "Arab" style of riding invokes multiple cultural anxieties:

Ginete: Hombre de a cavallo, que pelea con lança y adarga, recogidos los pies con estribos cortos, que no baxan de la barriga del cavallo. Esta es propia cavallería de aláraves, los quales vienen desnudos de piernas y braços, arremangada la manga de la camisa, y sin ninguna otra arma dura en el cuerpo, con sus turbantes en la cabeça y su alfanje o cimitarra colgando del hombro en el tahalí. Desta forma dizen haver sido las figuras que el desdichado rey don Rodrigo vio pintadas en el lienço de la torre encantada con un letrero que dezía: "Quando esta gente entrare en España, se perderá," y así se verificó con la venida de los aláraves ginetes. Este nombre puede ser griego, y valer tanto como desnudos y en la guerra aquel dezimos yr desnudo que no va guarnecido de hierro . . . y trayendo de aquí su origen, avíamos de dezir gymnetes; y por no llevar armas tales que puedan resistir el golpe de frente en frente, pelean de rodeo y muchas vezes quando van huyendo al parecer del contrario, le hieren y buelven sobre él, y otras hurtan el cuerpo al golpe, dexándose caer debajo de la barriga, o cuello del cavallo, sin perder la silla, y recibiéndole al soslayo en el adarga. Otros dizen que ginetes son cierta nación y casta de aláraves, dichos cenetas, o cenetes, que viven en las montañas de Africa, y son belicosos y grandes hombres de acavallo. Diego de Urrea dize que ginete se pudo dezir de cinete, que en terminación arábiga es *cinetum*, y sinifica ornamento, del verbo *ceyene*, hermosear o ser hermoso, por la gallardía de los ginetes quando salen de fiesta con sus turbantes y plumas, sus marlotas y borzeguíes y los jaezes de los cavallos ricos. El padre Guadix dize que ginete está corrompido de *genet*, que en arábigo vale soldado, o *chanet*. En el evangelio de San Juan, cap. 19, donde dize: *Venerunt ergo milites et primi quidem fregerunt crura et alterius*, etc.; en la versión arábiga, en lugar de *milites* está la palabra *genet* o *chenedt*.[18]

[*Ginete*: A man on horseback, who fights with a spear and a leather shield, his feet gathered into short stirrups, which do not reach below the belly of the horse. This is the proper horsemanship of Arabs, their legs and arms naked, their shirt sleeves rolled back, no armor on their body, their turbans on their heads and their cutlass or scimitar hanging from their shoulder in their swordbelt. It is said that such were the figures that the unfortunate king Don Rodrigo saw painted on the canvas in the enchanted tower, with a sign that said, "Spain shall be lost when these people come into it," and so it was with the coming of the *ginete* Arabs. This word may be Greek, and mean the same as naked, and in war we say he goes naked who is not protected by iron . . . and tracing its origin thence, we should say *gymnetes*, and because they do not carry arms such that can resist a head-on strike, they fight in roundabout ways and many times when they seem to their opponent to be fleeing they wound him and turn upon him, and other times they steer clear of a blow by falling below the horse's belly or neck without losing their seat, and instead receive it glancingly on their shield. Others say that *ginetes* are a certain nation and caste of Arabs, called *cenetas* or *cenetes*, who live in the mountains of Africa and who are bellicose and great horsemen. Diego de Urrea says that *ginete* may come from *cinete*, which with the Arabic ending is *cinetum*, and means ornament, from the verb *ceyene*, to beautify or be beautiful, for the grace of the ginetes when they come out on a feast day with their turbans and plumes, their *marlotas* and *borceguíes*, and the rich harnesses on the horses. Father Guádix says that ginete is a corruption of *genet*, which in Arabic means soldier, or *chanet*. In the Book of John, where it says, "*Venerunt ergo milites et primi quidem fregerunt crura et alterius*, etc." ["Then came the soldiers, and brake the legs of the first, and of the other, etc."], in the Arabic version instead of *milites* there is the word *genet* or *chenedt*.

Covarrubias's half-hearted effort to classicize the origin of *jinete*, by analogy to *gymnete*, attempts to foreground the nakedness of the Arab horsemen, who fight without armor. Yet these ostensibly vulnerable figures invoke for Covarrubias the legend of the benighted King Rodrigo's encounter with the prophecy of Moorish invasion, paradoxically the moment of Iberia's greatest Christian weakness. That first North African invasion is conflated with the much later arrival of the Zenetes in Spain, described in the *Crónica de Alfonso X*. In another vein, Covarrubias rewrites the tremendous agility and dexterity of the *jinetes*—in evidence during the *juegos de cañas*—as the cowardly avoidance of a straight fight. The *cañas*, which haunt this entire definition, complicate the purported Greek origin of *jinete*, as the etymology proposed by Urrea invokes precisely the ornament and spectacle of the games—the opposite of nakedness. The ethnic etymology (admitted by modern dictionaries,[19] and clearly operative in the *Crónica*) from *cierta nación y casta de aláraves* makes the *jineta* a North African practice, but this again is contradicted by the broad evidence of Spanish *jinetes*, as in the Lalaing citation and whole genre of *tratados* above. Finally, the emphasis on soldiers in Guadix's definition reintroduces the specter of Arab cavalry, and the appeal to no less a moment than the Crucifixion reads as a last attempt to emphasize the otherness and difference of the *jinete*, here the Jewish/Muslim tormenter of Christ.

Covarrubias's tour-de-force of definition is particularly striking given how common the *jineta* and the *cañas* were among the nobility in Spain, and the multiple cultural purposes they served in the newly unified nation. The *cañas* functioned both as performance and as military training. Thus the traveler Hyeronimus Münzer, who witnessed the sport in Granada, in 1494, noted their instructive and spectacular character: "In simulata illa pugna se exercitant, ut in vero prelio cum lanceis minus perhorrescant. . . . Numquam vidi tam pulchrum spectaculum"[20] ["with this simulacrum of battle the knights practice, so that they feel less fear in a real war with lances. . . . I have never seen such a beautiful spectacle"]. Much later, in a 1572 decree, Philip II included the *cañas* among the military exercises he exhorted Spanish gentlemen to undertake so as to be ready for war.[21] And even as late as 1599, in *De rege et regis institutione* (On the King and the Education of the King), Juan de Mariana recommended the *cañas* as good training for a prince, even as he recalled their Moorish origin: "inter se ex equis iaculentur Mauricae pugnae genere, quo alterius agminis pars facto impetum primum procurrit, mismisque in adversarius iaculorum imagine, pedum referunt ceduntque prementibus adversariis"[22] ["let them fight in the Moorish way, where part of one squad charges its opponent, and after having thrown reeds like darts, retreats"]. Mariana's emphasis on the *cañas* as a bodily discipline suggests a literal incorporation of Andalusi equestrian forms, as one more aspect of the Moorish *habitus* I discussed in chapter 1. A traditionally Spanish pursuit, the *cañas* are according to Mariana the perfect training for horsemanship and war.

As such, the *juegos de cañas* became an essential component of Spanish aristocratic celebrations, held to greet foreign royals or celebrate dynastic milestones, from the birth of the future Philip II in 1527 to the arrival in Spain of his bride, María of Portugal, in 1543.[23] The *cañas* were almost de rigueur as a welcome for visiting princes, who would appreciate the fantastic sartorial display and excellent horsemanship involved in such an event. Such were the games organized to celebrate the 1497 arrival in Spain of Princess Margaret of Austria to wed Prince Juan, son of Isabel and Fernando, and witnessed by an Italian traveler:

La regia magesta et il principe montati in su cavalli velocissimi, con le targe loro, vestiti a la morescha de salii et manti de brochato, cum diversi rechami et gale, con la testa velata al modo moresco.

Figure 10. Jan Cornelisz Vermeyen, *The Game of Canes* (1538). Private Collection.
Photograph: Photographic Survey, Courtauld Institute of Art.

Il conestabili, duchi de Alva, Biegera, Alburchech et marchese de Villafrancha
vestiti a la modesima foglia ma tutti de varii colori, et tanto richamente quanto sia
posibile. . . . Cum epsi erano multi altri conti et cavalieri, tutti cum salii et manti
de brocato et seta sopre seta, cum tanti recami de oro et argento, con si varie et
bella fogie, che era cosa de maraveglia.[24]

[His royal majesty and the prince rode on their very swift horses, with their shields,
dressed in the Moorish fashion with brocade mantles and doublets, with various
embroideries and ornaments, with their head veiled in the Moorish fashion.
    The Constable, and Dukes of Alva, Biegera, Albuquerque and Marquiss of Villa-
franca dressed in the same fashion but all in different colors, and as richly as
possible. . . . With them were many other counts and knights, all with brocade
doublets and mantles and silk over silk, with so much embroidery in gold and
silver, with such varied and beautiful fashions, that it was a marvelous thing.]

The appeal of the *cañas* for this foreign observer, as for many, lies in
the richly exotic attire of the contestants (Figure 10). A similar response is
clear in the account by Antoine de Lalaing of games held for Philip the
Fair, visiting Castile in 1501. The Flemish courtier notes that the knights
dress "à la morisque, bien gorgiasement" ["in the Moorish fashion, very
gorgeously"], with Moorish embroidery and head-wraps (*tocas*). Despite
the novelty and exotic appeal of the costume for Lalaing, however, he
perceives the sport itself as eminently Castilian: the knight skirmish "en

Figure 11. Juan de la Corte, *Fiesta en la Plaza Mayor* (1623). Museo Municipal de Madrid.

jettant leur cannes à la mode de Castille"[25] ["throwing their reeds in the Castilian fashion"]. Thus, although Ferdinand explains to Philip that "en ceste fachon font les Mores escarmouches contre les crestiens" ["thus do the Moors skirmish against the Christians"], the spectacle itself does not seem to have included any quadrille *not* dressed in Moorish garments, and the sport is identified as Castilian.

While these early examples took place not long after the fall of Granada, the *cañas* were still deemed the proper way to greet foreign princes more than a century later, when Charles I of England went on his ill-fated marital escapade to Madrid in 1623 (see the 1623 representation in Juan de la Corte, "Fiesta en la Plaza Mayor," Figure 11).[26] The continued popularity of the *cañas* within Spain and as marker of Spanish identity to foreigners suggests how deeply the Andalusi forms of the *djerid* and the *jineta* had been embraced. Crucially for our purposes, by the mid-sixteenth century the *juego de cañas* served to display Spanishness abroad.[27] Because they were distinctively Iberian, they represented Spain in a way that the more common jousts or classical pageants ubiquitous in Renaissance Europe (including Spain) never could.

The novelty and distinctness of the *cañas* were precisely the point in these self-representations, as at the games organized at Charles V's imperial coronation in Bologna in 1529. However Moorish, then, the *cañas* served to impress European observers with the luxury and pomp of Span-

ish festivities. Marco Antonio Magno rushed to write to the Venetian nobleman Marco Contarini of the games he witnessed in Bologna: "gli è
stato el [gioco] più bello, il più leggiadro, attilato, copioso et pomposo
che sia stato mai facto altra volta in Italia"[28] ["it was the most graceful,
elegant, sumptuous, and stately sport ever performed in Italy"]. The adu-
lation was not uniform, however, in that for some observers it confirmed
an orientalist perception of Spain. Il Galateo—no great lover of Spain—
found the games, with all their turning and fleeing, cowardly and unwor-
thy of strong men, a fitting sport for Moors.[29]

Yet overall Spaniards seem to have found the *cañas* an effective mode
of self-presentation, as at festivities at the entrance of Prince Philip (the
future Philip II) to Milan in 1548:

Estava aparejado para remate de las fiestas un juego de cañas, el qual se hizo en el
patio de palacio el día y fiesta de los Reyes. Fue cosa que en estremo pareció bien.
Diose gran contentamiento con esto a la Princesa de Molfeta y a su hija, y a todas
aquellas señoras y damas, por ser fiesta nueva y que pocas vezes se vee en aquella
tierra. Fueron seys las quadrillas, cada una de ocho cavalleros españoles.[30]

[A *juego de cañas* was prepared to cap the festivities, held in the palace courtyard
on the day of the Feast of the Epiphany. It was extremely well received. It gave
great pleasure to the Princess Molfeta and to her daughter, and to all those ladies
and gentlewomen, for it was a new celebration and one seldom seen in that land.
There were six quadrilles of eight Spanish knights each.]

Exotic Spain here serves as a spectacle to delight Italian ladies, in a display
enhanced by the costume and riding style of its knights, "los cuales con
muchos y muy ricos adereços, a lo morisco vestidos y en muy hermosos
cavallos españoles a la gineta con ricos jaezes y petrales entraron en la
carrera" (76) ["who with many and very rich adornments, dressed in the
Moorish fashion and on very beautiful Spanish horses, riding *gineta* style
with rich trappings entered the field"]. Games were held also in the Flemish city of Gant, birthplace of Charles V, which received the prince with a
full panoply of triumphal arches, inscriptions in classical languages, and
mythological allegories. In return, the Spaniards, dressed in Moorish finery, held their festive *cañas*, "con gran contentamiento y admiración de
todos los de aquella villa y generalmente de todos los cavalleros de aquellos
Estados, por ser para ellos cosa tan nueva y que no lo usan y pocas vezes
lo veen"[31] ["with great pleasure and admiration of all those in that city
and generally of all the knights from those States, as it was for them such
a new thing and one they do not have and which they seldom see"].

Perhaps most interesting for the long-term European construction of an exotic Spain were the *cañas* held by Philip II in London in 1554 to celebrate his marriage to Mary Tudor and England's return to the Catholic Church. The account, from a published letter to the Countess of Olivares, emphasizes both Philip's impatience with the delay in holding the games and the tremendous scale of the spectacle:

El domingo quiso el rey que el juego de cañas que ha tantos días que se deuia de auer hecho, que fuesse ese dia: y assi se boluio muy sereno, y se jugo en la plaça de palacio donde auia mas de doze mil personas viéndolo: y la Reyna y todos los señores y sus mugeres muy bien vestidos. . . . Los jugadores entraron por su orden. Don Juan de Benauides de terciopelo blanco y marlotas de damasco blanco, el albornoz con oro, bien costosas, y los vestidos assimesmo: diez. Y luego Luys Vanegass, de verde, con otros diez; ni mas ni menos las sedas y oro. Don Diego de Cordoua con sus diez donde yua el rey de recamado y oro, que eran los treynta de un puesto: a aquestos dio el Rey de vestir, y a sus trompetas y atabales al modo de España vestidos de seda blanca. . . . [*There follow the names of several more Spanish noblemen, each leading his own quadrille*] Entraron de dos en dos, y despues boluió cada quadrilla junta: y despues todos juntos salieron a tomar caballos y adargas y se començó el juego y duró un buen rato. Y se boluieron a salir como entraron, y assí se acabó la fiesta sin cayda ni desastre, y a todos parescio bien por ser cosa que no se auia visto en Londres.[32]

[On Sunday the King desired that the *juego de cañas*, which should have been held so many days earlier, take place on that day: and the weather became very serene, and the games were held in the palace courtyard before more than twelve thousand persons, and the Queen and all the lords and their ladies very well dressed. . . . The players entered in order. Don Juan de Benavides in white velvet and white damask *marlotas*, and a shield with gold on it, and all very costly, and ten dressed thus. And then Luis Venegas in green with another ten with no more or less in silks and gold. Don Diego de Córdoba with his ten, among whom was the King in embroidery and gold, who made up the thirty on one end; and the King gave these their costume, and also to his trumpeters and drummers, dressed in the Spanish fashion in white silk. . . . They came in two by two, and then each quadrille came together again, and then they all went for their horses and shields and the game began and lasted a good while. And they went out as they had come in, and thus the celebration ended with neither falls nor disasters. And it pleased everyone, for it was something never before seen in London.]

As in Gant, the "Spanish fashion" involves equestrian games markedly different from anything the natives have ever seen, both in their lavish display and in the exotic costumes (*marlotas*) and riding style involved. The games must have underscored for the English the continuities between al-Andalus and Philip's Spain, exacerbating the profound sense of national differences that characterized the visit.

Although the Andalusi origins of this equestrian game were not forgotten, as is clear from Mariana's descriptions, in the late-sixteenth and seventeenth century writers attempted to redeem the *cañas* by classicizing their origins, thus providing them with an impeccable imperial pedigree. This tradition—contested even in its day—linked the *cañas* to the martial games of Ascanius and his peers in Book 5 of the *Aeneid*, based on the equestrian drill of the Trojan boys. Thus Juan Rufo writes in a 1571 poem: "que quiere, a imitación de los troyanos, / jugar las cañas la caballería"[33] ["for the cavalry, like the Trojans, want to play cañas"]. This story of Trojan origins is particularly striking given that in the 1570s there were still actual Moriscos taking part in these games, whose presence would have recalled for the classicists the actual provenance of *jineta, marlotas,* and of course the *cañas* themselves.[34]

The classical origin story is repeated in Covarrubias, with no acknowledgment of any intervening Moorishness. In a long definition of *caña* that takes him from the Crucifixion to human frailty, to the history of writing and of music, and to the arrows of the Indians, Covarrubias notes:

En España es muy usado el jugar las cañas, que es un género de pelea de hombres de a cavallo. Éste llaman juego troyano, y se entiende averle traydo a Italia Julio Ascanio. Descrívele Virgilio, lib. 5, *Aeneidos*, tan por extenso que no quita punto del juego de cañas nuestro. Primero desembaraçan la plaça de gente, haze la entrada con sus quadrillas distintas, acometen, dan buelta, salen a ellos los contrarios.[35]

[In Spain the game of *cañas* is very common, which is a kind of combat of men on horseback. They call this the Trojan game, and it is understood to have been brought to Italy by Iulius Ascanius. Virgil describes it in Book 5 of the Aeneid, so extensively that not a thing is missing from our game of *cañas*. First they clear the parade ground of people, the different quadrilles make their entry, they charge, turn, the opponents charge them.]

Covarrubias then cites the relevant verses from Book 5 of the *Aeneid*, as though to settle the matter.

The *Aeneid* theory is expanded upon in the antiquarian Rodrigo Caro's *Días geniales o lúdicos* (written c. 1626), an ethnographic account of the feasts and games of Spain in dialogue form. Here, as in many of the sources, *cañas* are linked to bullfighting as quintessentially Spanish pursuits:

Don Pedro: Yo he tenido los juegos de cañas y toros, que son las fiestas más fre-
cuentes de que hoy usamos en España, por invención nuestra, y me fundo en la
afición notable y propensión que todos les tenemos; aunque he leído en la *Historia*
del Padre Juan de Mariana, de la Compañía de Jesús, que es cosa de los moros o
imitación de sus batallas, que tanto duraron en esta tierra.[36]

[Don Pedro: I have considered *juegos de cañas* and bullfights, which are the games
that we have most frequently in Spain today, as our invention, and I base myself
on the striking inclination and propensity we all have for them, although I have
read in the *History* of Father Juan de Mariana, of the Society of Jesus, that it is a
Moorish thing or imitation of their battles, which lasted so long in this land.]

Don Pedro's interlocutor, Don Fernando, claims that, with all due respect
to Mariana, he will prove that both traditions come from Rome and Troy,
and were practiced by young boys (59). He thus concurs with Mariana on
the martial and imitative quality of the games, but replaces Moors and
Spaniards with Greeks and Trojans:

Resta que digamos del juego de cañas, y de sus primeros inventores, que no fueron
los españoles, aunque más de jinetes se precien, sino Eneas el troyano, el cual,
estando en Sicilia, lo inventó, haciendo de él una viva representación de las batallas
en que él se había hallado entre los griegos y troyanos. (67)

[We must now address the *juego de cañas*, and its first inventors, who were not
Spaniards, although they are proudest of their horsemanship, but Aeneas the Trojan, who, while in Sicily, invented it, making of it a lively representation of the
battles between the Greeks and the Trojans in which he had found himself.]

The conflation of the *cañas* with the *juegos troyanos* via Virgil ties
Spain back to a Roman and imperial past that is both shared and contested
with other European nations, erasing the more immediate evidence of its
difference from Europe.[37] Thus the distinct effect of the games as a marker
of Spain's singularity gives way to the claim of a shared legacy. Yet this
attempt to redeem the pronounced Spanish taste for the sport by classicizing it never fully obscured the Andalusi origins of the *cañas*, as is evident
in the satirical poet and courtier Francisco de Quevedo's acerbic attack on
them as a "Moorish contagion" in the lines quoted above and elsewhere
in his "Epístola satírica": "¡Qué cosa es ver un infanzón de España, abrevi-
ado en la silla a la jineta, y gastar un caballo en una caña!"[38] ["What a
sight to see, a nobleman of Spain, abbreviated in the saddle, *jineta* style,
and wasting a horse on a *caña*!"]. Yet however problematic their origin,
and however dyspeptic they might have made the satirist Quevedo, the

cañas, like so many of the cultural practices I have described, had become fully Spanish. More important, because of the predilection for the games on the part of Spanish royalty, they had come to represent Spain for a variety of powerful aristocratic audiences across Europe.[39]

In the context of the frequent performance of *cañas* abroad, it is imperative to consider what was actually represented when Spaniards played Moorish games. As the practice of the *cañas* became established as Iberian within Spain, any sense of Moorish impersonation most likely disappeared for the Spaniards, to be replaced by the Andalusi habitus I have described earlier. Yet the stakes are very different when Spain thus represents itself to other Europeans. For foreign audiences, the collapse of semiotic or ludic distance as Spain plays Moorish games only reinscribes Spain's difference and exoticism: in this view, Spaniards are not just playing Moors or imitating them; they *are* Moors.[40] As I discuss more fully in Chapter 5, European prejudice against an ever more powerful Spain throughout the sixteenth century made such an elision appealing. Thus Ludovico Ariosto, despite his frequent calls to Charles V to lead Europe against the Turks, portrays in *Orlando Furioso* (1516, 1532) a fully Saracen Spain: there are no Spanish Christian champions in the poem because Spaniard *means* Moor in the world of the text. Spain's liminal position vis-à-vis Europe, as recorded in such texts, must thus necessarily inflect any reading of its relationship with the Moorishness within.

A similar semiotic instability operates, I submit, in the chivalric scene of Charles' imperial coronation at Aix-la-Chapelle (Aachen) in 1521. In his *Historia de la vida y hechos del Emperador Carlos V* (1604–1606), Prudencio de Sandóval notes the distinctive appearance of the Spaniards in the Emperor's entourage, which sets them apart from the Germans, Flemish, and Burgundians: "Tras esta caballería venía la del Emperador, que era un gran número de caballos maravillosos, y ricamente aderezados, a la brida y a la jineta, y en cada uno de ellos un paje, y algunos de los pajes tocados a la morisca"[41] ["After this cavalry came the Emperor's, a great number of marvelous horses, richly dressed, in the *brida* and in the *jineta* style, and on each of them a page, and some of the pages in Moorish headdresses"].

One could read both the *cañas* and the coronation scene, as I have done elsewhere, as ethnic cross-dressing—the performance of ersatz-Moorishness to construct a "fictive ethnicity"[42] for Spain as a nation that has conquered Islam. By fetishizing its visible manifestations in the context of ceremonial performances, one might argue, Spain offers up a manageable remnant of Moorishness as evidence of its triumph. Yet it is striking how late Spain continues to present itself in Moorish guise, and how it does so in international contexts where the exact nature of the relation between representer and represented is less easy to control. In Spain, greeting foreign dignitaries with a Moorish spectacle might represent a kind of metonymic model: where before we had Moors, now we have only their appurtenances. But the pages in Moorish headdress at Charles's coronation abroad pose a greater problem. They identify Spain with the Moors in a less elliptical fashion: in this context, Moor equals Spaniard. However much Charles himself, as a northern king lately come to Spain, might escape this characterization, the non-Iberian perception of his subjects as exotic and less than fully European gains traction.

Moreover, the Spanish turn to Moorish forms in the chivalric contexts I have described is so seamless, so effortless, that the more oppositional models of representing the other—quite pertinent, for example, to the *juegos de moros y cristianos*—hardly seem appropriate. Neither the ceremonial occasions nor the habitual manuals on horsemanship I have described emphasize the bodily difference of the other. Instead, when Spaniards play Moors, they do so in their own bodies, with no exaggeration or deformation, much less any sense of transgression.[43] Difference embraced, even embodied, is once again most apparent to those outside Spain, and to those occasional critics who would quarantine (Quevedo) or classicize (Covarrubias, Caro) Andalusi survivals.

The Knights in Granada

The equestrian traditions explored above occupy an important place in maurophile literature. The idealized Moor is often portrayed as a deft *jinete* or as a participant in *cañas* or other colorful equestrian games. In particular, Pérez de Hita's *Guerras civiles de Granada* paints in colorful detail the chivalric celebrations that animate the final years of the Nasrid court. Pérez de Hita's novel, published more than twenty years after the bloody War of the Alpujarras, and well into the fascination with the *romancero morisco* analyzed in Chapter 3, recounts the struggles of rival factions that led to the fall of Granada.[44] The *romancero* is everywhere in the text, with ballads generally presented as summaries or reprises of the action, even though in fact Pérez de Hita often derives his own narrative from preexisting verse. Though the chivalric entertainments are ostensibly the backdrop to the love affairs and violent rivalries of Granadan aristocratic clans, organized to distract enemies from their ill-will toward each other, the background tends to overwhelm the foreground of Pérez de Hita's text. Instead of the minute details of any one conflict or infatuation, what fires the imagination is the pomp and elegance of the decadent Nasrid court as expressed in its entertainments. For early modern readers, the material seems to have proved irresistible: the *Guerras civiles* went through over forty editions in Spanish in Iberia alone over the course of the sixteenth and seventeenth centuries, and the enthusiasm for it continued unabated in the eighteenth. There were also early translations into French, and later ones into English and German.[45]

Critics have long noted that Pérez de Hita's idealized Moorish knights are much like their chivalric Christian counterparts in their Petrarchan longing and Ariostan bluster. Their debt to chivalric predecessors is clearly recognized by readers beyond Spain, as in the early French translation that recommends Pérez de Hita's Moors as models for "la façon et la courtoisie qu'on y voit pratiquer ordinairement"[46] ["the fashion and courtesy one regularly sees practised there"], even as they remain negative political examples. Yet while much of the chivalric spectacle projects medieval and Renaissance conventions onto Moors, the description of entertainments such as the *cañas* grounds the idealization of maurophilia in a shared Iberian material culture, thus giving it a particular ideological force within Spain that is very different from its later, orientalist afterlife throughout Europe. What Spanish readers would have recognized in the *Guerras civiles* was a shared Iberian equestrian culture, with its attendant costume—a culture both Spanish and clearly derived from al-Andalus.[47] For readers elsewhere, literary depictions of Moors could never be as familiar, thus contributing to the exoticization of Spain.

The games and celebrations of the *Guerras civiles* bring together Moors and Christians at several levels. First, Pérez de Hita's own biography suggests material connections that result in an imaginative bond. The author, a *maestro zapatero* (master shoemaker) by trade, probably frequented Morisco artisans who worked in leather or silk.[48] He was also well versed in spectacle from his frequent assignments designing moveable carts (*carros*) as part of the pageantry for Corpus Christi and other festivals, an expertise that clearly informs his account of the panoply in Granada.[49] While the more allegorical and fanciful elements of the Granadan games are Renaissance constructions projected onto the Moors, the emphasis on horsemanship and elaborate attire reflects a well established Iberian association of things Moorish with chivalric pageantry, as in the ubiquitous *juegos de cañas* noted above. (Carrasco Urgoiti suggests that Pérez de Hita constructs a "magnifique tableau de moeurs chevaleresques qui est à la fois exotique et très espagnol par le luxe"[50] ["a magnificent tableau of chivalric manners, at once exotic and very Spanish in its luxury"]; I might argue that the Spanish would recognize it as "très espagnol," while French and other European readers would be the ones to find it exotic.) Second, Moorish and Christian knights actually come together in these festivities, in highly stylized encounters that ultimately privilege chivalry over domination and recall a shared investment in such demonstrations of chivalric skills. Last and perhaps most important, the festivities themselves, in particular the extended *juego de cañas* in the first part of the novel, emphasize aspects of Iberian culture that owe much to the Andalusi influence. Thus although the Moorish knights of the *Guerras civiles* may well be domesticated fantasies, their idealization features a shared culture that haunts Pérez de Hita's own post-Alpujarras moment.

Even the actual combats (as opposed to the mock-combats of the *cañas*) in the *Guerras civiles* are marked by panoply and visual spectacle. When the Maestre de Calatrava, one of the preeminent Christian knights, is to fight Muça, brother of the king of Granada, two hundred Moorish knights prepare to accompany him. Pérez de Hita's description reiterates the imagined audience's pleasure in the scene:

aun no eran los rayos del sol bien tendidos por la hermosa y espaciosa vega, quando el Rey Chico y su cavallería salió por la puerta que dizen de Bibalmaçan, llevando a su hermano Muça al lado, y todos los demás cavalleros con él, con tanta gallardía que era cosa de mirar la diversidad de los trajes y vestidos de los Moros cavalleros. Y los demás cavalleros que yvan de guerra no menos parecer y gallardía llevaban: parecían tan bien con sus adargas blancas y lanças y pendoncillos, con tantas divisas y cifras en ellos, que era cosa de mirar. (28–29)

[the rays of the sun had not yet fully bathed the lovely and spacious plain when the Young King and his cavalry came out of the gate that they call Bibalmaçan, with his brother Muça at his side, and all the other knights with him, with such elegance that the diversity of costume and dress among the Moorish knights was something to see. And the other gentlemen who were dressed in a warlike fashion were no less elegant and handsome: they looked so good with their white shields and lances and pennants, with so many emblems and figures, that it was something to see.]

Muça himself gives particular pleasure to his audience, whose side or allegiance is never specified: "Yva tan gallardo Muça que qualquiera que lo mirava recebía de verle grande contento" (29) ["Muça looked so gallant that any who looked at him took great pleasure in the sight of him"]. What gives such moments their force is the shared delight in the knight's appearance, not limited to viewers—or readers—of a certain camp. More-over, in this context the Moors have no special purchase on panoply: the Christians are just as elegant, "no menos aderezados que la contraria parte" (29) ["no less equipped than the other side"]. Maurophilia bathes the entire scene in a glow of heroic elegance.

The chivalric connection that functions as the logic of maurophilia is succinctly expressed in another episode of combat, in which the individual challenge to Malique Alabez by Don Manuel Ponce de León threatens to degenerate into an all-out battle (69–75). The knights compliment each other on their apparent mettle, and Alabez emphasizes that they share an exalted lineage (71). They join in furious battle, almost equally matched but not quite: the Christian must retain a slight advantage. Once they set aside their lances to fight on foot, their horses, on their own, join the *brava pelea* (73). But the most interesting moment comes when the many followers on each side join in, under the mutual impression that the other side is not playing by the rules. In the confusion, Don Manuel takes hold of Alabez's horse: "Y el primero que halló a la mano, fué el cavallo de Alabez, y echándole mano de las riendas, forçado de la necesidad en que se vía, no guardó el decoro que era obligado a tomar el suyo y dexar el ageno, aunque no era objeto notable, porque en la guerra todo se suffre" (73–74) ["And the first that he found was Alábez's horse, and taking hold of the reins, forced by the need in which he found himself, he did not keep that decorum which required him to take his own and leave anoth-er's, although this was not a great objection, because all is warranted in war"]. This unchivalrous grab is ignored by the Moorish knight, who, despite missing his own, superior steed, warns his foe that overwhelming reinforcements are on the way, stressing his chivalric obligation to the Christian knight: "Y toma este mi consejo, que aunque soy Moro, soy hidalgo, y soy obligado en ley de cavallero, aunque enemigo, a darte aviso" (74) ["And take this advice of mine, for though I am a Moor, I am noble, and obliged by the law of chivalry to warn you, though you are my enemy"].

The Moor's emphasis on chivalry here functions as an implicit rebuke to the Christian, who has sought the advantage when in a tight fix. Ponce de León, who gets the better of the horse trade, heeds the Moor's warning and recasts the exchange as chivalric pact: "para obligarte a que me busques, llevaré tu caballo, y tú lleva el mío, que es tan bueno como él; que cuando otra vez nos veamos destrocaremos" (74) ["to force you to seek me out, I will take your horse, and you take mine, which is as good as it, and when we next see each other we will undo the exchange"]. Beyond the murky ethics of the chivalric exchange, however, the equine chiasmus serves as a synecdoche for the broad cultural transfer at the frontier—of equestrian and martial techniques and the aristocratic celebrations that accompanied them.

The *Guerras civiles de Granada* features many scenes of such games, further reminders of a shared culture. Early in the text, a *juego de cañas* devised by the king to mend relations between embattled knights in Granada (41) is perverted by the villainous Zegrí clan, who decide to carry real lances instead of reeds and thus overwhelm their adversaries, the Abencerrajes, if they do not first succeed in provoking them by wearing their former colors as livery (54). Yet the Abencerrajes themselves are fully idealized, and dazzle in both *toros* and *cañas*—entertainments that would have seemed to readers quintessentially Spanish, however closely the text might associate them with Moors: "Los cavalleros Abencerrages andaban a cavallo por la plaça, corriendo los toros con tanta gallardía y gentileza que era cosa de espanto" (55) ["The Abencerraje knights rode on horseback through the parade ground, chasing the bulls with such bravery and elegance that it was an awesome thing"]. Not only are the Abencerrajes great horsemen, they are also favorites with the ladies, great friends to the common people and sympathetic to Christians (55)—it seems no wonder that the Zegríes resent them.[51]

The full force of the Zegríes' treachery comes through for readers who understand the delicate mechanism of the pseudocombat that is the *juego de cañas*. Pérez de Hita involves the reader in this shared understanding, interspersing tags such as "como es uso del juego" ["as is done in this game"] that depend on common knowledge. The entire intrigue presupposes that the reader knows how the game is played. At the moment of betrayal the Abencerrajes are "maravillados de aquel caso" (60)["marvelously surprised at this event"], yet although they grab their spears to face their enemies, the Zegríes have the advantage, for their weapons are real: "Mas los Zegríes llevaban lo mejor, por yr más bien adereçados que los Abencerrages" ["But the Zegríes were better off, for they were better prepared than the Abencerrages"]. The reader who recognizes the conventionality and rules of the *cañas* as mock-combat can best appreciate the magnitude of the Zegríes' betrayal of chivalry. Moreover, while the shared investment in chivalric forms transcends any difference between Moorish characters and Christian readers, the conflict in the text pits Moors against Moors, so that readerly sympathy cannot align itself along confessional divisions.

The shared Iberian nature of the Granadan celebration is evident, too, in the lengthy description of how the ladies dress for the occasion. Pérez de Hita spares no detail in describing the carefully worked materials of these imagined, wonderfully elaborate costumes. Rich embroidery and gems on silk *marlotas*, a lining of cloth of silver, stressed or slashed damask, fantastic *tocas*—all these details function as so many points of reference for his readers. Critics have noted that the novel describes many garments worn by Moriscos in Pérez de Hita's own time;[52] what is even more striking is the frequent Christian use of the same, as is evident from the historical accounts of the *juegos de cañas*.[53] As Correa notes in his new introduction to the *Guerras civiles* (xxix), the episodes recall Andrés de Bernáldez's description of Queen Isabel's arrival in the Christian camp during the war on Granada, similarly clad in Moorish finery, which I discussed in Chapters 2 and 3. The point is not to suggest that Pérez de Hita had read Bernáldez's *Memorias del reinado de los reyes católicos*, but rather to remind ourselves that the shared appreciation of such dress by Christian and Moorish nobles alike qualifies any supposed exoticism in Pérez de Hita's description. The costumes may well be lavish, but they are not in any way foreign to their Iberian readers, though they might be for later readers across Europe.

The next episode of equestrian games in the *Guerras civiles* features both *cañas* and a *juego de sortija*, which involved spearing a ring with a lance from a galloping horse. The games are organized, Pérez de Hita tells us, for the *día de San Juan*, the feast of St. John, June 24 (76). Yet what might seem a contrived superimposition of the Christian calendar on Muslims in fact reflects a simultaneous celebration of the summer solstice. As Rachel Arié notes, the feast of ᶜAnsāra was a seasonal celebration for Muslims and Mozarabs alike, and featured bonfires such as those of the famous "nights of San Juan."[54] Pérez de Hita underscores the coincidence: "El día de San Juan venido, fiesta que todas las naciones del mundo celebra[n]" (77) ["On the day of Saint John, a feast celebrated by all nations of the world"], and the date of the celebrations is recalled again in the popular ballad that "recapitulates" the events, but which actually long predates Pérez de Hita's own text:

La mañana de San Juan,
al punto que alboreava,
gran fiesta hazen los Moros,
por la vega de Granada.
Rebolviendo sus cavallos,
jugando van de las lanças
ricos pendones en ellas
labrados por sus amadas.
Ricas aljubas vestidas,
de oro y seda labradas;
el Moro que amores tiene
allí bien se señalava.

[On the morning of St. John, as the sun was rising, the Moors held a great celebration in the vale of Granada. Turning their horses, they play with their spears, with
rich pennants on them embroidered by their beloveds. Dressed in rich *aljubas*
[tunics], worked in gold and silk: the Moor who was in love, there distinguished
himself.]

The ballad foregrounds the much longer tradition of maurophilia in the
romancero, even as it reiterates the points of contact between Moors and
Christians in Pérez de Hita's text. With its apparatus of feasts, jousts, and
costumes, held on the shared feast-day of the summer solstice, the ballad
reveals the *Guerras civiles de Granada* as merely the uppermost layer of a
cultural palimpsest.

Even when Pérez de Hita turns to more conventional Renaissance
panoply, as in the elaborate *galeras* (literally galleys, but in this case floats
or cars) that each clan produces as part of the elaborate *juego de sortija,* he
introduces uncanny echoes between the Moors and their Christian counterparts. The Abencerrajes enter with a fantastic, hubristic display: a galley
with a crystal globe on its ram, and on the globe a golden sash with the
motto "Todo es poco" (96) ["Everything is too little"]. There is a striking
echo here of the famous motto of Charles V, "Plus ultra," evoked more
firmly when the narrator comments: "Bravo blasón, y solamente digno
que el famoso Alexandro o César le pusieran" (96) ["Brave blazon, and
worthy only to be displayed by the famous Alexander or Caesar"].
Though the narrator comes close to chastising the Abencerrajes for over-
reaching, and announces the role of their own hubris in their future down-
fall, the scene nonetheless prefigures in the heroic Moors the future ruler
of Spain. Ironic or otherwise, the emblem downplays the otherness of
Moors who are more proximate to Spain than even they realize.

The Exile and the Fall

The emphasis on shared cultural practices provides the material base for Pérez de Hita's maurophilia, but the most explicit ideological interventions of the text occur through the metaphorics of exile, precisely as they apply to the Abencerrajes. As I demonstrate in Chapter 3, the conventionality of exile as a Petrarchan metaphor for distance from the beloved is reliteralized in ballads from the last decades of the sixteenth century, when Granadan Moriscos were forcibly relocated throughout Castile as a result of the War of the Alpujarras, and when the very place of Moriscos in Spain was being heatedly debated. Elsewhere I have argued that Pérez de Hita's invented history of his own text's transmission, purportedly handed from its author, an exiled Moor in North Africa, to a Spanish-speaking rabbi, to an aristocratic Spanish patron and protector of Moriscos who commissions its translation (291), obliquely suggests his sympathy for victims of the Christian repression that followed the fall of Granada.[55] In the text itself, moreover, undeserved exile is a constant preoccupation. The Zegríes step up their conspiracy against the Abencerrajes by accusing the queen of Granada of adultery with one of them, and, to add yet another ostensible betrayal, remind the king of the proud motto on the crystal globe (170–71). The gullible king agrees to destroy the Abencerrajes, and lures them to the Alhambra, where they are beheaded one by one until a young page manages to warn those outside. The general bloodbath and civil unrest that ensue mark the beginning of the end for Granada, yet momentary order is achieved when the king defends his actions and banishes the remaining Abencerrajes from the city (186). Their allies protest, and counter the threat of exile with a dire warning about the depopulation of the city (187, 201).

    In a richly intertextual moment, the exile of the Abencerrajes invokes Pérez de Hita's hugely popular predecessor, the novella *El Abencerraje*, which I analyze in Chapter 2. There, the noble Abindarráez, a banished member of the clan, laments the unjust fate of his people and relates the bloody episode to his sympathetic Christian captor, Narváez. The echo reinforces the metaphorics of exile within the *Guerras civiles*, aligning both maurophile texts against contemporary repression through their recuperation of a legendary injustice. In the later text, the emphasis on the false accusation at the heart of the Abencerrajes' banishment and the warnings about its effects on the polity subtly refract the official debates of Pérez de Hita's own time, when the purported Morisco threat to the state was often

offered as an argument for their expulsion, the dangerous depopulation of
Moorish areas adduced against it.[56] Although the expulsion itself would
not begin until 1609, the aftermath of the War in the Alpujarras had provided ample precedent for the use of banishment as a tool of political
control, and the general expulsion of the Moriscos had been discussed as
a possible solution to their recalcitrance since at least the 1580s. The false
accusation against the Abencerrajes in the text obliquely qualifies the
claims that Moriscos were enemies of the Spanish state in the late sixteenth
century, despite Pérez de Hita's own assertion in Part II of the *Guerras
civiles* that the beleaguered Moriscos did turn to the Ottoman Turks for
assistance during the War of the Alpujarras. Moreover, in Part I the exiled
Abencerrajes are highly sympathetic to Christians, and would-be Christians themselves, further giving the lie to contemporary accusations of the
Moriscos' fundamental opposition to Christianization:

Finalmente, quedó que los Abencerrages saliessen de Granada, porque ellos mis-
mos lo pidieron assí a todos los de su vando; y era la causa, porque se querían
tornar Christianos y passarse en servicio del Rey Don Fernando, que de otra manera jamás salieran de Granada, porque tenían toda la gente común de su parte y
la flor de los cavalleros della. (205)

[Finally, it was agreed that the Abencerrages should leave Granada, for they themselves requested it of those in their camp, and the cause was that they wished to
turn Christian and pass into the King Don Fernando's service, for otherwise they
never would have left Granada, for they had all the common people on their side,
and the flower of its knights.]

In a daring twist, Pérez de Hita ascribes the Abencerrajes' desire to
leave Granada for Christian territory precisely to their desire for conversion, thus turning on its head the argument that Moriscos deserved expulsion for their continued perseverance in their Islamic faith. These
Abencerrajes are willing to suffer exile in order to become Christians and
subjects of the Christian king. Moreover, as their imagined letter offering
their services to Fernando (206) claims, the Abencerrajes will be instru-
mental in the conquest of their former home, thus both serving their new
king and taking their revenge. The king of Granada, by contrast, is re-
proached for banishing them, and warned that he will regret banishing
them "sin culpa" (208) ["though blameless"]. The Abencerrajes are
warmly welcomed by the Christians. In a lovely detail, the narrator notes
that Isabel makes the converted Moorish ladies "damas de su estrado"
(209) ["ladies of her *estrado*"], on which they presumably felt at home.

Pérez de Hita's yoking of a maurophilia based on a shared aristocratic culture to such unmerited yet paradoxically exemplary exile thus intervenes in the highly charged debate about the fate of the Moriscos. Significantly, the novel appears at a moment of rare optimism about the Morisco question, with the discovery in Granada of the famous syncretic gospels of the Sacromonte, the Morisco forgeries that endeavored to construct a shared Christian past for Moors in Spain.[57] And even as it charts the inevitable fall of Granada, the text evinces a strong nostalgia that centers on precisely the chivalric and material traditions that knit together Moors and Christians. The texture of maurophilia comes through most clearly in these laments, voiced by the narrator:

¡O Granada, Granada!: ¿qué desventura vino sobre ti? ¿Qué se hizo tu nobleza? ¿Qué se hizo tu riqueza? ¿Qué se hizieron tus passatiempos? ¿Tus galas, justas y torneos, juegos de sortija? ¿Qué [s]e hizieron tus deleytes, fiestas de San Juan? ¿Y tus acordadas músicas y zambras? ¿Adónde se escondieron los bravos y vistosos juegos de cañas, tus altivos zebohos en las alboradas, cantados en la huerta de Generalife? ¿Qué se hizieron aquellas bravas y bizarras libreas de los gallardos Abencerrages? ¿Las delicadas invenciones de los Gazules? ¿Las altas pruevas y ligerezas de los Alabezes? ¿Los costosos trajes de los Zegrís, y Gomeles, y Maças? ¿Qué se ha hecho, al fin, toda tu nobleza? (203–4)

[Oh Granada, Granada! What misfortune came upon you? What became of your nobility? What became of your riches? What became of your pastimes? Your galas, jousts, and tournaments, *juegos de sortija*? What became of your delights, your feasts of San Juan? And your remembered music and *zambra* dances? Where have your brave and showy *juegos de cañas* hidden, or your proud slippers in the *alborada* dance, sung in the orchard of the Generalife? What became of the fierce and gallant liveries of the brave Abencerrages? The delicate inventions of the Gazules? The great races and speed of the Alabezes? The costly costumes of the Zegríes, Gomeles, and Maças? What has become, in the end, of all your nobility?]

Although this elegiac recollection comes before the fall of Granada in the text, and the immediate antecedent is the civil war within it, the passage necessarily invokes also the disappearance of Nasrid Granada as a result of the Christian conquest. The plangent evocation of a ludic and festive Granada mourns not only its internal struggles but, more daringly, the destruction of its culture, if not its physical existence, by its new masters. What remains, and what Pérez de Hita deploys to such effect, is the set of chivalric aristocratic practices enthusiastically adopted by Christians—the very practices that make the lament, and maurophilia itself, so powerful for an Iberian audience. As I stressed at the outset, a more distanced, orientalizing reception of the same practices is certainly possible, as the embrace of the text in France and elsewhere shows, but its domestic consumption relies instead on a much more proximate understanding of what is mourned.

Beyond the plaint for Granada, the *Guerras civiles* ends with two seemingly contradictory postscripts, announced by the narrator immediately after he gives us the peculiar genealogy of his text:

Y pues ya avemos acabado de hablar de la guerra de Granada (digo de las civiles guerras della, y de los vandos de los Abencerrages y Zegrís), diremos algunas cosas del buen cavallero Don Alonso de Aguilar; cómo le mataron los Moros en Sierra Bermeja, con algunos romances de su historia; y pondremos fin a los amores del valeroso Gazul con la hermosa Lindaraxa. (291)

[And as we are now done with telling of the war of Granada (I mean of the civil wars within it, and of the factions of the Abencerrages and Zegrís), we will say some things about the good knight Don Alonso de Aguilar—how the Moors killed him in Sierra Bermeja, with some ballads on his story—and we will end the loves of the valiant Gazul and the beautiful Lindaraxa.]

Why does Pérez de Hita attempt to circumscribe his story to internal conflict, given that he has just narrated the culmination of the Christian conquest? The author seems to want to preserve Granada as a precinct of chivalric culture, deemphasizing the external conflict and moving to the wilder setting of the mountains for the alternative. The supplement to the story of Granada at the end of Part I is twofold. On the one hand, the narrator glides into the loves of Gazul and Lindaraxa as though nothing whatsoever had changed—Gazul hears of a *juego de cañas*, dresses in the accustomed livery, and then argues with his jealous beloved, who finally accepts him and sends him to the tournament as her knight. The narration is clearly secondary to the *romances* that Pérez de Hita wants to foreground here, as though to remind his readers of the enduring pleasures of maurophilia. As if to acknowledge the belated place of the episode within the text, the lovers, once married, convert to Christianity.[58]

On the other hand, Pérez de Hita concludes with a much harsher vision of conflict between Moors and Christians. In a sense, one could argue that Part II—the bloody and intimate account of the War of the Alpujarras, in which he fought—is itself such an alternative. But even in Part I the reader gets a taste of the violence that lies beyond chivalric convention. In contradistinction to all the noble Moors who want nothing more than to convert and serve the Catholic monarchs, after the fall of Granada "todos los lugares del Alpuxarra se tornaron a revelar y alçar" (306) ["all the places/towns of the Alpujarra once again rebelled and rose up"]. The anonymous, depersonalized rebellion announces a radical divergence in the representation of the conflict. It is now no longer a matter of singular chivalric exchanges but one of violent encounters between anonymous troops. King Fernando asks for a valiant knight to lead the counterattack, and Alonso de Aguilar volunteers in perfect chivalric mode: "Esta empresa, Cathólica Magestad, para mí está consignada, porque mi señora la reina me la tiene prometida" (307) ["This enterprise, your Catholic Majesty, is consigned to me, because my lady the queen has promised it to me"]. The force sent against the Moors is not individual, however, but corporate: one thousand infantry, and five hundred men on horseback. The Moors stop the Christians by rolling boulders down the mountains to crush them—nothing could be farther from the personal, idealized encounters earlier in the text. The few Christians who reach the top are immediately overwhelmed by a much larger Moorish force, and Aguilar is killed, though not before dispatching "more than thirty" of the enemy (308). Despite these last-minute heroics, however, the breakdown in chivalry appears complete, from the destruction of the horses at the foot of the mountains to the overwhelming difference in numbers. A ballad Pérez de Hita appends to the story emphasizes the change in register: one of the Christian knights, the *romance* tells us, is overrun by "mucha Mora canalla" (312) ["a lot of Moorish riff-raff"], and in none of the three ballads on the episode are any Moors named. The contrast with so many duels and chivalric encounters could not be more pronounced, both in the mode of combat and in its outcome—the complete rout of the Christians. The text ends on this both ominous and unconvincing note, in a last, feeble attempt to imagine the Moors' resignation as the only possible end to the standoff:

Esta fue la honrosa muerte del valeroso Don Alonso de Aguilar, y como avemos dicho, della les pesó mucho a los Reyes Cathólicos; los quales, como viessen la brava resistencia de los Moros, por estar en tan ásperos lugares, no quisieron embiar contra ellos por entonces más gente. Mas los moros de la Serranía, viendo que no podían vivir sin tratar en Granada, los unos se passaron en Africa y los otros se dieron al Rey Don Fernando, el qual los recibió con mucha clemencia. Este fin tuvo la guerra de Granada, a gloria de Dios nuestro Señor sea. (313)

[This was the honorable death of the courageous Don Alonso de Aguilar and, as we have said, the Catholic Monarchs were greatly saddened by it; who, seeing the fierce resistance of the Moors from such rugged places, did not send more men against them for the time being. But, seeing that they could not survive without dealing with Granada, some of the Moors in the mountains went to Africa and some gave themselves over to the King Don Fernando, who received them with great clemency. This was the end of the war in Granada, glory be to God our Lord.]

The abrupt end of the *Guerras civiles* thus reveals the tremendous pressures on the maurophile text: from actual and recent history, which fails to conform to chivalric paradigms, from the maurophobia of contemporary debates on the Morisco question, and from Moorish subjects who cannot be co-opted in either textual or political terms. Yet although the discordant ending acknowledges the limits of both authorial and political control over Moors, the overwhelming emphasis of the text—unlike its controversial and neglected second part—remains on the optimistic recuperation of a shared chivalric culture that enables an imaginative and material connection to Granada.

Beyond Pérez de Hita's singular though hugely influential text, the critical recovery of that chivalric culture seems essential if we are to place maurophilia in its proper context. In this vein, one might read back from the more extensive description of chivalric games in the *Guerras civiles* to the mentions of such traditions in the *romancero morisco*, as one more way to situate that corpus within its ideological framework. The attempts to classicize the origin of the *cañas* or to repudiate them altogether, much like the reaction against the ventriloquizing *romances* that I described in Chapter 3, show that although these practices were virtually hybridized, habitual, and willingly embraced by the Iberian nobility, there was nonetheless some consciousness that they conflicted with other, more orthodox understandings of Spain. Thus the dialectical relationship to Moorishness is not merely a matter of uncritical, internal acceptance versus pointed external exoticization; instead, as I have suggested throughout, for Spaniards as for other Europeans Moorishness remains an ongoing and conflictive dimension of Spain's national identity, long after the fall of Granada.

5

The Spanish Race

Allí habló el rey don Juan,
bien oiréis lo que decía:
"Si tú quisieras, Granada,
contigo me casaría;
daréte en arras y dote
a Córdoba y a Sevilla."
"Casada soy, rey don Juan,
casada soy, que no viuda;
el moro que a mí me tiene
muy grande bien me quería."
   —"Romance de Abenámar," anonymous, fifteenth century

[Then spoke the King Don Juan—you shall hear what
he said:
   "If you would consent, Granada, I would marry you.
I will give you for your dowry Cordoba and Seville."
   "I am married, King Don Juan. Married, and not yet
a widow. The Moor who possesses me loved me full
well."]

WITH THEIR EMPHASIS on the stuff of a shared material culture, maurophile texts recall for Spaniards the undeniable place of the Andalusi heritage in their own practices. Yet from the anonymous *romancero* to the
Abencerraje to the *Guerras civiles de Granada*, maurophilia trades also in
the powerful erotic charge of the Moor as love-object, or of a Moorish
desire in which the reader vicariously or voyeuristically participates. Often,
the conquest of territory is imagined as an erotics, conflating military and
sexual possession of a proximate enemy as in the epigraph above.[1] The
constant foregrounding of the attraction that Moors hold—for Christians
as for other Moors—is thus another of the genres' signal ideological interventions, particularly striking in contrast to the heightened anti-Morisco
rhetoric of the late sixteenth century. Yet even as the erotic vein of mauro-

philia provided a sympathetic alternative to the historical marginalization of Moriscos, outside Spain such imaginative couplings were put to very different rhetorical purposes. In the anti-Spanish pamphlets that circulated furiously throughout Protestant Europe in the last decades of the sixteenth century and that we have come to know as the Black Legend, Spaniards were imagined as a miscegenated race, tainted by Moorish and Jewish blood. This chapter juxtaposes the Black Legend construction of Spain, with a special emphasis on the English case, with a late example of maurophilia—the story of Ozmín and Daraja, from Mateo Alemán's picaresque *Guzmán de Alfarache* (1599), to show how miscegenation and assimilation, those two sides of an ideological coin, operate within and beyond Spain.

Black Spain

Whereas within the Peninsula the nation's pure, "gothic" identity was constantly complicated and challenged by a variety of cultural investments, whether self-conscious or inadvertent, Spain's enemies abroad ruthlessly exploited its Moorish past to construct the nation as a racial and religious other. Although the official discourse in Spain loudly renounced Moorishness, the westernmost reaches of Europe remained for many observers part of the Orient or Africa, and thus savage, cruel, or tyrannical. As I suggested in Chapter 4, the reception of Spanish maurophilia by foreign audiences contributed to the nation's perceived exoticism, despite the fact that, within Spain, Moorish forms were not necessarily exotic, though marked in some cases as regional or old-fashioned.[2] Yet, as I anticipated in the introduction to this study, the construction of an oriental Spain differs in an important way from the influential model proposed by Said for the nineteenth century: namely, this intra-European orientalism does not accompany colonial domination.[3] Instead, Spain is characterized as oriental in an effort to challenge its imperial domination over other emerging European nations, in particular its threat to Italy, France, the Netherlands, and England. In the cultural sphere, meanwhile, Spain's enduring engagement with Andalusi-derived practices serves to locate it beyond the pale of what is properly European. Even as Spain attempts to distance itself from its heritage, the admiring foreign accounts of Granada and Spanish local color early in the century gradually give way to a racializing discourse of essential Moorishness.

In much anti-Spanish propaganda—the various versions of the Black Legend—Spain is consistently associated with Islam, with Africa, with dark peoples. It is important to recover the essentializing blackness of this cultural mythology: critics typically read it metaphorically, with black as a figure for Spain's cruelty and greed in the New World, yet it often refers in unambiguous terms to Spain's racial difference, its *intrinsic* Moorishness. Beyond the frequent metaphorical association of blackness with evil in the early modern period, this discourse proposed a literal sense, in an attempt to render Spain biologically (if not visibly) black.[4] These characterizations deliberately misrepresent the racialization of difference within Spain. Certainly, Iberia's encounter with the New World led to much speculation about the color of peoples, and slave trading with Africa had established color as an index of ethnic difference even earlier. Yet, although racism based on physical appearance did exist, and blacks were singled out for their color, Moors were not reliably identifiable in this way.[5] The phenotypical notion of race was emphatically not the main focus for Spaniards in the sixteenth century, particularly where Moors were concerned. As the grim inventories for the sale and redemption of slaves during the Moorish uprising in the Alpujarras demonstrate, Moors came in all shades, from "color moreno," or "color negra," to "color blanco que tira un poco a membrillo cocho," and even, frequently, "color blanca" ["tawny," "black," "white tending to cooked quince," and "white"].[6] Sympathetic depictions of Moorish women in maurophile texts such as the *Guerras civiles de Granada* occasionally portray them as blonde, Petrarchan beauties indistinguishable from their European counterparts.[7] L. P. Harvey concludes, "It is likely that whatever differences might be visible at the level of individuals, at the level of the population as a whole they were insignificant."[8]

Spaniards were radically divided in their opinion of where the Moriscos had come from. Apologists for their expulsion, and even some of its opponents, generally attributed to them African origins, however long they might have resided in Spain, as does the sympathetic Pedro de Valencia: "son españoles como los demás que habitan en España, pues ha casi novecientos años que nacen y se crían en ella"[9] ["they are Spanish as all others who live in Spain, for they have been born and raised here for almost nine hundred years"]. Others, conversely, emphasized their Spanish and Christian origins as *converts* to Islam, or what was referred to during the Umayyad period as *muladíes*.[10] Thus in 1543 the bishop of Calahorra exhorted preachers to use gentle methods in proselytizing the Moriscos, "por ser nuestros próximos y ser tan antiguos españoles y muchos dellos descendientes de christianos"[11] ["as they are our neighbors and such ancient Spaniards and many of them descended from Christians"]. Moreover, many of the Moors and Turks encountered by Spaniards (as by other Europeans) in North Africa were European captives turned renegades, and therefore absolutely unmarked by bodily difference.[12] Thus, even if outside Spain the discourse of difference foregrounded skin color, and despite the existence of a trade in sub-Saharan black slaves, within Spain Moorishness emphatically does not equal blackness.

Instead, Spanish racial hysteria focused on covert cultural and religious practices, and on the much more ambiguous register of blood. The widespread consensus, amply reflected in satirical texts, was that *limpieza de sangre* (blood purity) was almost impossible to determine in any authentic fashion. Absent physical manifestations, how could one tell if any given subject was free of the Semitic or Moorish taint?[13] This ambiguity suggests the possibility of assimilation, passing, and other challenges to the official rhetoric of essentialized difference. In fact, certain former Muslims, particularly those whose families had belonged to the Nasrid nobility, were able to avoid stigmatization—not because, as the Black Legend would have it, Spain was "Moorish" or "African" in any uncomplicated way, but because the nuances of "racial" difference in the Peninsula differed so markedly from European accounts of it.[14]

The exacerbation of anti-Morisco feeling in the late sixteenth and early seventeenth centuries doubtless stemmed primarily from internal motivations—the bloody uprising in the Alpujarras, the economic appeal of Morisco property, the increasing perception that the forced converts and their descendants were unassimilable in religious or cultural terms. Yet I submit that it may have related also to European constructions of Spanish Moorishness, much as the earlier moments of Spanish maurophobia described in Chapter 1 were at least perceived as a response to earlier European versions of an excessively Moorish Spain. For the strident anti-Spanish pamphlets that were widely produced, translated, and circulated throughout the Netherlands, France, and England in the 1580s and 1590s moved from a rhetoric of religious difference within Christianity to a far starker vision of essential otherness.[15]

How did these conceptions of Spanish difference evolve? As critics have long noted, Spanish polemics on their own actions in the New World, signally Bartolomé de las Casas's *Breve historia de la destrucción de las*

Indias (1552) provided much of the grist for accusations of Spaniards' exceptional and cruelty.[16] As I noted briefly in Chapter 1, the racialization of Spanish difference existed much earlier, despite Spanish claims of religious homogeneity, as in Erasmus' notorious refusal in 1517 to visit a nation where "there are scarcely any Christians."[17] The overriding irony of the Peninsular expulsion of the Jews, of course, was the subsequent identification of Spaniards and Portuguese with Jews throughout Europe during the sixteenth century and beyond.[18] When the young protagonist of the picaresque *Guzmán de Alfarache* travels to Genoa to find his father, he is greeted everywhere with the double insult "Bellaco, marrano"[19] ["scoundrel, Jewish swine"]. The latter seems to have become a standard term for Spaniards.[20] Although many of these characterizations do not explicitly focus on race as bodily difference, their refusal to countenance the (ostensibly nominal) Christianity of the Spaniards they encounter makes Judaism or Islam into an essential taint.

The frequent Italian diatribes against the Spaniards, who had an increasing military presence in Italy in the sixteenth century, routinely describe them as *marranos*, infidel Moors, based on their violent behavior or appearance. After the sack of Prato in 1512, the town's poets refused to countenance the Spaniards' Christianity and even their humanity, describing them as "Spagnoli no, ma sí arrabiati cani, / nemici a Cristo"[21] ["not Spaniards but rabid dogs, enemies of Christ"] and "spagnoli no, ma rinnegate cani" ["not Spaniards but renegade dogs"]. Ariosto implicitly echoes these characterizations in his *Furioso*, where all Spaniards are simply Saracens. Dutch pamphlets also invoke Moorishness in decrying Spanish excesses, as in William of Orange's characterization of the duke of Alba as "this Moorish tiger-beast" with a "secret Muslim heart."[22] Yet the othering of Spain stems not just from these moments of violence but also from the perception of the nation's cultural indebtedness to al-Andalus, evident in Lalaing, Navagero, and other influential travelers, as noted in Chapter 1. The official ceremonial representation of Spain abroad often involved such "exotic" forms as the *juegos de cañas* or bullfights, also contributing to this impression. In the eyes of other Europeans, Spain's distinctive national identity was Moorish.

It is instructive in this regard to consider the accounts of the future Philip II's visit to London in 1554 for his marriage to Mary Tudor. The *relaciones* of Philip's visit suggest a profound suspicion on both sides, born of religious difference and of the prejudices involved in encountering uncouth Northern islanders, as the Spaniards saw it, or arrogant *dons* all too ready to rule Mary's subjects, in the eyes of the English. Fascinating documents for the history of Anglo-Spanish relations more generally, the accounts suggest how standard Spanish practices may have contributed to the sense of an oriental Spain that emerges from the Black Legend pamphlets. Most striking in this regard is the elaborate *juego de cañas* that Philip ordered to celebrate his marriage to the English queen, which I described in Chapter 4. The effect of such a spectacle must have been considerable. The account claims that the games were witnessed by twelve thousand spectators—an improbable number but indicative of the event's importance in the eyes of the chronicler. The "Spanish fashion" on display, while habitual for Iberian nobles, would have appeared quite exotic to the English audience: silk and damask *marlotas*, leather shields, and even the game itself, with its horsemen riding *a la jineta*, would have been markedly unfamiliar.

The sense of cultural dissonance comes through also in accounts of the encounter between Queen Mary and María Enríquez de Guzmán, the Duchess of Alba. The two versions of this ceremonial and very public event differ slightly in their details, yet both suggest imperfect communication and a great deal of attention to where and how the noble ladies would sit. In the first version, below, the ladies different preferences are patent:

ynbió la magestad de la reina las señoras damas de su cámara privadas suyas, la una era la condesa de Queldar y la otra la condesa de Pembruque, por la duquesa de Alba para que la acompañasen hasta palaçio porque quería venir a besar las manos de su magestad. Acompañó a la duquesa toda la corte. Su majestad de la rreina la esperó en una sala grande y enpeçando entrar los cavalleros se lebantó, y en entrando la duquesa salió hasta la mitad de la pieça a rreçivilla y allí allegó la duquesa a pedirle las manos de su magestad. Estubo gran rrato que no se las quiso dar la duquesa. Se las tomó por fuerça su magestad. La besó en el carrillo y luego latomó de la mano y de allí la llebó donde estava un dosel, y fue la lengua el Marqués de las Navas, porque la rreyna hablava en françes. Su magestad dixo a la duquesa si se quería asentar en alto o en baxo. La duquesa dixo que su magestad se asentase, que ella se asentaría en el suelo. Su magestad probó asentarse en el suelo. Y no pudo estar. Y luego mandó traer un banquillo cubierto de brocado [. . .] para la duquesa. La duquesa no le quería tomar y estubo un rrato porfiando hasta que se le hizo tomar.[23]

[Her Majesty the Queen sent the ladies of her chamber, one the Countess of Kildare and the other the Countess of Pembroke, for the Duchess of Alba to accompany her to the palace because she wanted to come kiss her Majesty's hands. The whole court accompanied the Duchess. Her Majesty the Queen waited for her in a large chamber and as the gentlemen began to enter she rose and as the

Duchess came in she advanced to the middle of the room to receive her and there
came the Duchess to beg for her Majesty's hands. For a long time the Duchess
would not give hers. Her Majesty took them by force. She kissed her on the cheek
and then took her by the hand to where there was a canopy, and the Marquis of
Navas translated, because the Queen spoke in French. Her Majesty asked the
Duchess whether she wanted to sit up high or down low. The Duchess said her
Majesty should sit, that she would sit on the floor. Her Majesty tried to sit on the
floor. And she could not take it. And then she asked for a small stool covered in
brocade for the Duchess. The Duchess did not want to take it and she insisted a
while until she forced her to take it.]

Presumably the duchess, accustomed to the *estrado*, is far more comfortable sitting on the floor, Moorish-fashion, than anywhere else. Though
Mary tries to sit like her, she finds it unbearable, and when she tries to
raise the duchess closer to her own level, the duchess demurs until forced
to sit on the low stool.

As aristocrats, these ladies should find common ground beyond national distinctions, but this version suggests a profound cultural and
courtly difference that comes between the two despite their best efforts.
Yet the second account of the same adumbrates cultural difference, suggesting instead a highly stylized exchange of courtesies, part of the protocol of a royal meeting:

[LA REINA] estaba en pie, y entrando la Duquesa por la puerta salió de su estrado
casi hasta la misma puerta, y allí se hincó de rodillas la Duquesa y le pidió la mano
con gran porfía, y la Reina se abajó casi tanto como ella, y la abrazó y jamás la
quiso dar la mano, y en levantándose la besó en la boca, según la costumbre que
acá usan las Reinas hacer con las Grandes Señoras de su sangre y no con otras. Y
tomóla de la mano preguntándole cómo venía y se había hallado en la mar, y
diciendo que se holgaba de verla. Y llevóla consigo al estrado do suelen tener una
silla alta, y la Reina llegando a la silla se asentó sobre la alhombra diciendo a la
Duquesa si se quería asentar allí. La Duquesa le suplicó que se asentase en su silla
y jamás quiso. Trujeron dos escabelos cubiertos de brocado pelo. Estonce sentóse
la Reina en uno cabe la silla, y mandó que se asentase la Duquesa en el otro. Ella
hizo una grande reverencia, y sentóse en el suelo, al lado, como allá se acostumbra,
y la Reina dejó el escabelo y sentóse en el alhombra con ella, no consintiéndola
levantar. La Duquesa porfió tanto que la Reina volvió a su escabelo y mandó que
ella tomase el que le daban, y ansí se asentó la Duquesa en el otro.[24]

[The Queen was standing, and when the Duchess entered through the door she
came forth from her *estrado* almost to the door itself, and there the Duchess knelt
before her and begged her for her hand, and the Queen lowered herself almost as
far and embraced her and would never give her her hand, and upon standing kissed

her on the mouth, as Queens here are wont to do with great ladies of their blood
and no others. And taking her by the hand she asked her how she was and how
she had fared at sea, saying she was glad to see her. And she took her with her to
the *estrado*, where they usually have a high chair, and the Queen reaching the chair
sat on the rug asking the Duchess whether she wanted to sit there. The Duchess
begged her to sit on her chair and never would accept. They brought in two stools
covered in brocade. Then the Queen sat on one next to the chair, and told the
Duchess to sit on the other. She made a great curtsy and sat on the floor, next to
her, as is the custom there, and the Queen left her stool and sat on the rug with
her, without allowing anyone to raise her. The Duchess insisted so much that the
Queen returned to her stool and told her to take the one offered, and thus the
Duchess sat on the other one.]

In this account, the two ladies attempt to outdo each other in courtesy
and deference. Any sense of their actual sitting preferences disappears amid
the highly formalized gestures of the protocol of the occasion. Mary's dais
is characterized as an *estrado*, while Mary herself seems to expect that the
duchess will want to sit on the floor.[25] The queen's familiarity with Spanish
customs makes perfect sense, of course, if we recall that her own mother,
Catherine of Aragon, was Spanish.

The variants in these accounts signal actual, important distinctions
between Spain and England while underscoring the need to treat those
distinctions with suspicion, especially given the way Spain's difference
would be magnified in the Black Legend discourse of Elizabeth's reign.
While I by no means wish to reinscribe the essentialized otherness that
Protestant pamphleteers ascribed to Spain, I find it instructive to reconstruct how Spain's cultural hybridity may have contributed to the discourse used against it.

The Black Legend pamphlets that appear from the 1570s on are far
less subtle in their account of Spanish difference. Over and over again,
Spain is racially conflated with the Moors, despite its own considerable
ambivalence about Moorish survivals and its deliberate self-construction
as vanquisher of Moors and victor of the Reconquista. While one might
construe the pamphlets as a corrective to Spain's own "blood" racism and
denial of its Semitic heritage, they were not penned in any humanist attempt at tolerance. Instead, ironically, they stigmatized Spain in Spain's
own terms, reinscribing the presence of Moors as a racial taint.

Though I focus here on English pamphlets, many of them were translations from Dutch or French originals, as the same set of virulent anti-
Spanish commonplaces circulated furiously throughout Protestant Eu-

rope. Although they shared the same discourse, the pamphlets also served particular local ends, as various consolidating nations resisted the encroachment of Habsburg power. As Eric Griffin points out for England, the pamphlets were quite effective at strengthening English identity in contradistinction to Spain, in a context of great anxiety about foreign influence or even invasion.[26] In this sense, their emphasis on the essential difference of Spain may say less about Spain than about English anxieties concerning recusants—*English* others capable of assimilating or passing, and who might easily cross over to Spain, whether physically or in their intimate allegiance. Yet, given the force of their racist othering, the pamphlets nonetheless had powerful consequences for Spain, for its perception throughout Europe, and even for its inclusion therein.

Thus "The Coppie of the Anti-Spaniard," translated from French in 1590, urges the nations of Europe to rally around France "and with one breath to goe and abate the pride and insolencie of these Negroes,"[27] invoking European racial solidarity against an African, black Spain. Conflating "Moors" and "Negroes" in this way is a powerful rhetorical gesture: not only does it construct Spain's difference as essential and easily identifiable, it substitutes the peoples of sub-Saharan Africa for the encroaching powers of North Africa and the Levant. As Nabil Matar usefully reminds us, English (and European) relations with these two groups were very different: "England's relations with sub-Saharan Africans were relations of power, domination, and slavery, while relations with the Muslims of North Africa and the Levant were of anxious equality and grudging emulation."[28] Here, then, the specific substitution of "Negro" for Moor seems not merely a misunderstanding, but a deliberate rhetorical ploy to diminish Spain.

Some of the pamphlets attempt to negotiate the apparent sameness of the Spaniards. After all, despite their *marlotas*, Phillip II and his entourage, as well as more recent envoys from Spain, were clearly white. The pamphlets make them the product of miscegenation: though they may appear light-skinned, they are tainted with Moorishness.[29] Thus Edward Daunce's "Brief Discourse of the Spanish State" (1590) foregrounds the accusation of racial impurity by claiming that Spaniards are genealogically "mingled with the Mores cruell and full of trecherie."[30] The theme of miscegenation returns in a striking moment of innuendo: during the eight centuries of Moorish occupation, Daunce insinuates, "we must not think that the Negroes sent for women out of Aphrick."[31]

This genealogical and racialist discourse appears often: as Griffin notes, *The Spanish Colonie, or briefe chronicle of the acts and gestes of the Spaniardes* (1583, the first English translation of Las Casas' *Brevísima relación*), ascribes the Spaniards' behavior to their "firste fathers the Gothes" and "their second progenitors the Saracens."[32] Edmund Spenser's *A View of the State of Ireland* (1596, printed 1633), which attempts to discredit any connection between Catholic Ireland and Spain, makes the purported taint explicit:

And yet after all those the Moores and barbarians breaking over out of Africa, did finally possess all Spain, or the most part thereof, and tread down under their foul heathenish feet whatever little they found there yet standing; the which, though afterward they were beaten out by Ferdinando of Aragon, and Elizabeth his wife, yet they were not so cleansed, but that through the marriages which they had made, and mixture with the people of the land during their long continuance there, they had left no pure drop of Spanish blood; no, nor of Roman or Scythian; so that of all nations under heaven I suppose the Spaniard is the most mingled, most uncertain, and most bastardly.[33]

Spenser's Irenius echoes Spanish anxieties about *limpieza de sangre* and the invisible taint of Semitic blood to English ends. Although he quickly demurs that "there is no nation now in Christendom, nor much further, but is mingled and compounded with others,"[34] the accusations of bastardy and unknowability suggest that Spain is exceptionally tainted. Though Mary Tudor was at least as "mingled" a subject as her Spanish husband, that is, his nation is the "bastardly" one, with Philip himself described in a contemporary French diatribe as "demi-More, demi-Juif, demi-Sarrazin."[35]

The mixed nature of the Spanish appears more obliquely in Shakespeare's *The Merchant of Venice*, in which Portia is courted by the Prince of Arragon. Lynda E. Boose cogently asks of the Spanish suitor: "Is Arragon to be understood as merely another member of the multitude of failed European suitors, or does his structural placement between the black Morocco and the white Bassanio, a Spaniard between a Moroccan and a Venetian, geographically imply that he occupies the space of the "white Moor?"[36] In Boose's reading, the Spaniard is not necessarily marked by color, but his full participation in Europe is cast into doubt by his imputed miscegenated blood. Thus, while the more sophisticated texts echo Spanish anxieties about hidden difference, they often revert to the more blatant accusations of an essential, visible otherness.

Far less understated is the representation of Spain's miscegenated blood in *Lust's Dominion; or, the Lascivious Queen* (1599/1600), which imagines the queen of Spain in an adulterous liaison with the Moorish villain Eleazar, who himself aspires to the Spanish throne.[37] At a symbolic level, Spanish blackness is moralized most explicitly in Thomas Middleton's political allegory *A Game at Chess* (1624), a *succès de scandale* on the stage that caused an international incident between Spain and England. Playing opposite a "white" England, Spain is none too subtly represented by the Black House, and its most notorious representative in London, Count Gondomar, by the Black Knight. As Gary Taylor notes, in Middleton's play "Blackness is Spanishness."[38] Although the allegory modulates the racial implications of white and black within the play, Spain's blackness nonetheless participates in the larger economy of color and race analyzed by Hall. Taylor reads the play as a major moment in the consolidation of color-based racism, yet he fails to interrogate the equation of Spain with blackness, echoing instead the prejudice of the early modern English: "Middleton's known sources for the play asserted that the Spanish were of mixed blood, as much Moorish African as European. Spaniards insisted on their 'pure blood,' but it was hard to deny the brownish complexions evident in many portraits from Golden Age Spain."[39]

References to Spain as Islamic appear not only in the Black Legend pamphlets, but in literary texts centrally concerned with questions of national identity, such as Spenser's *The Faerie Queene*, in which Philip II is famously figured as "Souldan."[40] The identification of Philip II in particular with Islam returns in histories such as Fulke Greville's *Life of Sir Philip Sidney* (c. 1612), in which the Spanish monarch makes an appearance as "Suleiman of Spain."[41] (The irony in this case is striking, since Greville's own subject is named after his godfather, the monarch vilified here). Although the identification of Spaniards with Turks has to do primarily with their perceived cruelty or tyranny, it invokes also the more generalized sense of a Spain that is other by blood. Indeed, the conflation of Turks with Moors and "Sarazens" (as in the French example above) suggests that this literature was more interested in the defamation of Spain than in geographical or historical precision.

As a whole, this racialist corpus makes the case that Spain cannot leave its Moorishness behind. However much it may imagine itself in contradistinction to the Moors defeated at Granada, the Black Legend constructs it as genealogically and essentially defined by Moorishness. Within Spain, in turn, much of the contemporary debate about the Moriscos revolved around whether Moorishness could be transcended. Could the Moriscos—by the late sixteenth century often the third or fourth generation born into Christianity, however superficial their faith—lose all marks of difference, or were they inherently unassimilable? The answers to this central question spanned the political spectrum, from calls for annihilation or expulsion to less frequent arguments for assimilation and intermarriage.[42]

Those who argued against the *estatutos de limpieza* noted that European attacks on Spanish *honra* were fed by Spain's refusal to consider baptized Moors or Jews full-fledged Christians. They contrasted self-defeating Spanish efforts to reveal Semitic stains with French or Italian dissimulation. Thus the humanist Pedro de Valencia argued that with the Spanish zeal for discovery "nos hemos querido infamar entre las demás naciones de Europa, que descendiendo ellas de no menor vio [*sic*] semejante mezcla, a los españoles solo nos valdonan Francia, y Ytalia, y tienen razón, porque la infamia es mala fama, y quitada la fama cesa la nota y la afrenta, y ellos acerca de sí han cubierto la fama, y nosotros conservámosla, descubrímosla con cuidado"[43] ["we have wished to defame ourselves among the other nations of Europe, for though they descend from no less a mix, only the Spaniards are insulted by France and by Italy, and they are right, for infamy is ill fame, and when the fame is gone so is the notice and affront, and they among themselves have covered over the fame, and we preserve it, carefully revealing it"]. The *romances* that deplored maurophilia also took up the issue of European perceptions, in their case as a reason to avoid more talk of Moors:

¿Ha venido a su noticia
que hay cristianos en España?
¿Quieren que diga el hereje
que en nuestra fe sacrosanta,
de los nombres de la pila
se nos sigue alguna infamia?[44]

[Has it come to (the maurophile poets') notice that there are Christians in Spain? Do they want the heretic to say that in our holy faith there is infamy in the names with which we are baptized?]

David Nirenberg notes the irony in the slights Spain received: the genealogical definitions that it had constructed for its "colectividades," he claims, "la habían convertido en un país híbrido" ["had transformed it into a hybrid country"].[45] While I would dispute the causality in Nirenberg's account, he is perceptive in noting how tied Spain's hybridity was to its defamation by other Europeans.

While Spaniards of various persuasions worry about the international effects of Spain's obsession with origins, maurophile literature is most directly concerned with the domestic acceptance of converts from Islam and their descendants. Thus the corpus argues for inclusion, via a complex negotiation of cultural and religious difference: given the Moriscos' cultural compatibility, which the texts often figure as erotic attraction, those who profess Christianity should be welcomed in Spain, they suggest. Thus in contrast to the external accusations of miscegenation, and the domestic fear of tainted blood, the textual erotics of maurophilia performs assimilation, affording inclusion within the nation.

Loving the Moor

Unlike both the Protestant pamphlets and the Spanish diatribes, arguments for Morisco assimilation necessarily treated difference as malleable and susceptible to change. During the first few years after the 1492 conquest, Hernando de Talavera, first archbishop of Granada, advocated a syncretic approach to proselytism that accommodated linguistic and cultural difference. Although Talavera's restraint was not the official policy for long, it suggested how medieval forms of tolerance might inform the new era, and how Moors might be persuaded to embrace Christianity in a gradual fashion.

These years also saw the conversion and assimilation of many families from the Nasrid aristocracy, whose status seems to have afforded them immediate entrée into Christian society.[46] In many cases these powerful élites served as essential intermediaries between the new Christian masters and the mass of the Moorish population, while achieving full social acceptance in Christian terms. Genealogies of the Granada Venegas family emphasized not only their recent unions with Christian captives but their remote origins in *taifa* rulers and, remarkably, an ancestral Christian nobility. Families such as the Granada Venegas would intermarry with *cristianos viejos* at the highest levels of Castilian society over the course of the sixteenth century, suggesting that there were important exceptions, born of rank and privilege, to the prevailing anxieties about Moorishness as a genealogical taint. Enrique Soria Mesa points out that these noble families often succeeded in being legally recognized as *hidalgos*, with all the privi-

leges of that class, and in bypassing the limitations the blood purity legislation entailed for most Moriscos.[47] Moreover, former Muslims who could
prove that they had converted to Christianity before the generalized
forced baptisms could claim the status of Old Christians.[48] These were
important exceptions to any racialist genealogy used against converts.

Intermarriage also provided an important qualifier to racialist understandings of Morisco difference. During the first part of the sixteenth century, official policy promoted intermarriage as the best way to ensure the
full Christianization of the newly converted. In certain cases the laws even
promised New Christians who married into Old Christian families all the
privileges of the latter.[49] Arguments for intermarriage persisted into the
early seventeenth century, when anti-Morisco sentiment had become
much more extreme and calls for their expulsion widespread. In his 1606
treatise on the Moriscos, Pedro de Valencia argued for "permixtión,"
which he glossed as "total mezcla, que no se puede discernir ni distinguir
qual es de aquesta, o aquella nación"[50] ["a total mix, in which it is impossible to discern or distinguish which is of this or that nation,"] and recommended also that "los que fueren naciendo de matrimonios de Cristianos
Viejos y Moriscos, no sean tratados ni tenidos por Moriscos, que a los
unos, ni a los otros no los afrentemos, ni despreciemos" ["those who
gradually are born to marriages of Old Christians and Moriscos should
not be treated as or held as Moriscos, and neither the ones nor the others
should be offended or despised"]. As Javier Castillo Fernández usefully
points out, historiography has largely neglected the large class of assimilated Moriscos (who might fall under Valencia's prescription), perhaps because they do not conform to the "clash of cultures" model.[51]

Despite the many voices raised against expulsion, it was finally decreed in 1609. The general expulsion decree of July 10, 1610, makes an
exception for Moriscas who had married Old Christians, and for children
born of the unions.[52] In his letter to Philip III protesting the expulsion,
Pedro Vaca de Castro, archbishop of Seville, argued for the rights of those
who had, after all, been united in Christian marriage, whether the Old
Christian was the husband or the wife.[53] While the number of intermar-
riages is uncertain, these sources suggest that they offered a path to assimilation that trumped essentialist understandings of difference. Actual,
institutionalized maurophilia on the part of an Old Christian spouse could,
for a good part of the sixteenth century, afford inclusion. For Moriscas
who had married Old Christians, that inclusion was still available when
the expulsions were decreed.[54]

The protracted controversies over Morisco assimilation underscore the ideological significance of idealizing maurophile productions. In fact, given the perceived correlation between class and assimilability, the genre's insistent portrayal of noble protagonists may represent the thin edge of the wedge for acceptance. The story of Ozmín and Daraja, from the first part of Mateo Alemán's 1599 picaresque *Guzmán de Alfarache*, foregrounds a sympathetic, aristocratic pair of lovers to reflect back on more than a century of maurophile tradition. The story is told to the *pícaro* Guzmán by a priest, to pass the time while riding from Seville to Cazalla. It evokes not only the Christian-Moorish friendships of *El Abencerraje* but also the ludic chivalric universe of the *Guerras civiles de Granada*, albeit in a slightly tarnished version. Much like the *Guerras civiles*, the story is set during the last years of the war on Granada, when the Moorish experience, despite the festive trappings of the texts, is one of loss and renunciation. But in Alemán's story the Moorish protagonists are located almost exclusively within the Christian world, where they must negotiate their cultural identity and, indeed, their very survival.

Daraja, the beautiful daughter of the *alcalde* of Baza, is taken captive by the Catholic Kings as the city falls. The location is striking: Baza was the area with the most voluntary conversions to Christianity in the last decade of the fifteenth century, one marked by particularly close relations between local élites and the Christian conquerors.[55] Daraja's bilingualism and the resulting difficulty in categorizing her are established immediately: "Tan diestramente hablaba castellano, que con dificultad se le conociera no ser cristiana vieja, pues entre las más ladinas pudiera pasar por una dellas" (216) ["She spoke Castilian so well, that one would be hard pressed to tell that she was not an Old Christian, for as one of the most fluent she could pass for one of them"].[56] Daraja's linguistic passing corresponds closely to the linguistic assimilation of many Moriscos by the late sixteenth century. In the aftermath of the 1609 expulsions, in fact, one official warned Philip III that *ladino* Moriscos were able to elude banishment by returning to Spain and moving to a new community, where, with their perfect Castilian, they were essentially unmarked.[57]

Daraja's ability to negotiate Christian culture proves essential to the story's progress. The queen becomes very fond of her and determines to acculturate and Christianize her through persuasion, offering to dress her in garments she will provide:

Siempre la reina la tuvo consigo y llevó a la ciudad de Sevilla, donde con el deseo que fuese cristiana, para disponerla poco a poco sin violencia, con apacibles medios, le dijo un día:

—Ya entenderás, Daraja, lo que deseo tus cosas y gusto. En parte de pago dello te quiero pedir una cosa en mi servicio: que trueques esos vestidos a los que te daré de mi persona, para gozar de lo que en el hábito nuestro se aventaja tu hermosura. (217)

[The queen kept her always by her side and took her to the city of Seville, where, in the hope that she should be a Christian, disposing her little by little without violence, and with peaceful means, she said to her one day:
"You must know, Daraja, how I look to your affairs and your pleasure. In partial payment I want to ask one thing of you in my service: to change that clothing for what I shall give you of my own, so that I can enjoy how our dress enhances your beauty.]

Daraja graciously acquiesces, and is dressed "a la castellana" (217). The irony here is acute: as I noted in chapter 3, wardrobe inventories inform us that Isabel's wardrobe was full of "Moorish" wear, from her *chapines* (platform shoes) to her *tocas de camino* (headwraps). The change of dress proposed here assumes a clearly marked difference that does not correspond to the sartorial hybridization evident in the period.

The question of dress and assimilation is similarly thematized for Daraja's betrothed, the noble Ozmín, who also passes easily for a Christian. When he goes in search of Daraja aided by a "moro lengua" (219) ["Moorish guide"], that is, a spy, the two dress in "traje andaluz" ["Andalusian costume"], which is enough to get them picked up as deserters from the Christian army. What exactly might such attire consist of circa 1490, and to what extent could it distinguish a Moor from a Christian? In fact, before they free themselves with a rich bribe, Ozmín claims to be the son of Luis de Padilla, the noble Christian who guards Daraja for the monarchs, and no one disputes his identity.

To reach Daraja, Ozmín will in turn assume a series of disguises that involve the transgression of class as well as religious divides. In order to penetrate the Padilla household, he spends a good portion of the text as a manual laborer, first as a bricklayer, then as a gardener. His plan succeeds exceedingly well, giving him ample opportunity to converse with Daraja "en algarabía" (224) ["in Arabic"]. The household eventually fills with rumors, and her captor Don Luis is left to wonder whether his attentive gardener is not in fact a Moor come to steal away his charge (225). When interrogated, Daraja adds more hybrid (and imaginary) identities to the mix: the gardener "Ambrosio," she explains, was a Christian captive brought up with Ozmín, and his closest companion: "era depósito de sus gustos, compañero de sus entretenimientos, erario de sus secretos y, en sustancia, otro él" (227) ["he was the repository of his pleasures, companion in his entertainments, coffer of his secrets, and, in essence, another of him"]. This fictive *otro él* suggests how fluid are the boundaries imagined here: nurture can make of a Christian captive another Ozmín, just as, presumably, captivity to Isabel and the Padillas is making a Christian of the captive Daraja. Lest there be any doubt, Daraja stresses the absolute amity and compatibility of the two doubles: "Ambos en todo tan conformes, que la ley sola los diferenciaba; que, por la mucha discreción de ambos, nunca della se trataron por no deshermanarse" (227) ["They were so like-minded/compatible in everything, that only their faith / the law distinguished them; and, as they were both so discerning, they never brought it up so as not to lose their likeness/rend their fraternal bond"].[58] The imaginary relationship between Ozmín and his Christian mirror-image, impeded only by the Law, suggests how much Moors and Christians share in this world—what comes between them is elided as long as possible for the sake of individual bonds.

The text relativizes religious difference and ironizes Christian motives for converting Moors by emphasizing the attraction Daraja holds for Christian suitors. Rodrigo de Padilla, son of Daraja's captor (and earlier impersonated by Ozmín), falls in love with her and approaches Ozmín—whom he takes to be Ambrosio the gardener, sometime Christian captive—for help. Rodrigo entreats "Ambrosio" to undertake Daraja's conversion so that he, a noble Old Christian, can marry her, and promises great rewards. The disguised Ozmín's equivocal answer suggests that religious difference is a matter of deictics, since all concerned have similar feelings about their own faith: "La misma razón con que has querido ligarme, señor don Rodrigo, te obligará que creas cuánto deseo que Daraja siga mi ley, a que con muchas veras, infinitas, y diversas veces la tengo persuadida. No es otro mi deseo sino el tuyo" (229) ["The same reason with which you have tried to bind me, lord Don Rodrigo, should make you believe how I long for Daraja to follow my faith, to which I have persuaded her many true, infinite and divers times. My desire is none other than yours"]. The narrator—a priest, it must be recalled—emphasizes the equivocation, lest the reader miss it: "No mintió el moro palabra en cuanto dijo, si hubiera sido entendido; mas con el descuido de cosa tan remota, creyó don Rodrigo no lo que quiso decir, sino lo que formalmente dijo" (230) ["The Moor did not lie in a word he said, if he had been understood, but unwitting of such a remote possibility, Don Rodrigo believed not what he meant to say, but what he formally said"]. Religious difference is thus both marked and relativized by the exchange.

If religious difference is carefully negotiated, cultural difference tends to disappear in the aristocratic world of the text. Though the story features the entertainments that Pérez de Hita and the *romances* made so central to maurophilia, the *juegos de caña* and bullfight here are Christian affairs. Daraja provides the occasion—they are held to assuage her great sadness (235)—yet no Moors take part, except for the disguised Ozmín, who covers his face and pretends to be a foreigner (236). The trappings of maurophilia are marshaled entirely on the Christian side, further complicating any absolute difference between them and the Moors. For Alemán, exquisite horsemanship is a regional trait: the riders on their *jineta* saddles seem one with the horse, he claims, "pues en toda la mayor parte del Andalucía, como Sevilla, Córdoba, Jerez de la Frontera, sacan los niños—como dicen—de las cunas a los caballos, de la manera que se acostumbra en otras partes dárselos de caña" (239) ["for in all the greater part of Andalucía, such as Seville, Cordoba, or Jerez de la Frontera, they place children, as they say, from their cribs on horseback, as they do elsewhere with hobbyhorses"]. The echo in *caballo de caña* of the very games related here only underscores local difference: where children in other cultures might ride hobbyhorses, Andaluces go straight to *juegos de caña*. Local style has so fully absorbed the Andalusi heritage that it is Christians who practice "Moorish" forms.

In this context of shared cultural practices, the narrative underscores the protagonists' literal and figurative ability to move from one camp to another. "Ambrosio" is sought out by Don Alonso, another Christian suitor for Daraja's hand, who wants his help in challenging Rodrigo. Ozmín/Ambrosio proceeds to tutor him not in the *cañas*, as one might expect, but in jousting. Given this double expertise—and particularly his striking ability on horseback "en ambas sillas" (242) ["on both saddles"], that is, *a la brida* and *a la jineta*, Alonso doubts Ambrosio's identity as a laborer. While he ostensibly questions only the gardener's class identity, his language betrays a soupçon of maurophilia: "Con el velo del vil vestido que vistes" (243) ["With the veil of the vile dress you wear"], he tells Ambrosio, he hides "oro finísimo y perlas orientales" ["the finest gold and Oriental pearls"]. Carefully ignoring such hints, Ambrosio claims instead that he is actually "Jaime Vives," a knight of Aragon, captured by the Moors and brought up with Ozmín. Though he adds one more layer of dissimulation, he echoes the general outline of Daraja's story of the

Christian mirror-image: the Moor, the putative captive claims, was "re-
trato mío, así en edad como el talle, rostro, condición y suerte" (244)
["my spitting image, in age as in size, visage, condition and fortune"]. He
adds to the fiction a love-object for Jaime Vives, Rodrigo's sister Doña
Elvira, explaining his need to penetrate the Padilla household and providing Daraja with her own mirror-image in a Christian lady.

Thus the novella complicates the distinctiveness of Christian and
Moorish identities, emphasizing their shared culture and experience.
Nonetheless it recognizes the kernel of religious difference that separates
them. The point is made obliquely, as the lovers are almost always under
surveillance and forced to equivocate. Resistance to religious assimilation
appears in Ozmín's ambiguous exchange with Rodrigo, cited above, and
again in Daraja's apparent meditation on the limits of social mobility.
Ozmín passes the ladies, dressed as a laborer and discreetly singing a
Moorish song, "que para quien sabía la lengua eran los acentos claros, y
para la que no y estaba descuidada, le parecía el cantar de lala, lala" (250)
["which could be clearly recognized by one who knew the language and
which seemed like 'lala, lala' to one who did not and was not paying attention"]. While Elvira praises the "savage's" innate and wasted talent, Daraja demurs:

—Agora sabes—dijo Daraja—que son las cosas todas como el sujeto en que
están y así se estiman. Estos labradores, por maravilla, si de tiernos no se trasplan-
tan en vida política y los injieren y mudan de tierras ásperas a cultivadas, desnudán-
dolos de la rústica corteza en que nacen, tarde o nunca podrán ser bien
morigerados: y al revés, los que son ciudadanos de político natural, son como la
viña, que, dejándola de labrar algunos años, da fruto, aunque poco; y si sobre ella
vuelven, reconociendo el regalo, rinde colmadamente el beneficio. Este que aquí
canta, no será poderoso un carpintero con hacha ni azuela para desalabearlo ni
ponerlo de provecho. (251)

["You know," said Daraja, "that all things are like the subject they are in and
are thus esteemed. Remarkably, these laborers, unless transplanted into an urbane
life while young and grafted and moved from rough to cultivated soils, denuding
them of the rustic bark with which they are born, may late or never be improved;
and, conversely, those citizens who are naturally urbane are like the vine, which,
untended for some years, gives fruit, though little, and if tended again, recognizing
the attention, gives an abundant reward. This one who sings here cannot be
straightened out nor made useful by a carpenter with axe or adze."]

Between his song and her words, the narrator explains, the lovers
understand each other perfectly. The hermeneutic prods underline how

social status stands in for religious difference in Daraja's careful speech on the limits of social mobility. She notes that subjects such as her talented gardener may be improved (with a possible echo of *moro* in *morigerado*?), but only if grafted early into an urbane or courtly life. Similarly, a noble subject may lose his or her excellence—or a Moor dissimulate his or her belief—only to regain it under the right circumstances. The carpenter who cannot straighten out Ozmín may be no other than Jesus himself, who cannot salvage a Moor long past the tender age. Daraja's words echo the language of agriculture from the Morisco debates, which argued that the Moriscos were like weeds choking the rightful Spanish crops.[59] Ironically, Daraja recommends habitual cultivation of the self for self-fashioning, while Ozmín is instead passing as a laborer, a gardener, and a Christian. Impersonation and hybridity, though very different alternatives, overlap in these characters' experience.

The same narrator who seems so attuned to the lovers' hidden meanings in this exchange takes up instead the more readily available discussion of class, launching into a powerful diatribe against peasants—the Old Christians par excellence, as Cavillac notes[60]—for their "odio natural" ["natural hate"] of their betters (251). By far the longest narratorial intervention, this passage introduces an unmotivated attack on Ozmín and Don Alonso by the village rabble. In self-defense, Ozmín kills the son of the *alcalde*, and is promptly arrested and condemned to hang. Attempts to challenge his sentence turn on his class: Rodrigo insists that to hang their servant "Ambrosio" is to disrespect him and his father, while Alonso claims that as a gentleman "Jaime Vives" cannot die for killing one so much his inferior; in the worst case, he should be beheaded, not hanged (256).

Despite these appeals, only royal intervention will save Ozmín. The diegesis reduces the fall of Granada to a background detail: "Cuando sucedieron estas cosas, ya Granada se había rendido" (254) ["When these things happened, Granada had already surrendered"].[61] It matters only in that it leads to the conversion of Ozmín and Daraja's fathers, bringing them into the fold, and frees the monarchs to pay attention to the lovers' plight. Ozmín is rescued from local justice at the eleventh hour, and reunited with Daraja before the sovereigns. Isabel offers them "uncoerced" baptism, which they, inevitably, accept, taking the names of the monarchs, who serve as their godparents.[62]

Yet the apparently orthodox resolution of this maurophile tale cannot undo its sustained dismantling of Moorish difference. Clearly, class trumps ethnicity or religion as the significant divide in the world of the text: noble Moors are as heroic and ideal as Christians, if not more so, and Daraja is constantly desired by the Christian side, even though the tale ends without actual exogamy. Dissimulation and accommodation are so prized—and effective—throughout the story that the sincerity of the conversion must be qualified, yet it nonetheless ensures a happy ending, projected into a future of the new converts' "ilustre generación" ["illustrious offspring," 259].[63] Most important, Ozmín and Daraja's origins do not diminish them in any way: conversion, however superficial and circumstantial, suffices to grant them inclusion in the Christian polity. No one in this universe worries about *limpieza de sangre*. The desire for Daraja shared by Ozmín and his multiple Christian counterparts leads to bifurcated outcomes: insofar as she represents the resistant, alluring otherness of Moorish Granada, the Christians conquer and domesticate her, but in her own person she is married to her original suitor, Ozmín, and achieves assimilation. Moreover, the shared culture that Christian and Moorish characters inhabit is already so marked by Andalusi forms that acculturation is relative: for these noble Moors, at least, Spanish culture does not seem foreign.

Moreover, part of what makes the tale of Ozmín and Daraja so unorthodox, so ideologically slippery, is its belatedness. Clearly, if the 1561 *Abencerraje* had ended with the conversion of its Moorish protagonists, Abindarráez and Jarifa, it would not hold the same interest as a powerful and ambiguous maurophile text. But by the time Alemán wrote his story, the legal repression of Moriscos, uprising in the Alpujarras, forced resettlements, and increasing calls for expulsion had made for a very different and far more radicalized situation. It is only in this later context that the conversion of the protagonists and their virtually forced abandonment of the religion to which they cleave for most of the text can in any way read as a maurophile resolution. Ozmín and Daraja represent that first, presumably most reluctant, generation of *nuevos convertidos de moros*; their idealization, their desirability, and, most important, their cultural compatibility offer the possibility of full assimilation for the descendants of "Fernando" and "Isabel."[64] In the political climate of the late 1590s, this inclusive stance towards Moorish origins would have offered an alternative, however compromised, to the arguments for expulsion.[65]

The narrative frame of Alemán's much longer picaresque also complicates the force of the novella. Recall that the story is narrated by a priest, although the *pícaro* Guzmán alerts us to his own hand in the retelling: "más dilatada y con alma distinta nos la dijo de lo que yo lo he contado"

(259) ["he told it to us longer and with a different soul than what I have recounted"]. About this *alma distinta* we can only speculate, but the *pícaro* may find enticing possibilities in the strategic transformation of the Moors that churchmen may have ignored or condemned. Here late maurophilia and the picaresque find common ground: both genres involve the reinvention of subjects and their abandonment of their origins. In this reading, the idealization of Ozmín and Daraja does not fool Guzmán for a minute: he recognizes them as kindred souls for their Protean self-fashioning and resourcefulness. As critics have noted, Ozmín's serial humble occupations further emphasize his connection to the *pícaro*.

Yet there are also more pointed connections between the novella and its frame. The *Guzmán* seems singularly preoccupied with exogamous attraction and *mestizaje*. The protagonist's own father—a *levantisco* or eastern type, possibly a Jew or Genoese—had been a renegade, married to a Moor whom he abandoned to return to Christianity (132–33). Guzmán is himself the product of a later adulterous union (144ff), though not one involving religious difference. Immediately before the tale of Ozmín and Daraja, Alemán gives us an extended comic meditation on animal hybridity and the irrepressibility of exogamous desire. Guzmán stays at an inn whose owner has ignored local prohibitions against crossing horses with donkeys (presumably due to the sterility of the resulting mules), and who decides to feed the boy the unfortunate issue, passing it off as lamb. Although the story may have its roots in folklore, its placement here is suggestive. Looking back on the episode, Guzmán airily notes that his own polite upbringing made the mule more distasteful to him than to his rude comrade, though hunger trumps this difference. When eggs are served, his companion laughs in recollection of an earlier alimentary transgression, when Guzmán was fed eggs so old that he felt chick bones crunching in his mouth (168–69). The nervous innkeeper begins to swear that he would not serve "gato por liebre" or "oveja por carnero" (195) ["cat for hare" or "mutton for lamb" and insisting on the "limpieza" of his establishment—claims promptly rebutted when Guzmán finds a large fresh blood stain and the body of the mule (198). Finally, while he is in the stables, his cape, a sign of social aspirations, disappears.

At every turn, the episode both erases and reinscribes difference: horse and donkey are, ultimately, alike enough to mate, whatever the law might say;[66] the hungry Guzmán is enough like his undiscerning companion, and the stewed mule enough like lamb, that only the innkeeper's guilt gives him away; the two inns are equally stained by the blood of innocents that should not be eaten; Guzmán without his fancy cape is just another *pícaro*. Compared to the transgressions and amalgams of this world, the passing and assimilation in the maurophile novella seem tame, if not honorable. While the strategic identities and flexibility of Ozmín and Daraja are more proper versions of what transpires in Guzmán's world, the lovers, unlike those whose honor is lost in the filth of the picaresque, remain untarnished. And, despite the extended furor in the frame about the benighted mule, miscegenation is never a concern in the novella when noble Christians desire Daraja.[67]

The appeal of the Moor as one argument for assimilation is reprised in a famous episode of the second part of *Don Quijote* (1615), published soon after the expulsions, which has been incisively analyzed by Francisco Márquez Villanueva and Carroll Johnson, among others.[68] The story of the Morisco Ricote and his daughter Ana Félix, beloved of the noble Don Gaspar Gregorio, allows Cervantes to go beyond Alemán to address explicitly the union between New and Old Christians.[69] Father and daughter are just as *ladino* as Daraja or Ozmín, though hardly aristocratic idealizations. They pass easily, moving in and out of Spain, and of religious, national, and even gender identities. So loyal is the Old Christian Don Gregorio to his Morisca beloved that he chooses to follow her into exile, undergoing a humiliating captivity in Algiers during which Ana disguises him as a woman to protect him from sodomy until she can arrange his escape back to Spain. Ricote and Ana, who is spectacularly disguised as a corsair captain, are eventually reunited on a galley off the coast of Barcelona, where the consummate outsider is revealed as the most Christian daughter of Sancho's old neighbor.[70]

Perhaps the most striking feature of their protracted adventures is the inconclusive ending: after a famously ironic debate about the merits of the Morisco expulsion, Ricote and his daughter are left waiting in Barcelona while their aristocratic patrons attempt to intercede for them at court and arrange their exemption from banishment. As the legislation reviewed above makes clear, the only reason Ana could not have remained was that Gregorio had not actually married her before the expulsion was announced. The proleptic force of his attachment is enough to deem her *Doña* Ana Félix,[71] but not yet enough to counter the expulsion. Thus the arbitrariness and implausibility of the decrees are made patent, while the lovers wait for their noble friends to bend the law.[72] And there they remain, eternally biding their time, long-term houseguests of the Catalan noble Don Antonio, and of the viceroy himself, availing themselves of

Christian hospitality for almost four hundred years now. Surely this inconclusive ending is itself a conclusion of sorts: it indicts the arbitrariness of the expulsions and suggests that no great harm proceeds from the inclusion in Spain of Moriscos who want nothing more than to assimilate.[73] De facto, Ricote and Ana Félix quietly remain, not only benignly overlooked but actively welcomed by the regional aristocracy.

Like the story of Ozmín and Daraja, the Ana Félix episode hinges on the desirability of Moorish or Morisco women who are adept at passing. Their appeal makes a metonymic argument for the inclusion of Moriscos in the Spanish polity, even though that inclusion seems to come at the cost of any distinct identity. Their challenge to essentializing or racialist accounts of Morisco difference, that is, paradoxically seems to require the disappearance of any distinctions, or at least so it would appear. Yet instead of imagining their cultural dissolution, we might recall the larger phenomenon that I have been tracing throughout this study: the persistence of a hybrid, *Mudéjar* Spain long after the fall of Granada. This, one might argue, is the culture that most easily assimilated Morisco subjects over the course of the cruel sixteenth century—a culture already marked not only by the idealizations of literary maurophilia but by a multitude of quotidian habits that rendered Moorishness quintessentially Spanish.

Whether embraced or stigmatized, therefore, Moorishness becomes an unavoidable component in the construction of Spain's national identity over the sixteenth century. Paradoxically, while critics who discuss early modern material culture seem only too willing to dismiss Moorish proclivities as a temporary fashion, Spain's enemies foreground its hybridity as a way to exclude it from the properly European. The construction of Spain is thus a complex negotiation between past and present, intra- and extra-European pressures, and fictive identities crafted both at home and abroad. The racialized, essentialized distinctions in the low register of Black Legend texts may be very different from the more strategic representation of commonalities between Moors and Christians in Spanish maurophilia, but they share an assumption that Spain's Moorishness must be addressed and rhetorically managed in any attempt to represent the nation.

Postscript: Moorish Commonplaces

GIVEN THE WIDESPREAD practices and constructions that I have traced throughout this book, it should come as no surprise that Moorishness continues to define ideas of Spain long after the expulsion of the Moriscos in the early seventeenth century. Whether as a domestic alternative to French cultural influence from the Enlightenment to the nineteenth century, or as the distinctive attraction of Andalusian tourism from the Romantics to our own time, Spain's Moorish identity proves remarkably resilient and useful in the long term.[1] As José Colmeiro and Lou Charnon-Deutsch have suggested, Moorishness colors other popular stereotypes about Spain and Andalucía, such as the dark, Oriental gypsy.[2] The gypsy, the flamenco, the Alhambra—these commonplaces anchor the external construction of Andalucía, whose romanticized local culture becomes in these discourses a synecdoche for Spain. Yet the replacement of a sober Castile by a festive Andalucía as the sine qua non of Spain, seamless though it might appear, has a long and complex history.[3] The perception and valuation of Moorishness varies for specific contexts, from the Napoleonic invasions to the development of high European Orientalism to Spain's own lamentable colonial adventures in North Africa. These different contexts nonetheless see recurring tensions between internal and external, sympathetic and hostile, views of the place of Moors and their culture within the nation. With the twentieth-century embrace of North Africa by an anti-European Franco, and the delicate contemporary repositioning of Spain in relation to an Islamic world associated with both immigration and terrorism, the dynamics have become ever more fraught.[4]

Part of the challenge in assessing this complex history is to question over-simplified understandings of Spain as heir of Al-Andalus, however benign they might seem. In this sense, even the most well-meaning arguments for ethnic tolerance in present-day Spain based on a shared genealogical past seem problematic, as do latter-day conversions to Islam by contemporary Andalusians "rediscovering" their ancestral spirituality.

Both within and beyond Spain, these efforts would seem to reinscribe
Spanish difference as they argue for cultural flexibility. Instead of essentializing identity, it seems crucial to foreground a shared culture and a shared
history, variously hybridized, as the rationale for Spain's engagement with
its North African neighbors. Yet this more sober project, often broached
both within Spain and from abroad, is complicated by the profound psy-
chic investments in a romanticized Andalucía that often characterize the
debates and their institutional context. As the work of anthropologist José
Antonio González Alcantud shows, the construction of a Moorish past
for Andalucía often involves rendering it an orientalized, exotic object of
desire.[5]

Moorishness has long held huge symbolic currency both within and
outside Spain. Well-known French and English Romantic fantasies, culmi-
nating with the cosmopolitan Washington Irving, celebrated the timeless
Spain of the Alhambra. In the late nineteenth-century, Moorishness took
on specific regional and national uses, embodying a folk Andalucía of eternally Moorish peasants, as in the vision of Archena, in the famous Valley
of Ricote near Murcia, by the local poet Vicente Medina:

Moriscos los atavíos
y moriscas las maneras
y moriscas las costumbres
      son en mi tierra.
. . . .
Las mujeres en el suelo
como las moras se sientan
y los hombres en cuclillas
se están horas enteras.

Los bailes, cosas de moros . . .
cosas de moros sus fiestas,
y de moros sus pasiones
y venganzas y peleas.

¿Qué le podría faltar
pa ser morisca a mi tierra?
Por no faltarle, ni el habla,
de palabras moras llena.

Murcia, Albacete, Alicante . . .
"Mi tierra morisca" es esa,
semejante a la de enfrente,
su hermana africana tierra.

El paisaje: Tierra de oro,
pueblos blancos y palmeras,
oasis, huertos, naranjos
y la mar azul-turquesa.[6]

[Moorish is the dress and Moorish the ways, and Moorish the customs of my land.
. . . The women sit on the floor like Moors, and the men spend hours squatting
down. The dances are Moorish, Moorish are their celebrations, and Moorish their
passions and vendettas and quarrels. What could my land be missing to be fully
Moorish, when even its language is full of Moorish words? Murcia, Albacete, Alicante. . . . That is "my Moorish land," just like its sister land in Africa, across the
way. The landscape: a golden land of white towns and palm trees, oases, groves,
orange trees, and the blue-turquoise sea.]

Medina's sense of the local is absolutely wrapped up in the exotic construction of a Moorish homeland. While there is no question that Archena
offers a distinctive local culture, this version expresses a highly romanticized longing for the past plenitude of Al-Andalus. The poet's own persona diverges into a native witness who can claim proximate, privileged
knowledge and a cosmopolitan traveler who delights in the difference of
Archena, here rendered satisfying precisely insofar as it meets Orientalist
expectations of heightened feeling and abundant local color. The "broth-
erhood" with Africa also takes on a more sinister significance when considered against the backdrop of Spain's own disastrous colonial expansion
into Morocco in the period.

In contradistinction to what he terms the "neo-Orientalist myth" of
Andalucía, González Alcantud argues that the contemporary cultural inheritance of Moorish forms is moderate, at best, and most pronounced
among what he terms "elementos desideologizados"[7] ["deideologized elements"]. While he is surely right to question the romantic claims of the
"Legado Andalusí" movement—the institutionalized celebration of
Moorish origins by the Andalucian government[8]—his emphasis on trace-
able forms ultimately discounts the long-term hybridization of Andalusi
forms into Spain, to the point where they are no longer recognizable as
anything but Spanish, and often extend beyond Andalucía.

Yet the romanticization that González Alcantud castigates is undeniable. At the regional level, the synecdochic focus on the Moors via the
"Legado Andalusí" project and other institutions recalls the place of the
mestizo in the imaginary of many Latin American nations. There, too, a
sanitized mythology idealizes groups consistently marginalized or persecuted in the present, as a historical commonplace stands in for any im-

proved place in society.[9] In Spain, the frequent recuperation of a glorious Moorish past for the nation coexists uneasily with a contemporary climate of anti-Islamic prejudice and closed borders, further complicated by tensions between regions with a very different investment in a shared past. From these various perspectives, the romanticization of Andalucía's Moorish past as a regional phenomenon is read either as a threat to properly national understandings of a fundamentally European Spain or, conversely, as a myth that threatens to overwrite the specific identities of *autonomías*—the increasingly autonomous regions of Spain—longing for more cultural and political distance from the nation.[10]

Daniela Flesler argues that Spanish anxieties about contemporary Moroccan immigration as a "return of the Moor" are managed through a series of distancing mechanisms.[11] Paradoxically, Moroccan immigrants both underscore and undermine Spain's hard-won European status. As a privileged destination and southern point of entry, Spain becomes the guardian of Europe's boundaries, but when Moroccans are imagined as iterations of Moorish invaders they recall the longstanding European location of Spain beyond Europe as an "African" nation. The cultural responses Flesler traces are varied: the Spanish version of differentialist racism holds that immigrants cannot be assimilated, given their cultural incompatibility.[12] Recreations of medieval Christian victories over Moors in the immensely popular *juegos de moros y cristianos*, meanwhile, both cater to a touristic fascination with Moorish Spain and render failed attempts at immigration (the repeated shipwreck of flimsy *pateras*) as so many thwarted invasions. As Flesler notes, the festivals both appropriate Moorishness and safely quarantine Moors in a fanciful medieval Spain.[13]

As Flesler's suggestive study demonstrates, Moorishness is thus acknowledged for certain sites, but cordoned off from competing versions of the nation. Consider two additional pieces of evidence for just how complex the various forms of institutional relations to the Moorish past are today: The city of Cáceres, in Extremadura, features among its attractions a Casa-Museo Arabe, the labor of love of a local resident who in the 1970s discovered Roman and Moorish ruins in his house and reconstructed them with enthusiastic assistance from Iraqi friends. The museum reproduces the domestic interior "as it might have looked under Arab domination" with a clear emphasis on the exotic: incense, colorful silks everywhere, and even the resident ghost of a lovelorn *mora*.[14] The reconstruction thus produces Moorishness as a difference within. Although the museum, in a city famed for the Renaissance palaces of New World conquistadors, clearly attempts to remind visitors of the widespread presence of Moors and Moriscos throughout Spain, it paradoxically circumscribes the Moorish influence to one highly fanciful interior while connecting it to a broader Arabic culture beyond Spain.

Contrast this to the much more sober house of Lope de Vega, most canonical of Spanish Golden Age playwrights, in Madrid. Lope's house, which displays furnishings from the period, features braziers, pillows on the floor, and a number of elements of what is clearly a Moorish heritage, yet there is no acknowledgment that the high Spanish culture here being celebrated owes anything to al-Andalus. Hybridization either goes unremarked—as fully realized habitus—or is swept under the rug.

The juxtaposition of these two very different institutions suggests an attempt to quarantine Moorish influence while mainstream Spanish culture, whether willfully or unconsciously, ignores its Moorish side. The situation becomes even more complicated when one considers the growth of regional identities in *autonomías* such as Catalunya or the Basque Country (Euskadi), imagined as fully European, in contradistinction to any orientalized version of Spain. Thus in a nation constantly debating its own identity, the presence of Moors is recognized, and even fetishized at the local level, but not as an integral, hybridized facet of Spanishness. By contrast, the critical recovery of hybrid practices that I limn in this book provides one way to challenge the commonplaces, such as touting Moorish exoticism for tourists, through which Spain has typically managed the legacy of al-Andalus, and also to go beyond purely regional understanding of Moorishness. This seems particularly urgent given how the celebration of Moorish heritage in the official discourse of tourism coexists with a marked racism against North African immigrants throughout Europe and with the exacerbation of anti-Muslim sentiment that marks the era of neoconservative warmongering and fundamentalist terrorism. Whereas the mere act of providing a genealogy for the celebration and marginalization of Moorishness will not create a place for North African immigrants within Spain, it may recall for Spaniards the complexities of their own maurophilia and maurophobia.

The cultural dynamic of simultaneous romanticization and containment to which I can only gesture here has important consequences also for Hispanism in the U.S. academy, my own locus of enunciation. Within Spanish departments, Moors remain an object of critical fascination, but the place of Moorish culture, like that of maurophilia, is carefully circumscribed to a literary margin and a bounded chronology—a curricular commonplace, if you will. Meanwhile, English and Comparative Literature departments—the most prestigious institutional locations for literary study in the U.S.—have partly overcome their resistance to a Hispanic culture traditionally imagined as somehow beyond Europe.[15] The development of ethnic studies and a new attention to the cultural production of the U.S. border with Latin America and the Caribbean has helped to bring the Hispanic world in from the margins. The transformation of "Golden Age" studies into a theoretically informed inquiry into early modernity, for its part, has ameliorated the marginalization of peninsular Iberia.

Yet these are still incipient and fragile advances, and it is important to recognize the long-term habits of thought that threaten to undermine them. The underlying suspicion of Hispanic culture in the U.S., I contend, stems not only from contemporary perceptions of a threatening other to the south, but from a much longer history of excluding Spain from Europe as an exotic, Moorish nation, whose purported ethnic otherness is reiterated with every new instance of the Black Legend. Thus the importance of a twofold intervention: while recovering the place of Moorishness in Spain in the sixteenth century and beyond, it is essential to emphasize also the constructedness of Spanish exoticism, as it served the purposes of imperial rivals and Protestant propagandists. Only this double move reveals the complexities of Spanish Moorishness, as it was variously experienced or overlooked within the nation, and deployed from without.

Notes

Introduction

1. I should note at the outset that throughout this book I alternate the more precise but cumbersome "Andalusi-derived" with the term "Moorish" since the latter most closely approximates the Spanish term *moro*, used in the period, and because it captures the ambiguity in how these practices relate to the Muslim religion, the various states of Al-Andalus, and an increasingly marginalized "race" of Moriscos. All translations are mine unless otherwise specified.

2. See among others Paul Julian Smith, *Representing the Other: "Race," Text, and Gender in Spanish and Spanish American Narrative* (Oxford: Clarendon, 1992), 45–56, and David Nirenberg, "El concepto de raza en el estudio del antijudaismo ibérico medieval," *Edad Media* 3 (2000): 39–60, especially 46–49, reprised in "Race and the Middle Ages: The Case of Spain and Its Jews," in *Rereading the Black Legend: The Discourses of Religious and Racial Difference in the Renaissance Empires*, ed. Margaret Greer, Walter Mignolo, and Maureen Quilligan (Chicago: University of Chicago Press, 2007), 71–87. John Beverley, for his part, notes that Castro's focus on religious "caste" ignored the many other kinds of exclusion in medieval and early modern Spain, and in particular that of the lower classes. See his "Class or Caste: A Critique of the Castro Thesis," in *Américo Castro, the Impact of His Thought: Essays to Mark the Centenary of His Birth*, ed. Ronald E. Surtz, Jaime Ferrán, and Daniel P. Testa (Madison: Hispanic Seminary of Medieval Studies, 1988), 141–49.

3. For a rich reevaluation of Castro's legacy in the context of contemporary Spanish cultural politics, see Eduardo Subirats, ed., *Américo Castro y la revisión de la memoria: el Islam en España* (Madrid: Libertarias, 2003).

4. The most explicit account of hybridity appears in the work of Homi Bhabha. See, for example, "Signs Taken for Wonders: Questions of Ambivalence and Authority Under a Tree Outside Delhi, May 1817," in *"Race," Writing and Difference*, ed. Henry Louis Gates, *Critical Inquiry* 12, 1 (1985): 144–65. The essay is reprinted in Bhabha's *The Location of Culture* (London: Routledge, 1994), 102–22. For the currency of the term in Iberian studies, see María Judith Feliciano and Leyla Rouhi's introduction to *Interrogating Iberian Frontiers*, ed. Barbara F. Weissberger with Feliciano, Rouhi, and Cynthia Robinson, *Medieval Encounters* 12, 3 (2006). For some potential problems with the term, see my "A Mirror Across the Water: Mimetic Racism, Hybridity, and Cultural Survival," in *Writing Race Across the Atlantic World, 1492–1763*, ed. Gary Taylor and Philip Beidler (London: Palgrave, 2005), 9–26. On Granada as a frontier society, see David Coleman, *Cre-*

ating Christian Granada: Society and Religious Culture in an Old-World Frontier City, 1492–1600 (Ithaca, N.Y.: Cornell University Press, 2003).

5. On the *mudéjar*, see Cynthia Robinson, "Mudéjar Revisited: A Prolegomena to the Reconstruction of Perception, Devotion and Experience at the Mudéjar Convent of Clarisas, Tordesillas, Spain (14th Century AD)," *Res* 43 (Spring 2003): 51–77; María Judith Feliciano Chaves, "Mudejarismo in Its Colonial Context: Iberian Cultural Display, Viceregal Luxury Consumption, and the Negotiation of Identities in Sixteenth-Century New Spain," Ph.D. dissertation, University of Pennsylvania, 2004; and Weissberger et al., eds., *Interrogating Iberian Frontiers.* For a careful assessment of the actual contemporary "heritage" of al-Andalus versus its romanticization, see José A. González Alcantud, "Mythos y techne: sobre las presuntas supervivencias moriscas en la contemporaneidad," in his *Lo moro: las lógicas de la derrota y la formación del estereotipo islámico* (Barcelona: Anthropos, 2002), 90–112.

6. "Yo había dicho muy poco sobre la extremadamente compleja y densa relación entre España y el islam, que ciertamente no se podía caracterizar simplemente como una relación imperial" ["I had said very little about the extremely complex and dense relationship between Spain and Islam, which certainly cannot be characterized simply as an imperial relationship"], Edward Said, "Prólogo a la nueva edición española," in *Orientalismo*, Spanish trans. María Luisa Fuentes (Barcelona: Debolsillo, 2003), 9; Said, *Orientalism* (London: Routledge, 1978). Note the asymmetry in Said's formulation between "Spain" and "Islam." For responses to Said, see José Colmeiro, "Exorcising Exoticism: *Carmen* and the Construction of Oriental Spain," *Comparative Literature* 54, 2 (2002): 127–43, and José A. González Alcantud, ed., *El orientalismo desde el sur* (Barcelona: Anthropos, 2006), especially his introduction, "El orientalismo: génesis topográfica y discurso crítico" (7–34) and "El canon andaluz y las fronteras imaginarias" (368–80), and Miguel Angel de Bunes Ibarra, "La emergencia del orientalismo en la edad moderna" (37–53).

7. Bunes Ibarra, "La emergencia del orientalismo," 44 and passim.

8. González Alcantud, "El canon andaluz y las fronteras imaginarias."

9. See Colmeiro, "Exorcising Exoticism," 129; Jesús Torrecilla, *España exótica: la formación de la imagen española moderna* (Boulder, Colo.: Society of Spanish and Spanish-American Studies, 2004); and Lou Charnon-Deutsch, *The Spanish Gypsy: The History of a European Obsession* (University Park: Pennsylvania State University Press, 2004).

10. Marcelino Menéndez Pelayo, *Orígenes de la novela*, vol. 1 (Madrid: Bailly, 1905), ccclxxxi, ccclxxxvi.

11. Georges Cirot, "La maurophilie littéraire en Espagne au XVIe siècle" (the essay continues in several parts under the same title), *Bulletin Hispanique* 40, 2 (1938)–46 (1944). Cirot cites as his predecessor Harry Austin Deferrari, whose 1927 University of Pennsylvania doctoral dissertation, "The Sentimental Moor in Spanish Literature Before 1600," argues that the literary Moors are historical because Moors had adopted *Christian* customs and in many cases were converted Christians. Despite his extensive contextualization, Deferrari nonetheless terms the period 1550–1600 "the height of the 'morisco' fad in Spanish literature" (55).

12. The exoticization of Spain based on the perceived excesses of its religious practices could certainly take up a book in its own right, but that is not my project here.

13. See my "Virtual Spaniards," *Journal of Spanish Cultural Studies* 2, 1 (March 2001): 13–26, and A. Katie Harris, *From Muslim to Christian Granada: Inventing a City's Past in Early Modern Spain* (Baltimore: Johns Hopkins University Press, 2007).

14. J. C. L. Simonde de Sismondi, *De la littérature du midi de l'Europe*, 4 vols. (Paris: Treuttel et Würtz, 1813), 4: 259–60.

Chapter 1. The Quotidian and the Exotic

1. The Capitulaciones were not unique in this; they were based on the medieval Castilian model of surrender treaties.

2. For a useful, exhaustive survey of travelers and their prejudices, see J. N. Hillgarth, *The Mirror of Spain, 1500–1700: The Formation of a Myth* (Ann Arbor: University of Michigan Press, 2000).

3. Colin Smith, "*Convivencia* in the *Estoria de España* of Alfonso X," in *Hispanic Medieval Studies in Honor of Samuel G. Armistead*, ed. Michael Gerli (Madison: Hispanic Seminary of Medieval Studies, 1992), 292. See also Juan Carlos Ruiz Souza, "Castilla y Al-Andalus: arquitecturas aljamiadas y otros grados de asimilación," *Anuario del Departamento de Historia y Teoría del Arte* (U.A.M.) 16 (2004): 17–43, 22.

4. I find useful in this context Pierre Bourdieu's account of the *habitus* as "principles which generate and organize practices and representations that can be objectively adapted to their outcomes without presupposing a conscious aiming at ends or an express mastery of the operations necessary in order to attain them," *The Logic of Practice*, trans. Richard Nice (Stanford, Calif.: Stanford University Press, 1990), 53. I am mindful of the fact that Bourdieu evolved his own exquisitely self-conscious practice in the context of the struggle against French colonialism in North Africa.

5. See María Judith Feliciano, "Muslim Shrouds for Christian Kings: A Reassessment of Andalusi Textiles in Thirteenth-Century Castilian Life and Ritual," in *Under the Influence: Questioning the Comparative in Medieval Castile*, ed. Cynthia Robinson and Leyla Rouhi (Boston: Brill, 2005), 101–31.

6. González Alcantud notes, "Es fácil imaginar respecto a la arquitectura popular, que tras los decretos de expulsión, el reparto de las propiedades de los moriscos hizo que se transmitiera íntegro y sin ninguna modificicación sustancial el patrimonio doméstico, y en especial las casas" ("Mythos y techné," 98) ["It is easy to imagine with respect to popular architecture that, after the expulsion decrees, the distribution of Morisco properties transferred the domestic tradition integrally and without any substantial modification, especially where houses themselves were concerned."]

7. Fernando Martínez Nespral notes that by the late seventeenth century

French travelers had become used to describing Spain as the antithesis of everything European. See Martínez Nespral, *Un juego de espejos: rasgos mudéjares de la arquitectura y el habitar en la España de los siglos XVI–XVII* (Buenos Aires: Nobuko, 2006).

8. Alberto Bartolomé Arraiza, "La vivienda en la segunda mitad del siglo XVI," in *Felipe II: un monarca y su época: las tierras y los hombres del rey* (Madrid: Sociedad para la Conmemoración de los Centenarios de Felipe II y Carlos V, 1998), 103–9. Laurent Vital in his account from 1517 admires Spanish houses but notes that they have very little furniture. Vital, *Premier voyage de Charles-Quint en Espagne*, in *Collection des voyages des souverains des Pays-Bas*, ed. M. Gachard, 4 vols. (Bruxelles: F. Hayez, 1874–82), 3: 252. Images of the *estrado* are available on the websites or catalogs for these museums; see http://www.museo-casa-natal-cervantes.org and Juan Manuel González Martel, *Casa Museo Lope de Vega: guía y catálogo* (Madrid: Real Academia Española, 1993). The *estrado* makes a frequent appearance in literary texts of the period. One of the most striking instances comes in Sancho's discussion with his wife about his daughter's marital fate, in Part II of *Don Quijote*. With a fascinating malapropism, Sancho imagines Sanchica elevated to a noble status "en un estrado de más almohadas de velludo que tuvieron moros en su linaje los *Almohadas* de Marruecos" ["on an *estrado* with more velvet pillows than there were Moors in the line of the Almohads/Pillows of Morocco"], Miguel Cervantes Saavedra, *El ingenioso hidalgo Don Quijote de la Mancha* (1605, 1615); ed. Martín de Riquer (Barcelona: Planeta, 1997), 598, my emphasis. Subsequent references to *Don Quijote* are in the text by page number only. The *estrado* also appears frequently as an aristocratic feminine space in the novellas of María de Zayas.

9. Bartolomé Arraiza, "La vivienda," 105.

10. Cited in Bartolomé Arraiza, "La vivienda," 105.

11. Antoine Lalaing, *Voyage de Philippe le Beau en Espagne*, in *Collection des voyages des souverains des Pays-Bas*, 4 vols., ed. M. Gachard (Bruxelles: F. Hayez, 1874–1882), 1: 121–318, 240.

12. Helen Nader, "Introduction," in *Power and Gender in Renaissance Spain: Eight Women of the Mendoza Family, 1450–1650*, ed. Nader (Urbana: University of Illinois Press, 2004), 9. Nader notes that the decoration of the palace, begun in 1485, included many Moorish elements: "In typical Castilian manner, the dukes did not distinguish among Muslim, ancient Roman, and modern European styles. Most surfaces of the rooms were decorated in Muslim style: tile floors and wainscoting and inlaid wood ceilings, while Flemish tapestries covered the upper walls" (9).

13. Louis Barrau-Dihigo, ed., "Voyage de Barthélemy Joly en Espagne (1603–1604)," *Revue Hispanique* 20, 58 (June 1909): 459–618, 561.

14. Martínez Nespral, *Un juego de espejos*, 123 and passim.

15. Andrea Navagero, *Viaggio fatto in Spagna et in Francia* (Venice, 1563), 9.

16. Martínez Nespral, *Un juego de espejos*, 149–55.

17. Vital, *Premier voyage de Charles-Quint en Espagne*, 251–52.

18. Lalaing, *Voyage de Philippe le Beau*, 203.

19. On Navagero's admiration for the Moorish gardens he saw in Spain, and their influence on Italian Renaissance gardens, see Christopher J. Pastore, "Ex-

panding Antiquity: Andrea Navagero and Villa Culture in the Cinquecento Veneto," Ph.D. dissertation, University of Pennsylvania, 2003, esp. 132–284.

20. Henri Cock, "Anales del año ochenta y cinco," in *Viajes de extranjeros por España y Portugal*, ed. J. García Mercadal, 6 vols., 2nd ed. (Salamanca: Junta de Castilla y León, 1999), 2: 464.

21. See Carmen Añón and José Luis Sancho, eds., *Jardín y naturaleza en el reinado de Felipe II* (Madrid: Sociedad Estatal para la Conmemoración de los Centenarios de Felipe II y Carlos V, 1998). In "Sevilla: los Reales Alcázares," one of the essays in that volume, Ana Marín Fidalgo describes several Renaissance and Mannerist gardens built in Seville, yet notes that their roots, and basic elements—the use of water, brick and tile, division into garden "compartments," walls with frequent openings—are clearly Moorish (335).

22. In discussing the continuity of gardens for a slightly earlier period, D. Fairchild Ruggles argues that "while agriculture is deeply affected by political strife, the actual practice more often than not transcends political, religious, and ethnic boundaries. . . . In general, agricultural innovations are quickly adopted when the benefits are recognized, provided the political and cultural climate allows it." Ruggles, *Islamic Gardens and Landscapes* (Philadelphia: University of Pennsylvania Press, 2008), xi.

23. William D. Phillips, Jr., *Enrique IV and the Crisis of Fifteenth-Century Castile, 1425–1480* (Cambridge, Mass.: Medieval Academy of America, 1978); Barbara F. Weissberger, *Isabel Rules: Constructing Queenship, Wielding Power* (Minneapolis: University of Minnesota Press, 2004).

24. Weissberger, *Isabel Rules*, 74.

25. Alfonso de Palencia, *Gesta Hispaniensa*, ed. and Spanish trans. Brian Tate and Jeremy Lawrance (Madrid: Real Academia de la Historia, 1998), 3.9. 17–19. Subsequent citations are in the text, by book, chapter, and line number.

26. On these soldiers, see Ana Echevarría Arsuaga, "La guardia morisca: un cuerpo desconocido del ejército medieval español," *Revista de Historia Militar* 45, 90 (2001): 55–78.

27. As the editors point out, the Latin wordplay on *ueneficio/beneficio* is untranslatable.

28. Phillips, *Enrique IV*, 87–90. Tate and Lawrance note in de Palencia, *Gesta Hispaniensa* that Pulgar, in his *Tratado de los reyes de Granada*, recognizes the longstanding tradition of entertaining Muslim kings at the Christian court (Book 3, n. 30, p. 130).

29. Tate and Lawrance confuse the issue when they refer to Enrique's "Islamofilia" (Book 3, n. 30, p. 130, and passim): surely the point is that the cultural hybridity did not necessarily indicate any deficiency in the subject's religious conformity, but was used to imply as much.

30. Malcolm Letts, ed. and trans., *The Travels of Leo of Rozmital Through Germany, Flanders, England, France, Spain, Portugal, and Italy, 1465–1467* (Cambridge: Hakluyt Society, 1957), 91–92, cited in Phillips, *Enrique IV*, 88.

31. Weissberger, *Isabel Rules*, 73. Weissberger is citing Alan Bray, *Homosexuality in Renaissance England* (London: Gay Men's Press, 1982).

32. Alain Milhou, "Desemitización y europeización en la cultura española

desde la época de los Reyes Católicos hasta la expulsión de los moriscos," *Cultura del Renaixement* II (1993): 35–60. See also Milhou, "La mutación de un país de frontera," in *Españas: 1492–1992*, ed. Jean-Pierre Dedieu (Paris: CNRS, 1991), 195–207.

33. Milhou, "Desemitización y europeización," 38.

34. On Italian constructions of the Spanish, see Arturo Farinelli, *Marrano (storia di un vituperio)* (Geneva: Olschki, 1925); Benedetto Croce, *Spagna nella vita italiana durante la Rinascenza* (Bari : G. Laterza & Figli, 1917); Sverker Arnoldsson, *La leyenda negra: estudios sobre sus orígenes* (Göteborg: Göteborgs Universitets Arsskrift, 1960).

35. Croce, *Spagna nella vita italiana*, 107 and ff., especially 113; Arnoldsson, *La leyenda negra*, 63–64.

36. Milhou, "Desemitización y europeización," 42.

37. Lalaing, *Voyage de Philippe le Beau*, 225.

38. Most historians ascribe the forced conversions of 1500–1502 to the general recrudescence of religious exclusionism under Archbishop Cisneros, and to the rebellions by Muslims in Granada when the original conditions of their surrender were not observed. L. P. Harvey argues that the Spanish policy was already evident in 1497, when Spain insisted that Portugal expel its Moors as the condition for a dynastic marriage. Harvey, *Muslims in Spain, 1500 to 1614* (Chicago: University of Chicago Press, 2005), 15–21.

39. Henry Charles Lea, *The Moriscos of Spain: Their Conversion and Expulsion* (Philadelphia: Lea Brothers, 1901, reprint New York: Burt Franklin, 1968), 81. Lea also contextualizes the complex agency behind Clement VII's 1524 papal brief to Charles, urging him to break with Fernando's oath not to expel the Muslims of Aragon and instead to force conversions and condemn any recalcitrant Muslims into slavery. Lea suggests that Charles asked Clement for the authorization, even though it was presented as the pope's initiative (82–85).

40. Milhou, "Desemitización y europeización," 38.

41. In two related articles, Ronald E. Surtz has studied the interesting case of Cristóbal Duarte Ballester, a Valencian tried by the Inquisition for the dual crimes of insufficient observance of Christianity and predilection for Moorish culture, as evidenced by his playing Moorish instruments and singing Moorish songs. Yet when one looks closely at this case it becomes clear that it is a permissive regard for Islam, not the mere singing, that alarms the Inquisition. Perhaps, then, as Surtz notes, it is in conjunction with religious dissidence maurophilia of any sort becomes suspect. Interestingly, as Surtz points out, when speaking Arabic and consorting with Moriscos Ballester was probably essentially indistinguishable from them. "Maurofilia y maurofobia en los procesos inquisitoriales de Cristóbal Duarte Ballester," in *Mélanges Luce López Baralt*, ed. Abdeljelil Temimi, 2 vols. (Zaghouan: Fondation Temimi, 2001), 2: 711–21, and "Crimes of the Tongue: The Inquisitorial Trials of Cristóbal Duarte Ballester," in *Interrogating Iberian Frontiers*, ed. Barbara F. Weissberger with María Judith Feliciano, Leyla Rouhi, and Cynthia Robinson, *Medieval Encounters* 12, 3 (2006): 519–32.

42. "Cédula sobre las músicas, cantos y bailes de los nuevamente convertidos," n. XLIV in Antonio Gallego y Burín and Alfonso Gámir Sandoval, *Los mori-*

scos del reino de Granada según el Sínodo de Guadix de 1554, ed. Darío Cabanelas Rodríguez (Granada: Universidad de Granada, 1968), 234.

43. Milhou, "Desemitización y europeización," 44.

44. Miguel Querol Gavaldá, in *La música en las obras de Cervantes* (Barcelona: Comtalia, 1948), 148, points out that Cervantes's joke seems to have led to an alternative definition for *albogues* in a number of dictionaries, despite the fact that there is no extant use of the term to denote the percussion instrument Don Quijote describes, beyond *Don Quijote* itself. Javier Irigoyen-García, in "La Arcadia hispánica: los libros de pastores españoles y la exclusión de lo morisco" (Ph.D. dissertation, University of Pennsylvania, 2008) notes that *albogues* would have appeared everywhere in the pastoral literature Don Quijote read, as they do in Cervantes's own pastoral *Galatea*. He thus reads this moment as deliberate "imposture" rather than actual ignorance on Don Quijote's or Cervantes's part (232–58).

45. For the pastoral as a genre that refuses the Moorishness of Spain, see Irigoyen-García, "La Arcadia hispánica."

46. Antonio de Nebrija, *Gramática castellana*, ed. Miguel Ángel Esparza and Ramón Sarmiento, (Madrid: Fundación Antonio de Nebrija, 1992). Nebrija discusses orthography and pronunciation in Book I, Chapter V, "De las letras I pronunciaciones de la Lengua castellana," 129–37.

47. Juan de Valdés, *Diálogo de la lengua*, ed. Juan M. Lope Blanch (Madrid: Castalia, 1984), 67.

48. For a comparison of Nebrija and Valdés, see Eric Beaumatin, "Langue de soi et phonèmes de l'Autre: Nebrija, Valdés, Quevedo," in *Les représentations de l'Autre dans l'espace ibérique et ibéro-américain*, ed. Augustin Redondo (Paris: Presses de la Sorbonne Nouvelle, 1991), 235–48.

49. Beaumatin, "Langue de soi," 242.

50. Felipe Maíllo Salgado, in *Los arabismos del castellano en la baja edad media* (Salamanca: Universidad de Salamanca, 1991), which traces the role of Arabic in Spanish until 1514, finds that the presence of Arabic-derived words corresponds closely to register: the higher the register, the less likely it is to find Arabisms, while they abound in satire and in representations of colloquial speech. He also notes that from the fifteenth century on, writers of Moorish or Jewish origins seem to be the ones intent on avoiding words derived from Hebrew or Arabic, even those fully integrated into Spanish, while writers less self-conscious about their own ethnic origins seem completely oblivious to such etymological distinctions (500). Maíllo Salgado suggests that Arabisms diminish in the sixteenth century as more European technical innovations are introduced into Spain and some of the referents for Arabisms disappear, but he does not emphasize the role of prohibitions against Arabic in this reduction (503). Also, as the examples from Valdés suggest, there were plenty of Arabic-derived elements that remained central to everyday existence in Spain.

51. Sebastien de Covarrubias, *Tesoro dela lengua castellana o española* (1611), ed. Martín de Riquer (Barcelona: Altafulla, 1998). 913.

52. See Walter Mignolo, *The Darker Side of the Renaissance: Literacy, Territoriality, and Colonization* (Ann Arbor: University of Michigan Press, 1995), Chap-

ter 1. For a contextualization of Aldrete in light of contemporary debates about the purported Christian past of Granada, see Kathryn A. Woolard, "Bernardo de Aldrete and the Morisco Problem: A Study in Early Modern Spanish Language Ideology," *Comparative Studies in Society and History* 44, 3 (July 2002): 446–80. Curiously, Woolard does not discuss Aldrete's own reflections on the role of Arabic in Spanish.

53. Bernardo Aldrete, *Del origen y principio de la lengua castellana o romance que oi se usa en España*, facsimile ed. Lidio Nieto Jiménez (Madrid: Visor, 1993), 363.

54. Strikingly, Aldrete's examples do not include any of the words singled out by Valdés.

Chapter 2. In Memory of Moors: History, Maurophilia, and the Built Vernacular

1. Juan de Mariana, *Historiae de Rebus Hispaniae* (Toleti: Typis Petri Roderici, 1592). There was a second Toledo edition in 1595, and an edition in Mainz in 1605. The Spanish translation, *Historia general de España*, was also published by Pedro Rodríguez in Toledo, 1601. For Spanish historiography in the sixteenth century, see Richard L. Kagan, "Clio and the Crown: Writing History in Habsburg Spain," in *Spain, Europe and the Atlantic World: Essays in Honour of John H. Elliott*, ed. Richard L. Kagan and Geoffrey Parker (Cambridge: Cambridge University Press, 1995), 73–99. Kagan points out that Mariana's immensely successful history followed a century's worth of failed attempts by royal chroniclers to write such a comprehensive account.

2. Roger Chartier, *Inscription and Erasure: Literature and Written Culture from the Eleventh to the Eighteenth Century*, trans. Arthur Goldhammer (Philadelphia: University of Pennsylvania Press, 2007), vii.

3. I take here Maurice Halbwachs's concept of memory forged in collective social frameworks, as opposed to that of isolated individuals. See "The Social Frameworks of Memory," in Halbwachs, *On Collective Memory*, ed. Lewis Coser (Chicago: University of Chicago Press, 1992), excerpts and translation of *Les cadres sociaux de la mémoire* (1925).

4. The notion of *lieux de mémoire* was famously proposed in the early 1980s by Pierre Nora, and developed in his encyclopedic anthology on contemporary France, *Les lieux de mémoire* (Paris: Gallimard, 1992). For a useful contextualization of Halbwachs and Nora, see Paul Ricoeur, *Memory, History, Forgetting*, trans. Kathleen Blamey and David Pellauer (Chicago: University of Chicago Press, 2004).

5. Peggy K. Liss emphasizes the role of chivalry in the final days of the war in her *Isabel the Queen: Life and Times*, rev. ed. (Philadelphia: University of Pennsylvania Press, 2004), 256–58. For Elizabeth, see Louis Montrose, "The Elizabethan Subject and the Spenserian Text," in *Literary Theory/Renaissance Texts*, ed. Patricia Parker and David Quint (Baltimore: Johns Hopkins University Press,

1986). Barbara Weissberger notes the striking similarities between the two queens' public images and the anxieties they produced in *Isabel Rules*.

6. Navagero, *Viaggio*, 27–28.

7. Juan Boscán, *Los cuatro libros del Cortesano, compuestos en italiano por el conde Baltasar Castellon, y agora nuevamente traduzidos en lengua castellana*, ed. Antonio María Fabié (Madrid: Rivadeneyra, 1873). The original Italian reads as follows:

> Sono molti che estimano la vittoria dei re di Spagna Ferrando ed Isabella contra il re di Granata esser proceduta gran parte dalle donne; ché il piú delle volte quando usciva lo esercito di Spagna per affrontar gli inimici, usciva ancora la regina Isabella con tutte le sue damigelle e quivi si ritrovavano molti nobili cavalieri innamorati; li quali finché giongeano al loco di veder gli nemici, sempre andavano parlando con le lor donne; poi, pigliando licenzia ciascun dalla sua, in presenzia loro andavano ad incontrar gli nimici con quell'animo feroce che dava loro amore, e 'l desiderio di far conoscere alle sue signore che erano servite da omini valorosi; onde molte volte trovaronsi pochissimi cavalieri spagnoli mettere in fuga ed alla morte infinito numero di Mori. (Baldassarre Castiglione, *Il libro del Cortegiano*, ed. Walter Barberis [Torino: Einaudi, 1998], 324–25).

8. Liss, *Isabel the Queen*, 257.

9. Andrés de Bernáldez, *Memorias del reinado de los reyes católicos*, ed. M. Gómez Moreno and J. de Mata Carriazo (Madrid: Real Academia de la Historia, 1962), 156. Subsequent citations are in the text, by page number only.

10. In *The Mendoza Family in the Spanish Renaissance, 1350–1550* (New Brunswick, N.J.: Rutgers University Press, 1979), Helen Nader makes a distinction between *caballero* and *letrado* chroniclers, arguing that the latter, who include Bernáldez, contrast with the chivalric perspective of the former (25–31). Yet my reading of Bernáldez suggests that his providential perspective is fully compatible with a chivalric tone, and even with his recognition of the Muslim enemy.

11. See Chapter 3 for a full discussion of "The Moorish Fashion."

12. See Claudio Guillén, "Literature as Historical Contradiction: *El Abencerraje*, the Moorish Novel, and the Eclogue," in his *Literature as System: Essays toward the Theory of Literary History* (Princeton, N.J.: Princeton University Press, 1971), 195–96, and George A. Shipley, "La obra literaria como monumento histórico: el caso de *El Abencerraje*," *Journal of Hispanic Philology* 2, 2 (Winter 1978): 118–19.

13. Francisco López Estrada, ed., *El Abencerraje (Novela y romancero)* (Madrid: Cátedra, 1996), 162. Unless otherwise specified, all citations from the text are to this edition by page number to *El Abencerraje*.

14. As I noted in Chapter 1, a number of laws against Morisco cultural practices had been passed by Charles V in 1526, although their enforcement was repeatedly postponed until the late 1560s. Philip II's 1557 bankruptcy led to new economic pressures, including a large increase in the silk tax in 1561. This proved devastating to the Granadan silk industry, which employed countless Moriscos. See Kenneth

Garrad, "La industria sedera granadina en el siglo XVI y su conexión con el levantamiento de las Alpujarras," *Miscelánea de estudios árabes y hebraicos* 5 (1956): 73–104.

15. See María Soledad Carrasco Urgoiti, "Las cortes señoriales del Aragón mudéjar y *El Abencerraje*," in *Homenaje a Casalduero: crítica y poesía*, ed. Rizel Pincus Sigele and Gonzalo Sobejano (Madrid: Gredos, 1972), 115–28.

16. Francisco López Estrada, "*El Abencerraje* de Toledo, 1561: Edición crítica y comentarios," *Anales de la Universidad Hispalense* 19 (1959): 31.

17. Israel Burshatin, "Power, Discourse, and Metaphor in the *Abencerraje*," *MLN* 99, 2 (March 1984), 209.

18. Burshatin, "Power, Discourse, and Metaphor," 197.

19. See the series of articles by Georges Cirot on "Maurophilie littéraire." Newer work on the pastoral in fact suggests that its idealizations, too, are compatible with precise ideological interventions. See Irigoyen-García, "La Arcadia hispánica."

20. Carrasco Urgoiti, "Las cortes señoriales"; Shipley, "La obra literaria."

21. Guillén, "Literature as Historical Contradiction," 170.

22. Guillén, "Literature as Historical Contradiction," 193.

23. Carrasco Urgoiti, "Las cortes señoriales," 119.

24. For references to the historical Rodrigo de Narváez in Spanish chronicles, see Francisco López Estrada's useful introduction to his edition of *El Abencerraje*, 43.

25. López Estrada, *El Abencerraje*, 44.

26. Burshatin argues that the Spanish attitude is compared favorably with the "Greek and Roman penchant for praising and writing down the slightest adventure of a man's life" ("Power, Discourse, and Metaphor," 199). The initial oppositional clause "sino que esta nuestra España" as well as the clause "que le paresce que cuanto se puede hacer es poco" suggest to me a more ambiguous valence.

27. Juan de Mena, *Laberinto de Fortuna*, ed. Louise Vasvari Fainberg (Madrid: Alhambra, 1976), 157. The text's popularity in the sixteenth century counters the notion that Spain did not adequately memorialize its heros; the topos appears repeatedly.

28. Cited in López Estrada's edition, 132 n.6.

29. In the preface to his much later history, Mariana repeats this topos of writerly disregard for heroism, describing Spain as "más abundante en hazañas que en escritores." *Historia general*, li.

30. Ricardo Krauel, "El esquema heroico de la historia de Abindarráez," *Romance Notes* 37, 1 (1996): 39–47, at 40.

31. Burshatin, "Power, Discourse, and Metaphor," 200. On the text's relation to the epic tradition, see also Kathleen Bollard, "Re-Reading Heroism in *El Abencerraje*," *Bulletin of Spanish Studies* 80, 3 (2003): 297–307.

32. There is a further irony in the fact that the title that rewards him mirrors the Moorish administration of the town: an *alcaide* or *alcalde*, Covarrubias notes, is "nombre arábigo, el que preside y gobierna algún lugar" (*Tesoro*, 72) ["an Arabic word for the one who presides over and governs a town"]. On the frontier, such mimetic phenomena abound.

33. *El Abencerraje*, 43–44.

34. I cite here from the version in López Estrada, *El Abencerraje y la hermosa Jarifa: cuatro textos y su estudio* (Madrid: Publicaciones de la Revista de Archivos, Bibliotecas y Museos, 1957), 377. For clarity, in subsequent references I refer to this edition as *Cuatro textos*.

35. Laura Bass, "Homosocial Bonds and Desire in the *Abencerraje*," *Revista Canadiense de Estudios Hispánicos* 24, 3 (Spring 2000): 453–71, 459. In "Re-Reading Heroism," Bollard underscores the differences between Narváez and Abindarráez, although she is careful to note how the *Diana* version makes them both more sentimental.

36. Bass, "Homosocial Bonds," 458–60 and Bollard, "Re-Reading Heroism," 305 both discuss the *escaramuza*, but primarily in terms of the two protagonists. I am more interested in the overwhelming numerical advantage of the Christians as a qualifier to Narváez's victory.

37. On Christian incursions into Moorish territory, see Julio Caro Baroja, *Los moriscos del Reino de Granada: ensayo de Historia Social*, 2nd ed. (Madrid: Istmo, 1976), 62–63.

38. See, among others, Walter Holzinger, "The Militia of Love, War, and Virtue in the *Abencerraje y la hermosa Jarifa*: A Structural and Sociological Reassessment," *Revista Canadiense de Estudios Hispánicos* 2, 3 (1978): 227–38, 228 and passim.

39. Bass, "Homosocial Bonds," 453–54 and passim.

40. Guillén discusses Narváez as exemplum in "Literature as Historical Contradiction," 208–17, and in an earlier version of the essay, "Individuo y ejemplaridad en el 'Abencerraje,' " in *Collected Studies in Honour of Américo Castro's Eightieth Year*, ed. M. P. Hornik (Oxford: Lincombe Lodge Research Library, 1965), 175–97.

41. It should be noted that the *Diana* edition, which makes no mention of the statue, does imagine descendants for Narváez, "cuyo linaje dura hasta aora en Antequera, correspondiendo con magníficos hechos al origen donde proceden" (López Estrada, *Cuatro textos*, 413.) Conversely, in the *Corónica* version Narváez specifically wishes Jarifa well with her pregnancy and emphasizes the continuation of the Moorish lineage: "Assimismo visitaréis a la hermosa Xarifa, y le daréis el parabién de su preñez, y le diréis como en estremo me he holgado de saber que está en términos de acrescentar un tan valeroso linage" (López Estrada, "*El Abencerraje* de Toledo," 30).

42. Shipley observes how striking it is that Narváez himself implicitly gives primacy to this "empresa tan generosa [y] digna" ("La obra literaria," 163–64) over "aquella empresa y guerra de Antequera" (131).

43. See Coleman, *Creating Christian Granada*; Harris, *From Muslim to Christian Granada*; and my "Virtual Spaniards."

44. Navagero, "Viaggio," 18.

45. Also, of course, the title of the 1995 novel by Salman Rushdie in which he addresses diaspora, exile, and many other themes resonant with Granada.

46. The text has been edited by Kenneth Garrad as "The Original Memorial of Don Francisco Núñez Muley," *Atlante* 2 (1954): 199–226.

47. Garrad, "Original Memorial," 219.

48. Garrad, "Original Memorial," 219–20.

49. Bernard Vincent, *1492: L'année admirable* (Paris: Aubier, 1991), 32.

50. Darío Cabanelas Rodríguez, "The Alhambra: An Introduction," in *Al-Andalus: The Art of Islamic Spain*, ed. Jerrilynn D. Dodds, exhibition catalog (New York: Metropolitan Museum of Art, 1992), 132.

51. Hieronymus Münzer, *Itinerarium Hispanicum Hieronymi Monetarii*, 1494–95, ed. Ludwig Pfandl, *Revue Hispanique* 48 (1920): 1–179, 46.

52. Cabanelas Rodríguez, "Alhambra," 132. Rafael López Guzmán notes that repairs continued throughout the sixteenth century, with a striking continuity in artisans, forms, and techniques, *Arquitectura mudéjar*, 2nd ed. (Madrid: Cátedra, 2000, 2005), 407.

53. Cited in Rafael López Guzmán, *Arquitectura mudéjar*, 407.

54. See Jerrilynn Dodds, "The Mudejar Tradition in Architecture," in *The Legacy of Muslim Spain*, 2 vols., ed. Salma Khadra Jayyusi (Leiden: Brill, 1994), 2: 595–96.

55. Navagero, *Viaggio*, 19. For Navagero's views on Granada, see Cammy Brothers, "The Renaissance Reception of the Alhambra: The Letters of Andrea Navagero and the Palace of Charles V," ed. Gülru Necipoglu, *Muqarnas* 11 (1994): 79–102.

56. Fernando Chueca Goitia, "El arte español en la época de Carlos V," in *Carolus V Imperator*, ed. Pedro Navascués Palacio (Barcelona: Lunwerg, 1999), 286.

57. Earl Rosenthal, *The Palace of Charles V in Granada* (Princeton, N.J.: Princeton University Press, 1985), 238. See also Brothers, "Renaissance Reception," 80–93. Certainly the period saw increasing importation of Renaissance styles, but, as I argue below, in most cases they were melded with local forms.

58. The architectural panorama in sixteenth-century Granada was very complex. While Charles's palace and the Cathedral seemed intended to mark a classicizing difference versus the Andalusi past, scores of local parish churches were being built in a hybrid Mudéjar style even after the expulsion of local Moriscos in 1570 (Coleman, *Creating Christian Grenada*, 70–72).

59. Brothers, "Renaissance Reception," 88–89. At the same time Brothers suggests a connection between the palaces in their association of hegemonic rule with pure geometric forms (90).

60. "Panel from the Mexuar, the Alhambra, Granada," Purificación Marinetto Sánchez, #119 in the exhibition catalog *Al-Andalus: The Art of Islamic Spain*, ed. Jerrilynn Dodds (New York: Metropolitan Museum of Art, 1992), 375.

61. Covarrubias, "Memoria," *Tesoro*, 798.

62. See the influential work of Fernando Chueca Goitia, whose *Invariantes castizos de la arquitectura española* (Buenos Aires: Dessat, 1947) nonetheless argued for the absolute Spanishness of "hispano-Muslim" or Mudéjar architecture.

63. The term Mudéjar was introduced by José Amador de los Ríos in his 1859 acceptance speech, "De la arquitectura mudéjar," to the Real Academia de las Bellas Artes de San Fernando, reprinted in his *El estilo mudéjar en la arquitectura* (Madrid: Imprenta de Manual Tello, 1872). For a good survey of the term's history

and of current debates, see López Guzmán, *Arquitectura mudéjar*. Mudéjar is also a term in wide general use, and describes literally hundreds of churches and other buildings admired throughout Spain. The Mudéjar architecure of the Aragonese city of Teruel, for example, has been designated part of UNESCO's World Heritage.

64. "Editors' Introduction," in *Under the Influence: Questioning the Comparative in Medieval Castile*, ed. Cynthia Robinson and Leyla Rouhi (Leiden: Brill, 2005), 5. See also Dodds, "Mudejar Tradition," 598.

65. López Guzmán, *Arquitectura mudéjar*, 17, my translation.

66. There has been some discussion as to whether Mudéjar applies also to Sicily and southern Italy, which experienced long periods of Arab settlement. See Gonzalo Borrás Gualis, "El arte mudéjar: estado actual de la cuestión," in *Mudéjar iberoamericano: una expresión cultural de dos mundos* (Granada: Universidad de Granada, 1993), 9–19, 19. On the problems with a formal understanding of Mudéjar as style, see Ruiz Souza, "Castilla y Al-Andalus," 32–34.

67. This is clearly the sense that applied by the late nineteenth century, when the academic term "neomudéjar" was deployed as a marker of national or regional identity in everything from railway stations to bullfighting rings to, perhaps most strikingly, the Spanish Pavilion at the 1889 Paris Universal Exposition.

68. Borrás Gualis, "El arte mudéjar," 18, my translation.

69. Borrás Gualis, "El arte mudéjar," 18, my translation. When applied to persons, "Mudéjar" referred to a Muslim who lived under Christian rule.

70. The critics who favor a narrower definition of the Mudéjar dismiss the New World examples as "survivals." See López Guzmán, *Arquitectura mudéjar*, 42–53.

71. López Guzmán, *Arquitectura mudéjar*, 57, my translation.

72. For a rich interdisciplinary account of the resulting cultural productions, see Robinson and Rouhi, *Under the Influence*. Robinson and Rouhi not only question the idea of influence, but problematize the notion of discrete, stable groups influencing each other in Iberia. See also Weissberger et al., *Interrogating Iberian Frontiers*.

73. López Guzmán, *Arquitectura mudéjar*, 386, my translation.

74. For a detailed account of the various stages in building and expanding the palace, see Vicente Lleó Cañal, *La Casa de Pilatos* (Madrid: Electa, 1998). Strikingly, Lleó Cañal calls the palace "a strange hybrid of medieval and Renaissance" (38) in an effort to fix chronologically elements that transcend the periodic divide. For the classicizing aesthetic within the palace, see Amanda Wunder, "Classical, Christian, and Muslim Remains in the Construction of Imperial Seville (1520–1635)," *Journal of the History of Ideas* 64, 2 (2003): 195–212. Wunder describes the transformation of Seville in the period as "a moment of synthesis, when imported innovations mixed with local traditions" (197).

75. Lleó Cañal, *La Casa de Pilatos*, 33.

76. Later remodelings included classical remains of local provenance, as a way to emphasize both the Renaissance and the local nature of the palace.

77. See Antonio Herrera Casado, *El palacio del Infantado en Guadalajara* (Guadalajara, Spain: Aache Ediciones, 2001), and Francisco Layna Serrano, *El pa-*

lacio del Infantado en Guadalajara, 2nd ed. (Guadalajara, Spain: Aache Ediciones, 1997).

78. Herrera Casado, *El palacio*, 37–42.

79. As Wunder puts it in discussing the classicizing ephemera that were often on display in Seville, "Ephemeral architecture might cloak the retrograde medieval city in a gilded mantle of Renaissance classicism, but the functional structures beneath the disguise stayed in place for everyday use" ("Classical, Christian," 208).

80. The most striking example of an effort to preserve Andalusi building practices is the *Breve compendio de la carpintería de lo blanco y tratado de alarifes* (Seville, 1633) by Diego López de Arenas, himself an *alarife* (master builder); see Wunder, "Classical, Christian," 208–11.

81. In assessing this question of agency for the Christianization of mosques in twelfth-century Toledo, Dodds observes: "But there is nevertheless a clear interest in some level of visual continuity on the part of patrons, or at least a curious abstinence on their part from distinguishing their new sacred buildings of Christian reconquest by any change in exterior visual vocabulary," ("Mudejar Tradition," 593). In the twelfth century, Dodds posits an "appealing meaning to this exotic new type of technique and ornament" (594). One might argue that by the sixteenth century, the meaningfulness had diminished along with the novelty, given the increasing hybridization in the intervening centuries, along with a "secularization of artistic form" (595).

82. See Pastore, "Expanding Antiquity," 136ff for a fascinating account of Navagero's own perception of Iberian Moorish gardens as part of Mediterranean antiquity. In this sense, there was no necessary contradiction between Moorish and classical elements.

83. Fernando del Pulgar, *Crónica de los Reyes Católicos*, ed. Juan de Mata Carriazo, 2 vols. (Madrid: Espasa-Calpe, 1943), 2: 96–98. The story seems important enough to merit its own chapter (153).

84. Mariana, *Historia general de España*, 2: 218. Mariana tells these stories of creative dissimulation just after narrating the king's reward to the count of Cabra of new arms, featuring a crowned king, surrounded by nine flags to signal those captured from the Moors, "todo a propósito de gratificar aquel servicio, y despertar a otros a emprender cosas grandes por la patria y la religión" ["all for the sake of rewarding that service, and to encourage others to take on great things for the fatherland and for religion"]. The juxtaposition ironizes the symbolic weight of the arms granted Cabra, but also suggests just how effectively the Christians gave meaning to the material.

Chapter 3. The Moorish Fashion

Epigraphs: Ramón Menéndez Pidal, *España y su historia*, 2 vols. (Madrid: Minotauro, 1957), 2: 276; Agustín Durán, ed., *Romancero general* (Madrid: Rivadeneyra: 1851), vol. 10, n. 244, p. 128. In my translation, I have purposely kept the Arabic-derived Spanish names for garments, rather than giving an English version, in order to convey the saturation by Moorish culture of which the poet complains.

1. For good introductory summaries of theories of fashion versus dress or costume, see Joanne Entwistle, *The Fashioned Body: Fashion, Dress, and Modern Social Theory* (Cambridge: Polity Press, 2000), esp. 40–111, and Daniel Leonhard Purdy's introduction to his anthology, *The Rise of Fashion: A Reader* (Minneapolis: University of Minnesota Press, 2004), 1–17.

2. I am thinking here of the fine work by Ann Rosalind Jones and Peter Stallybrass, *Renaissance Clothing and the Materials of Memory* (Cambridge: Cambridge University Press, 2000).

3. See Jones and Stallybrass, *Renaissance Clothing*, 1–2. By the 1640s, fashion would be described using the term *moda*, imported from the French.

4. Fernández de Oviedo, *Las quinquagenas de la nobleza de España* (1556; Madrid: Real Academia de la Historia, 1880), 175; cited in Carmen Bernís, *Indumentaria española en tiempos de Carlos V* (Madrid: CSIC, 1962), 31. See also Covarrubias's definition of *vestidura o vestido* (clothing or dress):

Todas las naciones han usado vestiduras propias, distinguiéndose por ellas unas de otras; y muchas han conservado su hábito por gran tiempo. A los españoles en este caso nos han notado de livianos, porque mudamos traje y vestido fácilmente. Y assí el otro que se hazía loco, o lo era, andava hecho pedaços y traya al ombro un pedaço de paño, y preguntándole porqué no se hazía de vestir, respondía que esperava a ver en qué paravan los trajes. Solo los labradores, que no salen de sus aldeas, han durado más en conservar el traje antiguo, aunque ya esto también está estragado. . . . No es instituto mío tratar de reformaciones, pero notorio es el excesso de España en el vestir, porque un día de fiesta el oficial y su muger no se diferencian de la gente noble. (*Tesoro*, 1003)

[All nations have had their own dress, which distinguishes them from others, and many have preserved their costume for a long time. In this regard, Spaniards have been noted as fickle, because we change habit and dress with such ease. And so a fellow who was mad or pretended to be, running around in rags with a cut of material over his shoulder, when asked why he did not have clothes made from it, would answer that he was waiting to see where fashion would end up. Only the peasants, who do not leave their towns, have kept the old costume for longer, but even this is now spoiled. . . . It is not my business to deal with reform, but the excess of dress in Spain is notorious: on a holiday, an official and his wife are indistinguishable from nobles.]

5. Carmen Bernís Madrazo, *Indumentaria medieval española* (Madrid: CSIC, 1956), "Modas moriscas en la sociedad cristiana española del siglo XV y principios del XVI," *Boletín de la Real Academia de la Historia* 144 (1959): 199–228; Ruth Matilda Anderson, *Hispanic Costume, 1480–1530* (New York: Hispanic Society of America, 1979); Rachel Arié, "Acerca del traje musulmán en España desde la caída de Granada hasta la expulsión de los moriscos," in her *Études sur la civilisation de l'Espagne* (Leiden: Brill, 1990), 121–41; Feliciano Chaves, "Mudejarismo in Its Colonial Context" and "Muslim Shrouds."

6. Arié, "Acerca del traje musulmán," 121–22. The existence of sumptuary laws that attempted to separate out Jews or Moors in earlier periods suggests that both the appearance and the dress of these groups was sufficiently similar that external signs of difference had to be imposed on them.

7. Bernís Madrazo, "Modas moriscas," 203. Feliciano Chaves notes also that "The generic term toca, so commonly found in Peninsular and colonial documentation of the sixteenth century, identified the same items of clothing as did the terms alfilem, ahareme, alfareme, almalafa, and almaizar found in Morisco historical documentation" ("Mudejarismo," 146).

8. The Trachtenbuch does depict some Moors in far more "exotic" costume. Feliciano Chaves points out that in some of the more striking images "the only 'exotic' elements are those provided by female clothing" ("Mudejarismo," 144).

9. Vital, *Premier voyage de Charles-Quint*, 149.

10. Bernís Madrazo, "Modas moriscas," 203.

11. Bernís Madrazo, "Modas moriscas," 204.

12. Feliciano Chaves, "Mudejarismo," 129.

13. Feliciano Chaves, "Mudejarismo," 129–33 and passim.

14. Bernís Madrazo, "Modas moriscas," 215–19. On the *juegos de cañas*, see Chapter 4 of this study.

15. Feliciano Chaves, "Mudejarismo," 142 n. 24, 154.

16. Feliciano Chaves, "Mudejarismo," 139–40. The importance of an "interwoven Iberian sartorial repertory," she observes, "is reduced to provide evidence of Castilian 'maurophilia,' or the taste for the 'exotic' and the consequent appropriation of 'Oriental luxury.'"

17. Anderson, *Hispanic Costume*, 92–97 for men, 215–17 for women. The embroidery on *camisas* is discussed on 189.

18. Bernís Madrazo, "Modas moriscas," 224–25.

19. While they do not use it in the Bourdieusian sense I intend here, Jones and Stallybrass juxtapose *habit*, in the sense of "the persistence of cultural patterns" to fashion understood as "the lability of an élite" (*Renaissance Clothing*, 6).

20. See especially Pierre Bourdieu, *Distinction: A Social Critique of the Judgement of Taste*, trans. Richard Nice (Cambridge, Mass.: Harvard University Press, 1984).

21. Marcy Norton, "Tasting Empire: Chocolate and the European Internalization of Mesoamerican Aesthetics," *American Historical Review* III, 3 (2006): 660–91.

22. Norton, "Tasting Empire," 670, 691.

23. Cf. Norton's account of how the Spaniards came to enjoy chocolate, in which she concludes that "Europeans inadvertently internalized Mesoamerican aesthetics" ("Tasting Empire," 18).

24. Feliciano Chaves, "Mudejarismo," 150.

25. Bernáldez, *Memorias*, 170.

26. Feliciano Chaves, "Mudejarismo," 161. Again, cf. the understanding of sodomy in Bray and my own analogy to maurophilia in Chapter 1.

27. As Francisco Núñez Muley reiterated in his *memorial*, which I discuss in Chapter 2, there were important distinctions between Muslim and local Granadan practices.

28. See the legislation collected in Gallego y Burín and Gámir Sandoval, *Moriscos del reino de Granada*.

29. "Cédula para que las cristianas viejas no se vistan a la morisca ni traigan almalafa" (Gallego y Burín and Gámir Sandoval, *Moriscos del reino de Granada*, 179).

30. Gallego y Burín includes these laws in his documentary appendix, but there is no textual sign of their particular concern with Moriscos.

31. Antonio León Pinelo, *Velos antiguos y modernos en los rostros de las mujeres: sus conveniencias y daños* (Madrid, 1641; Santiago de Chile: Centro de Investigaciones de Historia Americana, 1966), 168–69. I am grateful to Laura Bass and Amanda Wunder for sharing with me their work in progress on the *tapado*, as the fashionable half-veil of the late sixteenth and early seventeenth centuries was known.

32. León Pinelo, *Velos antiguos y modernos*, 166.

33. "Que los moriscos no traigan vestidos de Moros, sino que se conformen en los trages con los Christianos viejos" (1566) specifies that Moriscos should not "make or cut again *almalafas* or *marlotas*," *Leyes de la "Nueva" Recopilación que han sido comprendidas en la Novísima* in *Códigos españoles concordados y anotados* (Madrid: Antonio de San Martín, 1873), Título II, n. XVI (vol. II, p. 240).

34. Fray Damián Fonseca, *Relación de la expulsión de los moriscos del reino de Valencia* (Roma: Iacomo Mascardo, 1612; Valencia: Sociedad Valenciana de Bibliófilos, 1878), 117–18.

35. Cirot, "La maurophilie littéraire," *Bulletin Hispanique*. Cirot calls literary maurophilia "un phénomène curieux d'engouement collectif" (40, 2 [April–June 1938]: 150–57, 154) ["a curious phenomenon of collective infatuation"] and insists "La littérature se trouve ici en contradiction avec les faits" (156) ["literature here finds itself in contradiction with events"]. He ascribes maurophilia's choice of topic, in contradistinction to the pastoral or the chivalric, to "une raison littéraire: le besoin d'autre chose" (43, 3–4 [July–December 1941]: 289) ["a literary reason: the need for something else"].

36. María Soledad Carrasco Urgoiti's research has focused on the "Moorish novel" and the *romancero*. See, e.g., *El moro de Granada en la literatura: del siglo XV al XIX* (1956; Granada: Universidad, 1989) and *The Moorish Novel: "El Abencerraje" and Pérez de Hita* (Boston: Twayne, 1976).

37. Menéndez Pidal, *España y su historia*, 2: 277.

38. Menéndez Pidal, *España y su historia*, 2: 255. He notes that the collection was printed and reprinted several times in Huesca, Valencia, Burgos, Toledo, Lisbon, Madrid, Barcelona, Perpiñán, Zaragoza, and Alcalá de Henares.

39. See especially Carrasco Urgoiti, "Vituperio y parodia del romance morisco en el romancero nuevo," in *Culturas populares: diferencias, divergencias, conflictos: actas del coloquio celebrado en la Casa de Velázquez, los días 30 de noviembre y 1–2 de diciembre de 1983*, ed. Yves-René Fonquerne and Alfonso Esteban (Madrid: Universidad Complutense, 1986), 115–37, and "El romancero morisco de Pedro de

Padilla en su *Thesoro de varia poesía* (1580)," *Actas del XIV Congreso de la Asociación Internacional de Hispanistas*, ed. Isaías Lerner, Robert Nival, and Alejandro Alonso (Newark, Del.: Juan de la Cuesta, 2004), 2: 89–99.

40. Amelia García Valdecasas, *El género morisco en las fuentes del "Romancero general,"* (Valencia: Diputación Provincial de Valencia, 1987) 20.

41. Menéndez Pidal, *España y su historia*, 2: 278.

42. Ginés Pérez de Hita, *Historia de los bandos de Zegríes y Abencerrajes (Primera parte de las Guerras civiles de Granada)*, ed. Paula Blanchard-Demouge, facsimile edition with a preliminary study by Pedro Correa Rodríguez (Granada: Universidad de Granada, 1999), 256.

43. Durán, *Romancero general*, 234–36, pp. 122–24.

44. See Mladen Dolar, "Introduction: The Subject Supposed to Enjoy," in Alain Grosrichard, *The Sultan's Court: European Fantasies of the East*, trans. Liz Heron (London: Verso, 1998). They argue that the Western subject's jouissance in the fantasy of an erotic East comes from the renunciation of the erotic pleasure ascribed to the Other, and the subsequent difference of the Self. There is no such distancing in this corpus.

45. Durán, *Romancero general*, 56, p. 27. Durán does not attribute the ballad to Lope de Vega, but critics since then have generally done so. The force of my argument here does not depend on the specific authorship of Lope.

46. Ramón Menéndez Pidal, *Romancero hispánico* (Madrid: Espasa-Calpe, 1953) 2: 128.

47. Durán, *Romancero general*, 257, p. 136.

48. Harvey, *Muslims in Spain*, 294–300. Harvey is here following the earlier work of Henry Charles Lea.

49. Durán, *Romancero general*, 190, p. 99. The poem is satirized in 249, p. 131.

50. Durán, *Romancero general*, 244, p. 128.

51. Durán, *Romancero general*, 253, p. 134.

52. Gabriel Lasso de la Vega, *Manojuelo de romances* (1601; Madrid: Saeta, 1942), 102.

53. See also *romance* 131 in Lasso de la Vega's collection (364–67), in which he returns to this topos of the hired costumes. In this case, the *romancero* poets have produced a demand for so many Moorish costumes that there is nothing to rent for Carnival. Even this most dyspeptic of commentators, that is, cannot but acknowledge the phenomenal popularity of Moorish attire.

54. Lasso de la Vega, *Manojuelo*, 102–3.

55. Lasso de la Vega, *Manojuelo*, 103.

56. Durán edits them as their own class, which tends to erase the connection between them and specific *romances*, as in the Lope case above.

57. See Guillén, "Literature as Historical Contradiction," 170.

58. Carrasco Urgoiti notes the prevalence of these material details in "Vituperio y parodia."

59. Durán, *Romancero general*, 244, p. 128.

60. Durán, *Romancero general*, 245, p. 129. This conception of the pastoral

as the alternative to maurophile production is echoed in Menéndez Pidal's own succinct account of the *romancero morisco*: "Género tan singular llegó tardíamente a representar un mundo de añoranza ideal que, como el género pastoril, sirvió a fines del siglo XVI para disfrazar la intimidad de cada poeta" (*España y su historia*, 2: 278) ["This singular genre ultimately represented a world of idealized longing that, like the pastoral genre, served at the end of the sixteenth century to disguise each poet's private life"].

61. On the pastoral as an alternative to maurophilia, see Irigoyen-García, "La Arcadia hispánica."

62. Durán, *Romancero general*, 246, p.130.

63. Carrasco Urgoiti, "Vituperio y parodia," 132.

64. Carrasco Urgoiti, "Vituperio y parodia," 129.

65. Bourdieu, *The Logic of Practice*, 53.

Chapter 4. Playing the Moor

1. Philip J. Deloria, *Playing Indian* (New Haven, Conn.: Yale University Press, 1998).

2. There is an enormous bibliography on the *juegos de moros y cristianos*. See, most recently, Marlene Albert-Llorca and José Antonio González Alcantud, eds., *Moros y cristianos: representaciones del otro en las fiestas del Mediterraneo occidental* (Toulouse: Presses Universitaires du Mirail; Granada: Centro de Investigaciones Etnológicas Ángel Ganivet, 2003). For the *mauresque*, see the detailed entry in Christian Poché, *Dictionnaire des musiques et danses traditionelles de la Mediterranée* (Paris: Fayard, 2005), 262–65. The dance exists in distinct local versions not only throughout the Mediterranean but also in England, where it appears as the morris.

3. Francisco de Quevedo, "Epístola satírica y censoria contra las costumbres presentes de los castellanos," in Quevedo, *Poesía varia*, ed. James O. Crosby (Madrid: Catedra, 1981).

4. The 1726–37 *Diccionario de autoridades* (reprinted Madrid: Gredos, 1990) notes, "Juego o fiesta de a caballo, que introduxeron en España los Moros, el cual se suele executar por la Nobleza, en ocasiones de alguna celebridad" (128). For a minute description of the game, see "De como se ha de jugar a las cañas, y de la orden y concierto que en ello se ha de guardar," in Pedro de Aguilar, *Tractado de la cavalleria de la gineta* (1572), facsimile edition with an introduction by Angel Caffarena Such (Málaga: El Guadalhorce, 1960), 39–43. A version of the *cañas* has made its way to Argentina, where it exists as a *gaucho* game with light *boleadoras* instead of reed-spears.

5. Demetrio E. Brisset Martín, "Fiestas hispanas de moros y cristianos: historia y significados," *Gazeta de Antropología* 17 (2001): 17.

6. Rachel Arié, *España musulmana (siglos VIII–XV)*, vol. 3 of *Historia de España*, ed. Manuel Tuñón de Lara (Barcelona: Labor, 1982), 316–17.

7. Aguilar, *Tractado de la cavalleria*, 39.

8. In general I have adopted the modern spellings *jineta/jinete*, but have opted not to change the early modern spellings *gineta/ginete* in citations or translations from primary texts. *Brida* comes from the French *bride*, which also gives us the English *bridle*. On the *jineta*, see the very useful introductions to Cesáreo Sanz Egaña, ed., *Tres libros de la Jineta de los siglos XVI y XVII* (Madrid: Sociedad de Bibliófilos Españoles, 1951) and Caffarena Such's introduction to Aguilar. I am struck by the interest in the *jineta* during the Franco years. There is a marked privileging of Spain's difference, and a paradoxical embrace (at least by writers in Andalucía) of an othered Arab race, here both human and equine: "Es lo cierto que el arte de montar a la 'jineta', como antes hemos indicado, es introducido en España por los musulmanes en razón de sus propias características raciales y del tipo o raza del caballo árabe que en España ha enraizado" (xi) ["The truth is that the art of riding *jineta* style, as we have pointed out, is introduced into Spain by the Muslims due to their own racial characteristics and to the type or race of Arabian horse that has taken root in Spain"].

9. *Diccionario de autoridades*, 50. Sanz Egaña argues that the *jineta* was the riding style practiced since time immemorial on the Iberian peninsula, whatever its name, but does not provide any evidence to show that it predates the North African invasions (*Tres libros*, xi).

10. The *jineta* style of riding was also essential for bullfighting on horseback (Sanz Egaña, *Tres libros*, xvi). Although I cannot analyze the *toros* here, it is striking how often the *cañas* are paired with bullfighting as quintessentially Spanish entertainments. Arié claims that Granadan fights between bulls and dogs, a sport imported from the Maghreb, were the predecessors of the *corridas* (*España musulmana*, 316).

11. *Crónica del Rey Alfonso XI* in *Crónicas de los Reyes de Castilla*, ed. Cayetano Rosell, 3 vols. (Madrid: Atlas, 1953), I: 10.

12. Aguilar, "Prólogo" to *Tractado de la cavalleria* (n.p.). See also Hipólito Sánchez de Sopranis, *Juegos de toros y cañas en Jerez de la Frontera* (Jerez: Centro de Estudios Históricos Jerezanos, 1960), 3–4.

13. Lalaing, *Voyage de Philippe le Beau*, I: 225.

14. Spanish horses were famous throughout Europe. Note the OED definition of *jennet*, where the sense has migrated from the rider to his mount. The racialization of both is patent in the famous "grange" scene in *Othello* 1.1, where Iago taunts Brabantio with the miscegenation that will result from his daughter's elopement with the Moor: "you'll have your daughter covered with a Barbary horse; you'll have your nephews neigh to you; you'll have coursers for cousins and gennets for germans" (1.1.111–13). As the passage suggests, the jennet is often paired with the Barbary horse, or barb. While the racialization of the horses is not my topic here, it is striking to contrast the discourse of race as it applies to animals and people of North African origin in the period. See Irigoyen-García, "La Arcadia hispánica."

15. In Luis de Bañuelos y de la Cerda, *Libro de la jineta y descendencia de los caballos guzmanes*, ed. José Antonio de Balenchana (Madrid: Sociedad de Bibliófilos Españoles, 1877), Balenchana provides a bibliographic survey of the genre.

16. Bañuelos y de la Cerda, *Libro de la jineta*, "Prólogo," 3–7. Interestingly,

the author ascribes the excellence of the Spanish horses he most prizes, the "guz-manes," to a stallion purchased from Moorish ambassadors from Morocco, who of course appear riding "a la gineta." The horse, injured and spurned by the Moors, is bought by a series of Spaniards and finally destined to improve the local breed (12–14).

17. See Balenchana's introduction to Bañuelos y de la Cerda, *Libro de la jineta*, x–xi, and Sanz Egaña, *Tres libros de la Jineta*, xxxi–xxxv.

18. Covarrubias, *Tesoro*, 640. The definition of *jineta*, by contrast, never ad-dresses the riding style, focusing on a secondary definition, by analogy: *gineta*, in his spelling, is for Covarrubias only a shortened lance.

19. Joan Corominas, *Diccionario crítico etimológico castellano e hispánico* (Madrid: Gredos, 1980), gives: "JINETE: significó primeramente 'soldado de a caballo que peleaba con lanza y adarga, y llevaba encogidas las piernas, con estribos cortos', y procede del ár. vg. *zenêti* (ár. zanātî) 'individuo de Zeneta', tribu be-reber, famosa por su caballería ligera, que acudió en defensa del reino de Granada en el S. XIII" (517).

20. Münzer, *Itinerarium*, 64.

21. Cited in Sánchez de Sopranis, *Juegos de toros y cañas*, 26.

22. Juan de Mariana, "De exercitacione corporis," *De rege et regis instituti-one* (1599. Manz: Balthazar Lippus, 1605), Bk. II. Ch. V, 128–33, 130.

23. Anderson, *Hispanic Costume*, 27. See #116 in Jenaro Alenda y Mira, ed., *Relaciones de solemnidades y fiestas públicas de España* (Madrid: Rivadeneyra, 1903).

24. Hieronimi Vicecomitis, cited in Bernis, *Indumentaria española*, 201. See also #15–16 in Alenda y Mira, *Relaciones de solemnidades*.

25. Lalaing, *Voyage de Philippe le Beau*, 185–86.

26. Alenda y Mira, *Relaciones de solemnidades*, #779.

27. Feliciano Chaves, "Mudejarismo," 151.

28. This fascinating letter appears in Marino Sanuto, *I diarii di Marino Sa-nuto (1496–1533)*, ed. Rinaldo Fulin et al. (Venice: F. Visentini, 1879), 52: 352–55. The translation has been published as "Letter from Marco Antonio Marco to Marco Contarini, written at Bologna on 12 December 1529," Appendix 4 to *The Voyage of Sir Nicholas Carewe to the Emperor Charles V in the Year 1529*, ed. R. J. Knecht (Cambridge: Cambridge University Press, 1959).

29. Croce, *Spagna nella vita italiana*, 113–114.

30. Juan Christóval Calvete de Estrella, *El felicíssimo viaje del muy alto y muy poderoso Príncipe don Phelippe*, ed. Paloma Cuenca (Madrid: Sociedad Estatal para la Conmemoración de los Centenarios de Felipe II y Carlos V, 2001), 75.

31. Calvete de Estrella, *Felicíssimo viaje*, 204.

32. Muñoz, "Traslado de una carta que fue embiada del reyno de Ynglaterra a la muy illustre señora condesa de Oliuares, en que se da relacion como aquel reyno se ha reformado en la fe catholica y dado la obediencia al summo pontífice. Y las cerimonias con que esto se hizo, estando presente a todo el Príncipe nuestro señor: y las fiestas que para regocijar esto se hizieron" (1554), *Viaje de Felipe Seg-undo*, 137–39.

33. Juan Rufo, *Carta en tercetos a una dama*, lines 154–55, in Rufo, *Las seis-*

cientas apotegmas y otras obras en verso, ed. Alberto Blecua (Madrid: Espasa-Calpe, 1972), 322.

34. Paula Blanchard-Demouge cites *relaciones* of Moriscos playing *cañas* on p. lxxvi of her introduction to Pérez de Hita, *Guerras civiles de Granada*, which I discuss in the second part of this chapter.

35. Covarrubias, *Tesoro*, 291.

36. Rodrigo Caro, *Días geniales o lúdicos*, ed. Jean-Pierre Etienvre (Madrid: Espasa-Calpe, 1978), 58. Subsequent citations are in the text by page number.

37. On the Hapsburgs' use of the Virgilian tradition, see Marie Tanner, *The Last Descendant of Aeneas: The Hapsburgs and the Mythic Image of the Emperor* (New Haven, Conn.: Yale University Press, 1993).

38. Francisco de Quevedo. "Epístola satírica," 188.

39. Bullfights were also deemed Moorish by foreign observers. The seventeenth-century French traveler Antoine Brunel claimed that they displayed "an inveterate cruelty come from Africa and which has not returned there with the Sarracens." *Voyage d'Espagne curieux, historique et politique* (Paris, 1655), cited in Hillgarth, *Mirror of Spain*, 122.

40. An even more peculiar case is that recorded by Damián Fonseca in his 1612 *Relación de la expulsión de los moriscos*. Fonseca describes a *juego de cañas* played by Spaniards who arrived in North Africa on one of the first transports of exiled Moriscos. The strangest moment comes when the chronicler notes that the local Moors also play *cañas*, in a sort of mirroring mutual display that absolutely conflates the purported otherness behind the expulsions: "los demás caballeros que venían, escaramuçaron con la gente del Rey, con que alegraron la tierra, y fue mucho de ver la destreza con que al mismo tiempo dispararon la arcabuzería, mosquetería y los castillos. También escaramuçaron los Ginetes del Capitán Almançor con tanta ligereza, y buen garbo, que ponían admiración en los más pláticos de nuestros soldados" (112) ["and the other gentlemen all skirmished with the King's men (the soldiers in the *presidio*), with which they gladdened the land, and it was a thing to see with what skill they simultaneously fired the harquebuses, the muskets and the castles. The *Ginetes* of Captain Almançor also skirmished with such speed and elegance that they aroused admiration in the most experienced of our soldiers"].

41. Prudencio de Sandóval, *Historia de la vida y hechos del Emperador Carlos V* (1604–1606), ed. Carlos Seco Serrano (Madrid: BAE, 1955), 1: 452. Bernís Madrazo cites also two attendants dressed in white satin, in the Moorish style, at Charles's later coronation by the pope in Bologna (*Indumentaria española*, 28).

42. The term comes from Étienne Balibar, "The Nation Form: History and Ideology," in Étienne Balibar and Immanuel Wallerstein, *Race, Nation, Class: Ambiguous Identities*, trans. Chris Turner (London: Verso, 1991), 86–106.

43. There are some interesting exceptions to this general rule in the late fifteenth-century chronicle *Hechos del condestable don Miguel Lucas de Iranzo*. At Christmas, in the year 1463, the knights play the *juegos de cañas* as part of a larger dramatic representation, with those who play Moors wearing fake beards. Juan Mata Carriazo, ed., *Hechos del condestable don Miguel Lucas de Iranzo (crónica del siglo XV)* (Madrid: Espasa-Calpe, 1940), 98. At the *juegos* held to celebrate the

birth of the Condestable daughter Luisa, those playing Moors wear fake beards and also appear "tiznados"—wearing some sort of blackface—to accentuate difference (259). But these exaggerated representations seem more akin to the *juegos de moros y cristianos* than to the more common version of *cañas*. On the problem of Morisco racial difference, see Chapter 5. I am grateful to Teófilo Ruiz for these references.

44. Pérez de Hita would also write a controversial second part of the *Guerras civiles*, on the Alpujarras uprising itself, not published until 1604. As I argue in *Mimesis and Empire: The New World, Islam, and European Identities* (Cambridge: Cambridge University Press, 2001), chapter 2, the very yoking of the two parts under the same title makes the Moriscos part of the Spanish polity, and the idealization of Moors that characterizes Part I haunts the war that Pérez de Hita defiantly terms a *civil* conflict.

45. See the list of editions compiled by Blanchard-Demouge in her edition of Pérez de Hita, *Guerras civiles*, xcvii–cxviii. On the relationship between the 1595 text and its "second part," see Fuchs, *Mimesis and Empire*, chapter 2.

46. "Préface au lecteur," *L'histoire des guerres civiles de Grenade*, anonymous French translation (Paris: Toussaincts, 1608), reproduced in *Guerras civiles*, cxvi. On French interest in Spanish maurophilia, see María Soledad Carrasco Urgoiti, "Les fêtes équestres dans *Les Guerres civiles de Grenade de Pérez de Hita*," in *Les fêtes de la Renaissance*, ed. Jean Jacquot et Elie Konigson (Paris: CNRS, 1975), 299–312.

47. Blanchard-Demouge is generally recognized as the first critic to reverse the negative nineteenth-century verdicts on the *Guerras civiles* for its "fancifulness." Through a careful marshaling of chronicles and *relaciones de fiestas*, Blanchard-Demouge locates the text in its historical context. See especially her conclusions on lxxxvi. My reading of material culture in Pérez de Hita is obviously indebted to her invaluable contributions.

48. Carrasco Urgoiti, "Les fêtes équestres," 301.

49. The slight documentary record on Pérez de Hita's life includes several municipal decrees to pay him for *carros* and *invenciones*. See Joaquín Espín Rael, *De la vecindad de Pérez de Hita en Lorca desde 1568 a 1577* (1922), reprinted with documents as *Aportaciones documentales para una biografía de Ginés Pérez de Hita*, ed. Manuel Muñoz Barberán and Juan Guirao García (Lorca: Ayuntamiento de Lorca: 1975).

50. Carrasco Urgoiti, "Les fêtes équestres," 307.

51. In a fascinating moment, one of the Zegríes describes the Abencerrajes as *mestizos* (136), as though their idealized regard for Christians were reflected in a racial hybridity.

52. Juan Martínez Ruiz's exhaustive archival study, "La indumentaria de los moriscos según Pérez de Hita y los documentos de la Alhambra," *Cuadernos de la Alhambra* 3 (1967): 55–124, relies on inventories in the Archivo de la Alhambra of goods confiscated from Moriscos who rebelled or left Spain.

53. See also the accounts of *juegos de cañas* and other royal entertainments in Blanchard-Demouge's introduction, lxx–lxxv.

54. Arié, *España musulmana*, 311–12.

55. See Fuchs, *Mimesis and Empire*, 59–60.

56. See Harvey, *Muslims in Spain*, 297–301 for examples of these often viru-lent debates. The official proclamations for the expulsion rely heavily on the Moris-co threat to the state for their justification. I transcribe here from the order of expulsion for Andalucía, Granada, and Hornachos, issued in Seville in 1612, as reproduced in Harvey (402):

> El REY: Por cuanto la razón de bueno y christiano govierno obliga en con-ciencia expeler de los Reinos y Repúblicas las cosas que causan escándalo [y] daño a los buenos súbditos, y peligro al Estado, y sobre todo ofensa y desser-vicio a Dios nuestro Señor, aviendo la experiencia mostrado que todos estos inconvenientes a causado la residencia de los Christianos nuevos Moriscos en los reinos de Granada y Murcia y Andaluzía, porque demás de ser y proceder de los que concurrieron en el levantamiento del dicho Reyno de Granada, cuyo principio fue matar con atrozes muertes y martirios a todos los Sacer-dotes y Christianos viejos que pudieron de los que entre ellos bivían, llaman-do al Turco que viniesse en su favor y ayuda. Y aviéndolos sacado del dicho Reino, con fin de que, arrepentidos de su delito, biviessen Christiana y fiel-mente, dándoles justas y convenientes órdenes y preceptos de lo que devían hazer, no solo no los han guardado, ni cumplido con las obligaciones de nuestra Santa Fe, pero, mostrado siempre aversión a ella, en grande menos-precio y ofensa de Dios nuestro señor, como se ha visto por la multitud dellos que se han castigado por el Santo Oficio de la Inquisición. Demás de lo qual, han cometido muchos robos y muertes contra los Christianos viejos, y no contentos con esto, han tratado de conspirar contra mi Corona Real y estos Reinos, procurando el socorro y ayuda del Turco.

> [THE KING: Whereas the reason of a good and Christian state obliges it in good conscience to expel from the Kingdoms and Republics those things that cause scandal and harm to the good subjects, and danger to the Sate, and above all offense and disservice to God our Lord, and experience having shown that the residence of the New Christian Moriscos in the kingdoms of Granada and Murcia and Andaluzía causes all these problems, because aside from being and coming from those who participated in the uprising of the said kingdom of Granada, the beginning of which was to kill with atrocious deaths and martyrdoms all the Priests and Old Christians they could of those who lived among them, calling on the Turk to come to their aid and favor. And having removed them from said Kingdom, so that, repenting of their crime, they could live in a Christian and loyal manner, and giving them just and convenient orders and precepts for what they were to do, not only have they not kept them, nor fulfilled the obligations of our Holy Faith but instead always shown aversion to it, scorning and offending God our lord, as is evi-dent from the multitude of them that have been chastised by the Holy Office of the Inquisition. Aside from which, they have committed many thefts and murders against Old Christians, and, not content with this, have tried to

conspire against my Royal Crown and these Kingdoms, procuring the succor and aid of the Turk.]

I cite this document at some length to provide a sense of how forceful an intervention maurophilia was against such discourses, and how adroitly Pérez de Hita turns conspiracy and exile into calumnies of which his proto-Christian Abencerrajes are accused.

57. There is an enormous bibliography on the *plomos*. See my "Virtual Spaniards"; the various essays on the topic in *Al-qantara* 23, 2 (2002); and, most recently, Harris, *From Muslim to Christian Granada*.

58. Although I read Pérez de Hita's emphasis on conversion as a moral defense of the Moriscos, Michel Cavilllac argues that "le thème de la conversion fait partie du processus politique et n'implique pas de profondes raisons spirituelles" ["the theme of conversion is part of the political process and does not imply deep spiritual reasons"], "*Ozmín y Daraja* à l'épreuve de l'*Atalaya*," *Bulletin Hispanique* 92, 1 (1990): 141–84, 158 n.39.

Chapter 5. The Spanish Race

1. For the related uses of Petrarchism in the context of European imperial expansion, see Roland Greene, *Unrequited Conquests: Love and Empire in the Colonial Americas* (Chicago: University of Chicago Press, 1999). On the Abenámar ballads and the conceptualization of the frontier, see Sizen Yiacoup, "Memory and Acculturation in the Late Medieval and Early Modern Frontier Ballad," *Journal of Romance Studies* 4, 3 (Winter 2004): 61–78.

2. María Soledad Carrasco Urgoiti provides a useful account of the circulation of maurophile texts in France and Spain, in "La 'Historia de Ozmín y Daraja' de Mateo Alemán en la trayectoria de la novela morisca," reprinted in her *Estudios sobre la novela breve de tema morisco* (Barcelona: Bellaterra, 2005).

3. It should be noted, of course, that Spain embarks on its own colonial project in North Africa in the period, with its own attendant orientalism, and that this colonization continues for centuries. See Bunes Ibarra, "La emergencia del orientalismo."

4. On the multiple cultural meanings of blackness in England, in particular, see Kim Hall, *Things of Darkness: Economies of Race and Gender in Early Modern England* (Ithaca, N.Y.: Cornell University Press, 1995). As she notes in her introduction, "the culture recognized the possibilities of this language for the representation and categorization of perceived physical differences" (4); "I argue that descriptions of dark and light, rather than being mere indications of Elizabethan beauty standards or markers of moral categories, became in the early modern period the conduit through which the English began to formulate the notions of "self" and "other" so well known in Anglo-American racial discourses" (2). In her *English Ethnicity and Race in Early Modern Drama* (Cambridge: Cambridge University Press, 2003), Mary Floyd-Wilson has argued for the contradictory dis-

courses of "geohumoralism" as a complicating factor in the valuation of different ethnicities in the period. See also Sujata Iyengar, *Shades of Difference: Mythologies of Skin Color in Early Modern England* (Philadelphia: University of Pennsylvania Press, 2005) and Gary Taylor, *Buying Whiteness: Race, Culture, and Identity from Columbus to Hip-Hop* (New York: Palgrave, 2005).

5. Bernard Vincent concludes as much in "¿Qué aspecto físico tenían los moriscos?" *Actas del II Coloquio Historia de Andalucía: Andalucía Moderna* (Córdoba: Monte de Piedad y Caja de Ahorros de Córdoba, 1983), 2: 335–40. For color-based racism in medieval and early modern Spain, see James H. Sweet, "The Iberian Roots of American Racist Thought," in *Constructing Race: Differentiating Peoples in the Early Modern World, William and Mary Quarterly* 54, 1 (January 1997): 143–66. While Sweet's reconstruction of the antecedents of modern racisms is important, I disagree with his assessment that "nearly all [Moors] were distinguishable from white Christians by their physical appearance" (150), and his account of *limpieza de sangre* as "based on skin color" (160) is highly misleading.

6. Nicolás Cabrillana, *Documentos notariales referentes a los moriscos 1569–71*, coll. from Archivo Histórico Provincial de Almería (Granada: Universidad de Granada, 1978). The reference to "membrillo cocho" ("cooked quince") comes from Document 304, the others are repeated throughout the collection. See also the 1573 Cordoban census cited in Vincent, "¿Qué aspecto físico," 336–37.

7. See Pérez de Hita's depiction of the blonde Maleha in the second part of the *Guerras civiles de Granada*, or Cervantes's fable of Spanish soldier-poets courting a blond Moor in North Africa in "El amante liberal."

8. Harvey, *Muslims in Spain*, 10.

9. Pedro de Valencia, *Tratado acerca de los moriscos de España* (1606), facsimile ed. by Joaquín Gil Sanjuan (Málaga: Algazara: 1997), 76–81.

10. From the Arabic *muwallad*, which means born and raised among Arabs, half-breed; half-caste; half-blood. It was used for Christians who converted to Islam and also for the Muslim offspring of a mixed marriage. L. P. Harvey points out that for a later period the term *elche* is more common, although it suggests that the converts are "outsiders to the community that has adopted them." Harvey, *Islamic Spain, 1250 to 1500* (Chicago: University of Chicago Press, 1990). Controversies over the Granadan *elches* erupted in the years after the fall of Granada, as these relatively recent converts to Islam—renegades from the Christian point of view—proved to be the thin edge of the wedge: could they be "rescued" from Islam, if other Muslims could not be compelled to turn Christian? Harvey, *Muslims in Spain*, 30–33; see also Deferrari, "Sentimental Moor," 20–21, where he reviews earlier sources on Christian conversions to Islam.

11. Cited in Florencio Janer, *Condición social de los moriscos de España: causas de su expulsión y consecuencias que esta produjo en el orden económico y político* (Madrid: Real Academia de la Historia, 1857), 233.

12. Hence the common references in English texts of the period to "white Turks" or "white Moors."

13. One of the most famous examples of this kind of satire is Cervantes's biting *entremés*, "El retablo de las maravillas," in which a trio of rogues convince

an audience of small-town notables that they can only prove their *limpieza* by asserting that they can see the imaginary spectacle staged before them.

14. On passing and national identity, see my *Passing for Spain: Cervantes and the Fictions of Identity* (Urbana: University of Illinois Press, 2003).

15. For the English construction of Spain as a racial other, see Eric Griffin, "From Ethos to Ethnos: Hispanizing 'the Spaniard' in the Old World and the New," *Early Modernities, New Centennial Review* 2, 1 (Spring 2002): 69–116, esp, 95–101, and my own "Spanish Lessons: Spenser and the Irish Moriscos," *Studies in English Literature* 42, 1 (Winter 2002): 43–62. Although Griffin chooses the term "ethnos," he is really concerned with "incipient racialist thought" (102) and the "ethno-essentializing spirit."

16. On the Black Legend, see most recently Hillgarth, *Mirror of Spain*, and Margaret Greer, Maureen Quilligan, and Walter Mignolo, eds., *Rereading the Black Legend: The Discourses of Religious and Racial Difference in the Renaissance Empires* (Chicago: University of Chicago Press, 2007). For the origins of the Black Legend in Italy and Germany, see Arnoldsson, *Leyenda negra*.

17. Erasmus, *Opus epistolarum*, ed. P. S. Allen and H. M. Allen, vol. 3 (Oxford: Oxford University Press, 1913), n. 798, cited in Hillgarth, *Mirror of Spain*, 161.

18. On the perception of Iberians as Jews and Jews as Iberians, see Hillgarth, *Mirror of Spain*, 160–94, 236–40, and Edmund Campos, "Jews, Spaniards, and Portingales: Ambiguous Identities of Portuguese Marranos in Elizabethan England," *ELH* 69, 3 (Fall 2002): 599–616.

19. Mateo Alemán, *Guzmán de Alfarache*, ed. José María Micó (Madrid: Cátedra: 1997), 378. Subsequent citations are in the text by page number.

20. Hillgarth, *Mirror of Spain*, 236. See also Farinelli, *Marrano*.

21. *Tre narrazioni del sacco di Prato* (1512), cited in Croce, *Spagna nella vita italiana*, 232.

22. Cited in Hillgarth, *Mirror of Spain*, 313, 316.

23. "Relación de lo ocurrido en el viaje del Rey a Inglaterra, 1554," Biblioteca de El Escorial, ij-U-4, fol. ccccxlviii–ccccxlix.

24. "Carta primera de lo sucedido en el viaje de S. A. a Inglaterra, año de 1554," Muñoz, *Viaje de Felipe Segundo*, 98–99.

25. The connection makes sense when one considers that Covarrubias defines *tarima* (dais), the low platform on which a throne was often placed, by reference to the ladies' *estrado*: "El estrado que acostumbran poner a los reyes y príncipes, de madera, el qual cubren con paños de seda o brocado, y sobre él la silla y sitial. También llaman estrado en el que se asientan las damas, cubierto de tapetes y cogines o almohadas. Algunos quieren que este nombre sea arábigo" (*Tesoro*, 954–55) ["The *estrado* usually placed for kings and princes, made of wood and covered with cloths of silk or brocade, and on it the chair and ceremonial seat. They also call *estrado* the place where the ladies sit, covered in carpets and cushions or pillows. Some say that this name is Arabic"].

26. Griffin, "Ethos to Ethnos," 97.

27. "The Coppie of the Anti-Spaniard" (London: John Wolfe, 1590), 35.

28. Nabil Matar, *Turks, Moors, and Englishmen in the Age of Discovery* (New York: Columbia University Press, 1999), 7–8.

29. Edmund Spenser's 1596 *A View of the Present State of Ireland*, which attempts to discredit any connection between Catholic Ireland and Spain, describes the latter as being "of all nations under heaven . . . the most mingled, most uncertayne and most bastardly," Spenser, *A View of the Present State of Ireland*, ed. W. L. Renwick (Oxford: Clarendon, 1970), 59.

30. Edward Daunce, "A Brief Discourse of the Spanish State, with a Dialogue annexed intituled Philobasilis" (London: Richard Field, 1590), 36 and passim.

31. Daunce, "Brief Discourse," 31.

32. *The Spanish Colonie* (London: William Brome, 1583), q2a, cited in Griffin, "Ethos to Ethnos," 95.

33. Spenser, *View of the Present State*, 44.

34. Spenser, *View of the Present State*, 44.

35. (Antoine Arnauld), *L'Anti-Espagnol* (1590), 22, cited in Hillgarth, *Mirror of Spain*, 237. On the modern racialization of Catherine of Aragon, see Griffin, "Ethos to Ethnos," 72–78.

36. Lynda E. Boose, "The Getting of a Lawful Race: Racial Discourse in Early Modern England and the Unrepresentable Black Woman," in *Women, "Race," and Writing in the Early Modern Period*, ed. Margo Hendricks and Patricia Parker (New York: Routledge, 1994), 35–54, 39.

37. On the play's dating and authorship, see Charles Cathcart, "*Lust's Dominion; or, the Lascivious Queen*: Authorship, Date, and Revision," *Review of English Studies* 52 (2001): 360–75.

38. Taylor, *Buying Whiteness*, 136.

39. Taylor, *Buying Whiteness*, 134.

40. See Fuchs, "Spanish Lessons," 55–58.

41. Fulke Greville, *The Prose Works of Fulke Greville, Lord Brooke*, ed. John Gouws (Oxford: Clarendon, 1986), 60. I am grateful to Benedict Robinson for this reference.

42. For a good survey of the more moderate positions and of the juridical objections to the idea of expulsion, see Francisco Márquez Villanueva, *El problema morisco (desde otras laderas)* (Madrid: Libertarias, 1991), 118–28.

43. Valencia, *Tratado*, 140.

44. Durán, *Romancero general*, 245, p. 129.

45. Nirenberg, "Concepto de raza," 59.

46. On the noble Granadan families who converted to Christianity, see Enrique Soria Mesa, "Una versión genealógica del ansia integradora de la élite morisca: el *Origen de la Casa de Granada*," *Sharq al-Andalus* 12 (1995): 213–21, and "De la conquista a la asimilación: la integración de la aristocracia nazarí en la oligarquía granadina. Siglos XV–XVII," *Areas* 14 (1992): 51–64.

47. Soria Mesa, "De la conquista," 57, 62–64.

48. Javier Castillo Fernández, "Luis Enríquez Xoaida, el primo hermano morisco del Rey Católico (análisis de un caso de falsificación histórica e integración social)," *Sharq al-Andalus* 12 (1995): 235–53, 240. See also James B. Tueller, *Good*

and Faithful Christians: Moriscos and Catholicism in Early Modern Spain (New Orleans: University Press of the South, 2002).

49. See, e.g., the king's instructions to the archbishop of Granada, December 10, 1526, urging that Old Christians marry New Christians, and the queen's 1530 letter promising rewards to New Christians of either sex who married Old Christians, both reproduced in Gallego y Burín and Gámir Sandoval, *Los moriscos del reino de Granada*, 213.

50. Valencia, *Tratado*, 136–37.

51. Castillo Fernández, "Pero han quedado en la sombra masas de moriscos residentes en zonas de población mixta como ciudades y grandes pueblos situados en zonas llanas donde la aculturación era ya importante (una buena parte conocía y utilizaba el castellano). . . . La pregunta es si este olvido de los historiadores ha sido inconsciente o simplemente estas categorías no encontraban acomodo dentro del rígido esquema de conflicto de culturas" (Castillo Fernández, "Luis Enríquez Xoaida," 236) ["But masses of Moriscos residing in mixed-population zones such as cities and large towns, situated in plains where acculturation was already marked (a good number knew and used Spanish), have remained in the shadows. . . . The question is whether this forgetting on the part of historians has been unconscious or whether it is simply that these categories could not be accommodated within the rigid schema of the clash of cultures"]. See also his "La asimilación de los moriscos granadinos." Tueller's recent *Good and Faithful Christians* goes some distance toward redressing this oversight. Conversely, David Coleman (*Creating Christian Granada*, 51–52) argues that, by contrast to colonial Mexico or Peru, in Granada there was no significant intermarriage, given that the repopulation of the city by immigrants included both men and women. Yet he acknowledges important exceptions to the rule among the élite, and does not confront the problem of the invisible assimilated masses posed by Castillo Fernández. In a sense, Coleman seems to be seeking a visible, racially distinct mark of what he problematically calls "miscegenation," and thus fails to recognize how similar were the New and Old Christians intermarrying in Granada.

52. The law clarifies: "advirtiendo que no se ha de entender este vando ni han de ser expelidos, los Christianos viejos casados con Moriscas, ellos, ellas, ni sus hijos," reproduced in Harvey, *Muslims in Spain*, 408.

53. "En las mujeres casadas con christianos viejos y a los hijos dellos, christianos viejos son ellos y sus padres y abuelos y nietos de tales. Y sus mujeres, aunque moriscas, deven gozar de los privilegios de sus maridos y padres. Casáronse ellos de buena fe con permisión de V. M. y según sus leyes y las de la Santa Madre Yglesia. ¿Por qué les han de quitar sus mujeres ni quien puede? Qualquiera dellos que se vaya o absente, aunque fuese morisco con christiana vieja, parece que dividía el matrimonio, y luego verná en duda si valió o no, por averse casado de diferente ley, y luego otros muchos daños" ["In the case of women married to Old Christians and their children, they are Old Christians as are their parents and grandparents and their grandchildren. And their wives, although Moriscas, must enjoy the privileges of their husbands and fathers. They married in good faith with your Majesty's permission and according to your laws and those of the Holy Mother Church. Why should their wives be taken from them and who can do such a thing?

Any of them who leaves or absents him or herself, though it be a Morisco [married to] an Old Christian woman, would seem to divide the marriage, and thence will come many doubts whether it was valid or not, for having married a different faith/law, and many other harms"], cited in Antonio Domínguez Ortiz and Bernard Vincent, *Historia de los moriscos: vida y tragedia de una minoría* (Madrid: Revista de Occidente, 1978), 281.

54. A letter by the Count of Salazar notes the rash of marriages that occurred as a way to forestall expulsion: "Havido gran cantidad de casamientos de Moriscas con Christianos viexos para quedasse y algunos graçiosisimos; aora han dado en descasarse muchos y ellos se meten a frailes y ellas a monjas" ["There have been a great number of marriages of Moriscas to Old Christians so that they may stay and some very comical; now many of them are undoing the marriages and the men become friars and the women nuns"], cited in Henri Lapeyre, *Geografía de la España morisca*, trans. Luis C. Rodríguez García (Valencia: Diputación de Valencia, 1986), 327.

55. Castillo Fernández, "Luis Enríquez Xoaida," 238–39. It is also striking that the governor of Baza after the Christian conquest was Enrique Enríquez de Guzmán—the noble name that the *pícaro*'s grandmother and mother will adopt and he takes on.

56. It is difficult to render the whole sense of *ladino* in my translation. After a century of Spanish presence in the New World, the word, which had long described Moors fluent in Spanish, may also have acquired connotations of *mestizaje* and Spanish acculturation beyond language use. Michel Cavillac argues that Daraja "se comporte apparemment comme une 'convertie' en puissance" ["apparently behaves as a potential 'convert'"], *"Ozmín y Daraja,"* 146.

57. Letter from Pedro de Arriola to Philip III, November 22, 1610: "Muchos Moriscos de los expedidos del Andaluzia y Reyno de Granada se van bolviendo de Berberia en navios de Françeses que los echan en esta costa de donde se van entrando la tierra adentro y he sabido que los mas dellos no buelben a las suyas por temor de ser conosçidos y denunçiados, y como son tan ladinos residen en qualquier parte donde no los conosçen como si fuessen christianos viejos" ["Many Moriscos of those expelled from Andalucía and the Kingdom of Granada gradually return from Barbary in French ships that cast them on this shore, whence they gradually move inland and I've been told that most of them do not return to their own lands for fear of being recognized and denounced, and as they are so *ladinos* they reside in any place where they are not known as though they were Old Christians"], in Lapeyre, *Geografía de la España morisca*, 321.

58. Translating Alemán's text is particularly challenging here, for the relation between Ozmín and Ambrosio is imagined in terms of both a willed and a given similarity; that is, of both what depends and does not depend on their own agency.

59. Thus Pedro Aznar Cardona argues after the fact that the Moriscos needed to be expelled to preserve the "viña catholica de España" ["Catholic vine of Spain"], and that Felipe III "mandó arrancar de rayz, y decepar tan malas plantas infructuosas, de amargos y mortales efectos" ["ordered than such fruitless plants, with such bitter and mortal effects, be extirpated and pulled out by the roots"], *Expulsión justificada de los Moriscos Españoles* (Huesca: Pedro Cabarte,

1612), II.3v, II.4r. There is an additional irony in the image of the "fruitless" plants, given that much of the anti-Morisco discourse focused on their supposedly unnatural fertility.

60. Cavillac, "*Ozmín y Daraja*," 160.

61. Cf. "ganada es Granada" in Parmenio's famous leveling speech in Fernando de Rojas's *La Celestina*.

62. There seem to be historical models for this resolution. María Jesús Rubiera Mata suggests that the Catholic monarchs may have served as godparents to the baptism of an élite Moorish couple, Abu Zayyan Ibn 'Abd al-Haqq and his wife, the daughter of Muley Haçen, who received their names. Rubiera Mata, "La familia morisca de los Muley-Fez, príncipes meriníes e infantes de Granada," *Sharq al-Andalus* 13 (1996): 159–67, 163.

63. Hortensia Morell neatly ties the "impostura" of the conversion to the larger narrative stance of the condemned *pícaro* narrator of the *Guzmán*: "Este final ambiguo, entre cerrado y abierto, coincide entonces con el de la narración de su autobiografía por Guzmán: cierra lo acontecido en un patrón de simulación e impostura pasadas y abre la alternativa del porvenir" ["This ambiguous ending, somewhere between open and closed, thus coincides with Guzmán's narration of his autobiography: it sums up what has happened in a pattern of past dissimulation and imposture and opens up future alternatives"], "La deformación picaresca del mundo ideal en *Ozmín y Daraja* del *Guzmán de Alfarache*," *La Torre* 13, 87–88 (1975): 101–25, 115. See also Judith A. Whitenack, "The *alma diferente* of Mateo Alemán's 'Ozmín y Daraja,'" *Romance Quarterly* 38, 1 (1991): 59–71, in which the critic notes the striking absence of any comment from the narrator on the conversions (64–67), and Carrasco Urgoiti, "La 'Historia,'" 110–11.

64. Bernard Vincent has noted that among the most common names given to Moriscos are precisely Fernando and Isabel, Juan and Juana, suggesting that high officials, and perhaps the royal family itself, presided over collective baptisms. Vincent, *Minorías y marginados en la España del siglo XVI* (Granada: Diputación de Granada, 1987), 40.

65. Even a defender of the expulsions such as Juan de la Puente paradoxically recognizes an intrinsic Spanishness to the Moriscos, claiming that they are "Moros en lo secreto, en lo público Christianos, y Españoles en la sangre" ["secret Moors, public Christians, and Spaniards by blood"], in *Conveniencia de las dos Monarquías Católicas, la de la Iglesia Romana y la del Imperio Español* (Madrid: Imprenta Real, 1612), Book 3, ch. 3, p. 22.

66. Cf. Covarrubias's definition of *mulato*: "el que es hijo de negra y de hombre blanco, o al revés: y por ser mezcla extraordinaria la compararon a la naturaleza del mulo" ["the offspring of a black woman and a white man, or the other way around, and because it is an extraordinary mix they compared it to the nature of the mule"].

67. Cavillac reads Daraja's multiple Christian suitors, and the story's resolution more generally, as a possible rebuke to the *limpieza de sangre* legislation ("*Ozmín y Daraja*," 152ff).

68. Francisco Márquez Villanueva, "El morisco Ricote o la hispana razón de estado," in his *Personajes y temas del "Quijote"* (Madrid: Taurus, 1975); Carroll B.

Johnson, "Ortodoxia y anticapitalismo en el siglo XVII: el caso del morisco Ricote" in *Hispanic Studies in Honor of Joseph H. Silverman*, ed. Joseph Ricapito (Newark, Del.: Juan de la Cuesta, 1988), 285–96.

69. As Angel González Palencia first noted, Ricote seems to be named for the Valley of Ricote, the last place from which Moriscos were expelled, in 1614. See his "Cervantes y los moriscos," *Boletín de la Real Academia Española* 27 (1947–48): 107–22. For the fullest treatment of Ricote's name, see Márquez Villanueva, "El morisco Ricote," 229–335. See also F. J. Flores Arroyuelo, *Los últimos moriscos (Valle de Ricote, 1614)* (Murcia: Academia Alfonso X El Sabio, 1989).

70. I offer a reading of this scene of anagnorisis in my *Passing for Spain*, 38–45.

71. Miguel Cervantes Saavedra, *El ingenioso hidalgo Don Quijote de la Mancha* (1605, 1615), ed. Martín de Riquer (Barcelona: Planeta, 1997), 1047.

72. It is striking to consider in this context the 1614 resolution by the Council of State calling for an end to the expulsions, which seems to recognize the futility of an endless inquisition into the purity of Spanish subjects, all of whom in some measure participate in the identity being ostracized:

Heviendose acabado la expulsion de los Moriscos de Bal de Ricote y otros lugares del Reyno de Murcia que era sola la poblacion conocida que dellos havia quedado en España, se ba platicando en el Conssejo sobre lo mucho que conviene al servicio de Dios y de V.Md. que cesen ya las delaciones y juridiciones que ay en esta materia de expulsion y que teniendola por concluyda se trate solamente de que no buelban los que han salido . . . y a todas las justicias que no admitan ninguna delacion de Moriscos, si no fuere de los que huvieren buelto o bolvieren, como esta dicho, para castigarlos conforme a los bandos, y que los que el dia de oy no hoviessen salido de España, aunque esten sus causas pendientes, no sean molestados ni se hable en ello, porque si esto no se ataja, es cosa que nunca tendra fin, ni los agravios y ynconbenientes que dello resultarian; de que ha parecido al Consejo dar quenta a V.Md. para que se sirva de mandar lo ver y proveer los [*sic*] que mas fuere su real voluntad. (Lapeyre, *Geografía de la España morisca*,329)

[Now that we have completed the expulsion of the Moriscos from the Valley of Ricote and other places in the Kingdom of Murcia, which was the only known population remaining in Spain, the Council is discussing how much it behooves the service of God and of your Majesty that the denunciations and jurisdictions in this matter of the expulsions should cease and that, considering it done, it should be endeavored only that those who have left should not return . . . and all justices should be ordered not to admit any more denunciations of Moriscos, except those who have returned or may return, so as to punish them according to the decrees, and those who have to this day not left Spain, even though their cases may be pending, should be let alone and this should not be mentioned, because if this is not cut short, it will never end, and neither will the grievances and problems that result from it, all of which the Council thought to tell your Majesty so that you may order that it be looked into and decree according to your royal will.]

73. For a different reading of Ricote's intentions, see Richard Hitchcock, "Cervantes, Ricote and the Expulsion of the Moriscos," *Bulletin of Spanish Studies* 81, 2 (2004): 175–85.

Postscript: Moorish Commonplaces

1. See Torrecilla, *España exótica*, esp. 98–110.
2. See Enrique Baltanás, "La gitanofilia como sustituto de la maurofilia: del romancero morisco al *Romancero gitano* de Federico García Lorca," in *Flamenco y nacionalismo: aportaciones para una sociología política del flamenco*, ed. Gerhard Steingress and Enrique Baltanás (Seville: Universidad de Sevilla, 1995), 207–22; Colmeiro, "Exorcising Exoticism"; and Charnon-Deutsch, *Spanish Gypsy*, 47, 92.
3. On Andalucía as a stand-in for Spain itself, see Torrecilla, *España exótica*, 25 and passim, and Charnon-Deutsch, *Spanish Gypsy*, 184.
4. On the contemporary geopolitical stakes and their twentieth-century antecedents, see Hishaam D. Aidi, "The Interference of al-Andalus: Spain, Islam, and the West," *Social Text* 24, 2 (2006): 67–88.
5. See, among other studies, González Alcantud, *Lo moro*, and the collection, González Alcantud, ed., *El orientalismo desde el sur*.
6. Vicente Medina, "Mi tierra morisca," in Medina, *Aires murcianos* (1898), ed. Javier Díez de Revenga (Murcia: Academia Alfonso X el Sabio, 1985), 321–28.
7. González Alcantud, *Lo moro*, 109.
8. El Legado Andalusí is a powerful cultural institution, organized by the Junta de Andalucía, which promotes the region based on its heritage, through exhibits, publications, and tourism. Its website, www.legadoandalusi.es, features such attractions as the "Ruta de los Nazaríes" and the "Ruta de Washington Irving."
9. See J. Jorge Klor de Alva, "The Postcolonization of the (Latin) American Experience," in *After Colonialism: Imperial Histories and Postcolonial Displacements*, ed. Gyan Prakash (Princeton, N.J.: Princeton University Press, 1995).
10. For the resistance to the Moorish heritage in Spanish twentieth-century historiography, on the one hand, and its erasure amid contemporary neo-nationalisms in Spain, see Subirats, ed., *Américo Castro*, especially Juan Goytisolo, "Américo Castro en la España actual" (23–37) and Subirats, "La península multicultural" (39–49).
11. Daniela Flesler, *The Return of the Moor: Spanish Responses to Contemporary Moroccan Immigration* (West Lafayette, Ind.: Purdue University Press, 2008). Beyond the points I summarize here, Flesler provides a compelling analysis of contemporary Spanish film and novels dealing with immigration and/or the Moorish past.
12. Flesler, *Return of the Moor*, 5 and passim.

13. Flesler, *Return of the Moor*, 65–76.

14. For more information on the museum, Casa Museo Arabe Yusuf al Burch, see the detailed description at http://www.caceresjoven.com/paginas/turismo/museos/museo8.asp

15. See Walter Cohen, "The Uniqueness of Spain," in *Echoes and Inscriptions: Comparative Approaches to Early Modern Spanish Literatures*, ed. Barbara A. Simerka and Christopher B. Weimer (Lewisburg, Pa.: Bucknell University Press, 2000), 17–29.

Bibliography

El Abencerraje (Novela y romancero). Ed. Francisco López Estrada. Madrid: Cátedra, 1996.

Aguilar, Pedro de. *Tractado de la cavalleria de la gineta*. 1572. Facsimile edition with an introduction by Angel Caffarena Such. Málaga: El Guadalhorce, 1960.

Aidi, Hishaam D. "The Interference of al-Andalus: Spain, Islam, and the West." *Social Text* 24, 2 (2006): 67–88.

Albert-Llorca, Marlene, and José Antonio González Alcantud, eds. *Moros y cristianos: representaciones del otro en las fiestas del Mediterraneo occidental*. Toulouse: Presses Universitaires du Mirail; Granada: Centro de Investigaciones Etnológicas Ángel Ganivet, 2003.

Aldrete, Bernardo. *Del origen y principio de la lengua castellana o romance que oi se usa en España*. Facsimile edition ed. Lidio Nieto Jiménez. Madrid: Visor, 1993.

Alemán, Mateo. *Guzmán de Alfarache*. 2 vols. Ed. José María Micó. Madrid: Cátedra: 1997.

———. *Ortografía castellana*. 1609. Ed. José Rojas Garciadueñas. México, D.F.: Colegio de México, 1950.

Alenda y Mira, Jenaro, ed. *Relaciones de solemnidades y fiestas públicas de España*. Madrid: Rivadeneyra, 1903.

Amador de los Ríos, José. *El estilo mudéjar en la arquitectura*. Madrid: Imprenta de Manual Tello, 1872.

Anderson, Ruth Matilda. *Hispanic Costume, 1480–1530*. New York: Hispanic Society of America, 1979.

Añón, Carmen, and José Luis Sancho, eds. *Jardín y naturaleza en el reinado de Felipe II*. Madrid: Sociedad Estatal para la Conmemoración de los Centenarios de Felipe II y Carlos V, 1998.

Arié, Rachel. "Acerca del traje musulmán en España desde la caída de Granada hasta la expulsión de los moriscos." *Études sur la civilisation de l'Espagne*. Leiden: Brill, 1990. 121–41.

———. *España musulmana (siglos VIII–XV)*. *Historia de España*, vol. 3. Ed. Manuel Tuñon de Lara. Barcelona: Labor, 1982.

Ariosto, Ludovico. *Orlando Furioso*. 1516, 1532. Vicenza: Mondadori, 1976.

Arnoldsson, Sverker. *La leyenda negra: estudios sobre sus orígenes*. Göteborg: Göteborgs Universitets Arsskrift, 1960.

Aznar Cardona, Pedro. *Expulsión justificada de los Moriscos Españoles*. Huesca: Pedro Cabarte, 1612.

Balibar, Étienne, and Immanuel Wallerstein. *Race, Nation, Class: Ambiguous Identities.* Trans. Chris Turner. London: Verso, 1991.

Baltanás, Enrique. "La gitanofilia como sustituto de la maurofilia: del romancero morisco al *Romancero gitano* de Federico García Lorca." In *Flamenco y nacionalismo: aportaciones para una sociología política del flamenco*, ed. Gerhard Steingress and Enrique Baltanás. Seville: Universidad de Sevilla, 1995. 207–22.

Bañuelos y de la Cerda, Luis de. *Libro de la jineta y descendencia de los caballos guzmanes.* Ed. José Antonio de Balenchana. Madrid: Sociedad de Bibliófilos Españoles, 1877.

Barrau-Dihigo, Louis, ed. "Voyage de Barthélemy Joly en Espagne (1603–1604)." *Revue Hispanique* 20 (June 1909): 459–618.

Bartolomé Arraiza, Alberto. "La vivienda en la segunda mitad del siglo XVI." *Felipe II: un monarca y su época: las tierras y los hombres del rey.* Madrid: Sociedad para la Conmemoración de los Centenarios de Felipe II y Carlos V, 1998. 103–9.

Bass, Laura. "Homosocial Bonds and Desire in the *Abencerraje.*" *Revista Canadiense de Estudios Hispánicos* 24, 3 (Spring 2000): 453–71.

Beaumatin, Eric. "Langue de soi et phonèmes de l'Autre: Nebrija, Valdés, Quevedo." In *Les représentations de l'Autre dans l'espace ibérique et ibéroaméricain*, ed. Augustin Redondo. Paris: Presses de la Sorbonne Nouvelle, 1991. 235–48.

Bernáldez, Andrés de. *Memorias del reinado de los reyes católicos.* Ed. M. Gómez Moreno and J. de Mata Carriazo. Madrid: Real Academia de la Historia, 1962.

Bernís Madrazo, Carmen. *Indumentaria española en tiempos de Carlos V.* Madrid: CSIC, 1962.

———. *Indumentaria medieval española.* Madrid: CSIC, 1956.

———. "Modas moriscas en la sociedad cristiana española del siglo XV y principios del XVI." *Boletín de la Real Academia de la Historia* 144 (1959): 199–228.

Beverley, John. "Class or Caste: A Critique of the Castro Thesis." In *Américo Castro: The Impact of his Thought*, ed. Ronald E. Surtz, Jaime Ferrán, and Daniel P. Testa. Madison: Hispanic Seminary of Medieval Studies, 1988. 141–49.

Bhabha, Homi. *The Location of Culture.* London: Routledge, 1994.

———. "Signs Taken for Wonders: Questions of Ambivalence and Authority Under a Tree Outside Delhi, May 1817." In *"Race," Writing and Difference*, ed. Henry Louis Gates. *Critical Inquiry* 12, 1 (1985): 144–65. Reprinted in Bhabha, *The Location of Culture.* London: Routledge, 1994.

Bollard, Kathleen. "Re-Reading Heroism in *El Abencerraje.*" *Bulletin of Spanish Studies* 80, 3 (2003): 297–307.

Boose, Lynda E. "'The Getting of a Lawful Race': Racial Discourse in Early Modern England and the Unrepresentable Black Woman." In *Women, "Race" and Writing in the Early Modern Period*, ed. Margo Hendricks and Patricia Parker. New York: Routledge, 1994. 35–54.

Borrás Gualis, Gonzalo. "El arte mudéjar: estado actual de la cuestión." *Mudéjar iberoamericano: una expresión cultural de dos mundos.* Granada: Universidad de Granada, 1993. 9–19.

Boscán, Juan. *Los cuatro libros del Cortesano, compuestos en italiano por el conde Baltasar Castellon, y agora nuevamente traduzidos en lengua castellana.* Ed. Antonio María Fabié. Madrid: Rivadeneyra, 1873.

Bourdieu, Pierre. *The Logic of Practice.* Trans. Richard Nice. Stanford, Calif.: Stanford University Press, 1990.

———. *Distinction: A Social Critique of the Judgement of Taste.* Trans. Richard Nice. Cambridge, Mass.: Harvard University Press, 1984.

Brisset Martín, Demetrio E. "Fiestas hispanas de moros y cristianos: historia y significados." *Gazeta de Antropología* 17 (2001).

Brothers, Cammy. "The Renaissance Reception of the Alhambra: The Letters of Andrea Navagero and the Palace of Charles V," ed. Gülru Nocipoglu. *Muqarnas* 11 (1994): 79–102.

Bunes Ibarra, Miguel Ángel de. "La emergencia del orientalismo en la edad moderna." In *El orientalismo desde el sur*, ed. José A. González Alcantud. Barcelona: Anthropos, 2006. 37–53.

Burshatin, Israel. "Power, Discourse, and Metaphor in the *Abencerraje.*" *MLN* 99, 2 (March 1984): 195–213.

Cabanelas Rodríguez, Darío. "The Alhambra: An Introduction." In *Al-Andalus: The Art of Islamic Spain*, ed. Jerrilynn D. Dodds. New York: Metropolitan Museum of Art, 1992. 127–33.

Cabrillana, Nicolás. *Documentos notariales referentes a los moriscos 1569–71.* Coll. from Archivo Histórico Provincial de Almería. Granada: Universidad de Granada, 1978.

Caffarena Such, Angel. Introduction to Pedro de Aguilar, *Tractado de la cavalleria de la gineta* Facsimile edition. Málaga: El Guadalhorce, 1960.

Calvete de Estrella, Juan Christóval. *El felicíssimo viaje del muy alto y muy poderoso Príncipe don Phelippe.* Ed. Paloma Cuenca. Madrid: Sociedad Estatal para la Conmemoración de los Centenarios de Felipe II y Carlos V, 2001.

Campos, Edmund. "Jews, Spaniards, and Portingales: Ambiguous Identities of Portuguese Marranos in Elizabethan England." *ELH* 69, 3 (Fall 2002): 599–616.

Caro, Rodrigo. *Días geniales o lúdicos.* Ed. Jean-Pierre Etienvre. Madrid: Espasa-Calpe, 1978.

Caro Baroja, Julio. *Los moriscos del Reino de Granada: ensayo de historia social.* 2nd ed. Madrid: Istmo, 1976.

Carrasco Urgoiti, María Soledad. "Las cortes señoriales del Aragón mudéjar y *El Abencerraje.*" In *Homenaje a Casalduero: crítica y poesía*, ed. Rizel Pincus Sigele and Gonzalo Sobejano. Madrid: Gredos, 1972. 115–28.

———. *Estudios sobre la novela breve de tema morisco.* Barcelona: Bellaterra, 2005.

———. "Les fêtes équestres dans *Les Guerres civiles de Grenade de Pérez de Hita.*" In *Les fêtes de la Renaissance*, ed. Jean Jacquot and Elie Konigson. Paris: CNRS, 1975. 299–312.

———. *The Moorish Novel: "El Abencerraje" and Pérez de Hita.* Boston: Twayne, 1976.

———. *El moro de Granada en la literatura: del siglo XV al XIX.* 1956. Granada: Universidad, 1989.

———. "El romancero morisco de Pedro de Padilla en su *Thesoro de varia poesía* (1580)." In *Actas del XIV Congreso de la Asociación Internacional de Hispanistas*, ed. Isaías Lerner, Robert Nival and Alejandro Alonso. Newark, Del: Juan de la Cuesta, 2004. 2: 89–99.

———. "Vituperio y parodia del romance morisco en el romancero nuevo." In *Culturas populares: diferencias, divergencias, conflictos: actas del coloquio celebrado en la Casa de Velázquez, los días 30 de noviembre y 1–2 de diciembre de 1983*, ed. Yves-René Fonquerne and Alfonso Esteban. Madrid: Universidad Complutense, 1986. 115–37.

Casa Museo Arabe Yusuf al Burch. http://www.caceresjoven.com/paginas/turismo/museos/museo8.asp

Castiglione, Baldassarre. *Il libro del Cortegiano.* Ed. Walter Barberis. Torino: Einaudi, 1998.

Castillo Fernández, Javier. "La asimilación de los moriscos granadinos: un modelo de análisis." In *Disidencias y exilios en la España moderna*, ed. Antonio Mestre Sanchís and Enrique Giménez López. Alicante: Universidad de Alicante, 1997. 347–62.

———. "Luis Enríquez Xoaida, el primo hermano morisco del Rey Católico (análisis de un caso de falsificación histórica e integración social)." *Sharq al-Andalus* 12 (1995): 235–53.

Cathcart, Charles. *"Lust's Dominion; or, the Lascivious Queen*: Authorship, Date, and Revision." *Review of English Studies* 52 (2001): 360–75.

Cavillac, Michel. *"Ozmín y Daraja* à l'épreuve de l'*Atalaya.*" *Bulletin Hispanique* 92, 1 (1990): 141–84.

Cervantes Saavedra, Miguel. *El ingenioso hidalgo Don Quijote de la Mancha.* 1605, 1615. Ed. Martín de Riquer. Barcelona: Planeta, 1997.

———. *Don Quixote.* Trans. Edith Grossman. New York: Ecco, 2005.

Charnon-Deutsch, Lou. *The Spanish Gypsy: The History of a European Obsession.* University Park: Pennsylvania State University Press, 2004.

Chartier, Roger. *Inscription and Erasure: Literature and Written Culture from the Eleventh to the Eighteenth Century.* Trans. Arthur Goldhammer. Philadelphia: University of Pennsylvania Press, 2007.

Chueca Goitia, Fernando. "El arte español en la época de Carlos V." In *Carolus V Imperator.* Ed. Pedro Navascués Palacio. Barcelona: Lunwerg, 1999. 253–415.

———. *Invariantes castizos de la arquitectura española.* Buenos Aires: Dossat, 1947.

Cirot, Georges. "La maurophilie littéraire en Espagne au XVIe siècle." *Bulletin Hispanique* 40, 2 (April–June 1938)–46 (1944).

Cock, Henri. "Anales del año ochenta y cinco." In *Viajes de extranjeros por España y Portugal*, ed. J. García Mercadal. 6 vols. 2nd ed. Salamanca: Junta de Castilla y León, 1999. 2: 453–602.

Códigos españoles concordados y anotados. 12 vols. Madrid: Antonio de San Martín, 1873.

Cohen, Walter. "The Uniqueness of Spain." In *Echoes and Inscriptions: Compara-*

tive Approaches to Early Modern Spanish Literatures, ed. Barbara A. Simerka and Christopher B. Weimer. Lewisburg, Pa.: Bucknell University Press, 2000. 17–29.

Coleman, David. *Creating Christian Granada: Society and Religious Culture in an Old-World Frontier City, 1492–1600*. Ithaca, N.Y.: Cornell University Press, 2003.

Colmeiro, José. "Exorcising Exoticism: *Carmen* and the Construction of Oriental Spain." *Comparative Literature* 54, 2 (2002): 127–43.

"The Coppie of the Anti-Spaniard." London: John Wolfe, 1590.

Coromimas, Joan. *Diccionario crítico etimológico castellano e hispánico*. Madrid: Gredos, 1980.

Covarrubias, Sebastián de. *Tesoro de la lengua castellana o española*. 1611. Ed. Martín de Riquer. Barcelona: Altafulla, 1998.

Croce, Benedetto. *Spagna nelle vita italiana durante la Rinascenza*. Bari: G. Laterza & Figli, 1917.

Crónica del Rey Alfonso XI. In *Crónicas de los Reyes de Castilla*, vol. 1. Ed. Cayetano Rosell. Madrid: Atlas, 1953.

Daunce, Edward. "A Brief Discourse of the Spanish State, with a Dialogue annexed intituled Philobasilis." London: Richard Field, 1590.

Deferrari, Austin. "The Sentimental Moor in Spanish Literature Before 1600." Ph.D. dissertation, University of Pennsylvania, 1927.

Deloria, Philip J. *Playing Indian*. New Haven, Conn.: Yale University Press, 1998.

Diccionario de autoridades. 1726–37. Madrid: Gredos, 1990.

Dodds, Jerrilynn, ed. *Al-Andalus: The Art of Islamic Spain*. Exhibition catalog. New York: Metropolitan Museum of Art, 1992.

———. "The Mudejar Tradition in Architecture." In *The Legacy of Muslim Spain*, ed. Salma Khadra Jayyusi. 2 vols. Leiden: Brill, 1994.

Dolar, Mladen. "Introduction: The Subject Supposed to Enjoy." In Alain Grosrichard, *The Sultan's Court: European Fantasies of the East*, trans. Liz Heron. London: Verso, 1998. ix–xxvii.

Domínguez Ortiz, Antonio, and Bernard Vincent. *Historia de los moriscos: vida y tragedia de una minoría*. Madrid: Revista de Occidente, 1978.

Durán, Agustín, ed. *Romancero general*. Madrid: Rivadeneyra, 1851.

Echevarría Arsuaga, Ana. "La guardia morisca: un cuerpo desconocido del ejército medieval español." *Revista de Historia Militar* 45, 90 (2001): 55–78.

Entwistle, Joanne. *The Fashioned Body: Fashion, Dress, and Modern Social Theory*. Cambridge: Polity Press, 2000.

Espín Rael, Joaquín. *Aportaciones documentales para una biografía de Ginés Pérez de Hita*. Ed. Manuel Muñoz Barberán and Juan Guirao García. Lorca: Ayuntamiento de Lorca, 1975.

Farinelli, Arturo. *Marrano (storia di un vituperio)*. Geneva: Olschki, 1925.

Feliciano Chaves, María Judith. "Mudejarismo in Its Colonial Context: Iberian Cultural Display, Viceregal Luxury Consumption, and the Negotiation of Identities in Sixteenth-Century New Spain." Ph.D. dissertation, University of Pennsylvania, 2004.

———. "Muslim Shrouds for Christian Kings: A Reassessment of Andalusi Tex-

184 Bibliography

tiles in Thirteenth-Century Castilian Life and Ritual." In *Under the Influence: Questioning the Comparative in Medieval Castile*, ed. Cynthia Robinson and Leyla Rouhi. Boston: Brill, 2005. 101–31.

Feliciano Chaves, María Judith, and Leyla Rouhi. "Introduction." In *Interrogating Iberian Frontiers*, ed. Barbara F. Weissberger with María Judith Feliciano Chaves, Leyla Rouhi, and Cynthia Robinson. *Medieval Encounters* 12, 3 (2006): 317–28.

Flesler, Daniela. *The Return of the Moor: Spanish Responses to Contemporary Moroccan Immigration*. West Lafayette, Ind.: Purdue University Press, 2008.

Flores Arroyuelo, F. J. *Los últimos moriscos (Valle de Ricote, 1614)*. Murcia: Academia Alfonso X El Sabio, 1989.

Floyd-Wilson, Mary. *English Ethnicity and Race in Early Modern Drama*. Cambridge: Cambridge University Press, 2003.

Fonseca, Fray Damián. *Relación de la expulsión de los moriscos del reino de Valencia*. Roma: Iacomo Mascardo, 1612. Valencia: Sociedad Valenciana de Bibliófilos, 1878.

Fuchs, Barbara. *Mimesis and Empire: The New World, Islam, and European Identities*. Cambridge: Cambridge University Press, 2001.

———. "A Mirror Across the Water: Mimetic Racism, Hybridity, and Cultural Survival." In *Writing Race Across the Atlantic World, 1492–1763*, ed. Gary Taylor and Philip Beidler. New York: Palgrave, 2005. 9–26.

———. *Passing for Spain: Cervantes and the Fictions of Identity*. Urbana: University of Illinois Press, 2003.

———. "Spanish Lessons: Spenser and the Irish Moriscos." *Studies in English Literature* 42, 1 (Winter 2002): 43–62.

———. "Virtual Spaniards." *Journal of Spanish Cultural Studies* 2, 1 (March 2001): 13–26.

Gallego y Burín, Antonio, and Alfonso Gámir Sandoval. *Los moriscos del reino de Granada según el Sínodo de Guadix de 1554*. Ed. Darío Cabanelas Rodríguez. Granada: Universidad de Granada, 1968.

García Valdecasas, Amelia. *El género morisco en las fuentes del "Romancero General"*. Valencia: Diputación Provincial de Valencia, 1987.

Garrad, Kenneth. "La industria sedera granadina en el siglo XVI y su conexión con el levantamiento de las Alpujarras." *Miscelánea de estudios árabes y hebraicos* 5 (1956): 73–104.

González Alcantud, José A. "El canon andaluz y las fronteras imaginarias." In *El orientalismo desde el sur*, ed. José A. González Alcantud. Barcelona: Anthropos, 2006. 368–80.

———. *Lo moro: las lógicas de la derrota y la formación del estereotipo islámico*. Barcelona: Anthropos, 2002.

———. "El orientalismo: génesis topográfica y discurso crítico." In *El orientalismo desde el sur*, ed. José A. González Alcantud. Barcelona: Anthropos, 2006. 7–34.

González Martel, Juan Manuel. *Casa Museo Lope de Vega: guía y catálogo*. Madrid: Real Academia Española, 1993.

González Palencia, Ángel. "Cervantes y los moriscos." *Boletín de la Real Academia Española* 27 (1947–48): 107–22.

Goytisolo, Juan. "Américo Castro en la España actual." In *Américo Castro y la revisión de la memoria: el Islam en España*, ed. Eduardo Subirats. Madrid: Libertarias, 2003. 23–37.

Greene, Roland. *Unrequited Conquests: Love and Empire in the Colonial Americas.* Chicago: University of Chicago Press, 1999.

Greer, Margaret, Maureen Quilligan, and Walter Mignolo, eds. *Rereading the Black Legend: The Discourses of Religious and Racial Difference in the Renaissance Empires.* Chicago: University of Chicago Press, 2007.

Greville, Fulke. *The Prose Works of Fulke Greville, Lord Brooke.* Ed. John Gouws. Oxford: Clarendon, 1986.

Griffin, Eric. "From Ethos to Ethnos: Hispanizing 'the Spaniard' in the Old World and the New." *Early Modernities, New Centennial Review* 2, 1 (Spring 2002): 69–116.

Guillén, Claudio. "Individuo y ejemplaridad en el 'Abencerraje.'" In *Collected Studies in Honour of Américo Castro's Eightieth Year*, ed. M. P. Hornik. Oxford: Lincombe Lodge Research Library, 1965. 175–97.

———. *Literature as System: Essays Toward the Theory of Literary History.* Princeton, N.J.: Princeton University Press, 1971.

Halbwachs, Maurice. *On Collective Memory.* Ed. and trans. Lewis A. Coser. Chicago: University of Chicago Press, 1992.

Hall, Kim. *Things of Darkness: Economies of Race and Gender in Early Modern England.* Ithaca, N.Y.: Cornell University Press, 1995.

Harris, A. Katie. *From Muslim to Christian Granada: Inventing a City's Past in Early Modern Spain.* Baltimore: Johns Hopkins University Press, 2007.

Harvey, L. P. *Islamic Spain, 1250 to 1500.* Chicago: University of Chicago Press, 1990.

———. *Muslims in Spain, 1500 to 1614.* Chicago: University of Chicago Press, 2005.

Herrera Casado, Antonio. *El palacio del Infantado en Guadalajara.* Guadalajara, Spain: Aache, 2001.

Hillgarth, J. N. *The Mirror of Spain, 1500–1700: The Formation of a Myth.* Ann Arbor: University of Michigan Press, 2000.

Hitchcock, Richard. "Cervantes, Ricote and the Expulsion of the Moriscos." *Bulletin of Spanish Studies* 81, 2 (2004): 175–85.

Holzinger, Walter. "The Militia of Love, War, and Virtue in the *Abencerraje y la hermosa Jarifa*: A Structural and Sociological Reassessment." *Revista Canadiense de Estudios Hispánicos* 2, 3 (1978): 227–38.

Irigoyen-García, Javier. "La Arcadia hispánica: los libros de pastores españoles y la exclusión de lo morisco." Ph.D. dissertation, University of Pennsylvania, 2008.

Iyengar, Sujata. *Shades of Difference: Mythologies of Skin Color in Early Modern England.* Philadelphia: University of Pennsylvania Press, 2005.

Janer, Florencio. *Condición social de los moriscos de España: causas de su expulsión y consecuencias que esta produjo en el orden económico y político.* Madrid: Real Academia de la Historia, 1857.

Johnson, Carroll B. "Ortodoxia y anticapitalismo en el siglo XVII: el caso del morisco Ricote." In *Hispanic Studies in Honor of Joseph H. Silverman*, ed. Joseph Ricapito. Newark, Del.: Juan de la Cuesta, 1988. 285–96.

Jones, Ann Rosalind, and Peter Stallybrass. *Renaissance Clothing and the Materials of Memory.* Cambridge: Cambridge University Press, 2000.

Kagan, Richard L. "Clio and the Crown: Writing History in Habsburg Spain." In *Spain, Europe and the Atlantic World: Essays in Honour of John H. Elliott*, ed. Richard L. Kagan and Geoffrey Parker. Cambridge: Cambridge University Press, 1995. 73–99.

Klor de Alva, Jorge J. "The Postcolonization of the (Latin) American Experience." In *After Colonialism: Imperial Histories and Postcolonial Displacements*, ed. Gyan Prakash. Princeton, N.J.: Princeton University Press, 1995.

Knecht, R. J., ed. *The Voyage of Sir Nicholas Carewe to the Emperor Charles V in the Year 1529.* Cambridge: Cambridge University Press, 1959.

Krauel, Ricardo. "El esquema heroico de la historia de Abindarráez." *Romance Notes* 37, 1 (1996): 39–47.

Lalaing, Antoine. *Voyage de Philippe le Beau en Espagne.* In *Collection des voyages des souverains des Pays-Bas.* 4 vols. Ed. M. Gachard. Bruxelles: F. Hayez, 1874–1882. 1: 121–318.

Lapeyre, Henri. *Geografía de la España morisca.* Trans. Luis C. Rodríguez García. Valencia: Diputación de Valencia, 1986.

Lasso de la Vega, Gabriel. *Manojuelo de romances.* 1601. Madrid: Saeta, 1942.

Layna Serrano, Francisco. *El palacio del Infantado en Guadalajara.* 2nd ed. Guadalajara, Spain: Aache Ediciones, 1997.

Lea, Henry Charles. *The Moriscos of Spain: Their Conversion and Expulsion.* Philadelphia: Lea Brothers, 1901. Reprint New York: Burt Franklin, 1968.

León Pinelo, Antonio. *Velos antiguos y modernos en los rostros de las mujeres: sus conveniencias y daños.* Madrid, 1641. Santiago de Chile: Centro de Investigaciones de Historia Americana, 1966.

Letts, Malcolm, ed. and trans. *The Travels of Leo of Rozmital through Germany, Flanders, England, France, Spain, Portugal, and Italy, 1465–1467.* Cambridge: Hakluyt Society, 1957.

Leyes de la "Nueva" Recopilación que han sido comprendidas en la Novísima in *Códigos españoles concordados y anotados.* Madrid: Antonio de San Martín, 1873.

Liss, Peggy K. *Isabel the Queen: Life and Times.* Rev ed. Philadelphia: University of Pennsylvania Press, 2004.

Lleó Cañal, Vicente. *La Casa de Pilatos.* Madrid: Electa, 1998.

López Estrada, Francisco. "*El Abencerraje* de Toledo, 1561: edición crítica y comentarios." *Anales de la Universidad Hispalense* 19 (1959): 1–60.

———, ed. *El Abencerraje y la hermosa Jarifa: cuatro textos y su estudio.* Madrid: Publicaciones de la Revista de Archivos, Bibliotecas y Museos, 1957.

López Guzmán, Rafael. *Arquitectura mudéjar.* 2nd ed. Madrid: Cátedra, 2000–2005.

Lust's Dominion; or, the Lascivious Queen. 1657. Ed. J. Le Gay Brereton. Louvain: Uystpruyst, 1931.

Maíllo Salgado, Felipe. *Los arabismos del castellano en la baja edad media*. Salamanca: Universidad de Salamanca, 1991.

Mariana, Juan de. *Historiae de Rebus Hispaniae*. Toleti: Typis Petri Roderici, 1592. Spanish translation *Historia general de España*, trans. Pedro Rodríguez, 1601.

———. *Obras del Padre Juan de Mariana*. Ed. Francisco Pí y Margall. 2 vols. Madrid: Atlas, 1950.

———. *De rege et regis institutione*. 1599. Manz: Balthazar Lippus, 1605.

Marin Fidalgo, Ana. "Sevilla: los Reales Alcázares." In *Jardín naturaleza en el reinado de Felipe II*, ed. Carmen Añón and José Luis Sancho. Madrid: Sociedad Estatal para la Conmemoración de los Centenarios Felipe II y Carlos V, 1998.

Marinetto Sánchez, Purificación. "Panel from the Mexuar, the Alhambra, Granada." In *Al-Andalus: The Art of Islamic Spain*. Ed. Jerrilynn Dodds New York: Metropolitan Museum of Art, 1992.

Márquez Villanueva, Francisco. *Personajes y temas del "Quijote"*. Madrid: Taurus, 1975.

———. *El problema morisco (desde otras laderas)*. Madrid: Libertarias, 1991.

Martínez Nespral, Fernando. *Un juego de espejos: rasgos mudéjares de la arquitectura y el habitar en la España de los siglos XVI–XVII*. Buenos Aires: Nobuko, 2006.

Martínez Ruiz, Juan. "La indumentaria de los moriscos según Pérez de Hita y los documentos de la Alhambra." *Cuadernos de la Alhambra* 3 (1967): 55–124.

Mata Carriazo, Juan. ed. *Hechos del condestable don Miguel Lucas de Iranzo (crónica del siglo XV)*. Madrid: Espasa-Calpe, 1940.

Matar, Nabil. *Turks, Moors, and Englishmen in the Age of Discovery*. New York: Columbia University Press, 1999.

Medina, Vicente. *Aires murcianos*. 1898. Ed. Javier Díez de Revenga. Murcia: Academia Alfonso X el Sabio, 1985.

Mena, Juan de. *Laberinto de Fortuna*. Ed. Louise Vasvari Fainberg. Madrid: Alhambra, 1976.

Menéndez Pelayo, Marcelino. *Orígenes de la novela*. Vol. 1. Madrid: Bailly, 1905.

Menéndez Pidal, Ramón. *España y su historia*. 2 vols. Madrid: Minotauro, 1957.

———. *Romancero hispánico*. 2 vols. Madrid: Espasa-Calpe, 1953.

Mignolo, Walter. *The Darker Side of the Renaissance: Literacy, Territoriality, and Colonization*. Ann Arbor: University of Michigan Press, 1995.

Milhou, Alain. "Desemitización y europeización en la cultura española desde la época de los Reyes Católicos hasta la expulsión de los moriscos." *Cultura del Renaixement: Homenatge al pare Miquel Batllori. Manuscrits* 11 (1993): 35–60.

———. "La mutación de un país de frontera." In *Españas: 1492–1992*, ed. Jean-Pierre Dedieu. Paris: CNRS, 1991. 195–207.

Montrose, Louis. "The Elizabethan Subject and the Spenserian Text." In *Literary Theory/Renaissance Texts*, ed. Patricia Parker and David Quint. Baltimore: Johns Hopkins University Press, 1986. 303–40.

Morell, Hortensia. "La deformación picaresca del mundo ideal en *Ozmín y Daraja* del *Guzmán de Alfarache*." *La Torre* 13, 87–88 (1975): 101–25.

Muñoz, Andrés. *Viaje de Felipe Segundo a Inglaterra por Andrés Muñoz y relaciones varias relativas al mismo suceso.* Ed. Pascual de Gayangos. Madrid: Sociedad de Bibliófilos Españoles, 1877.

Münzer, Hieronymus. *Itinerarium Hispanicum Hieronymi Monetarii.* 1494–95. Ed. Ludwig Pfandl. *Revue Hispanique* 48 (1920): 1–179.

Nader, Helen. "Introduction." In *Power and Gender in Renaissance Spain: Eight Women of the Mendoza Family, 1450–1650,* ed. Helen Nader. Urbana: University of Illinois Press, 2004. 1–26.

———. *The Mendoza Family in the Spanish Renaissance, 1350–1550.* New Brunswick, N.J.: Rutgers University Press, 1979.

Navagero, Andrea. *Viaggio fatto in Spagna et in Francia.* Venice, 1563.

Nebrija, Antonio de. *Gramática castellana.* Ed. Miguel Ángel Esparza and Ramón Sarmiento. Madrid: Fundación Antonio de Nebrija, 1992.

Nirenberg, David. "El concepto de raza en el estudio del antijudaismo ibérico medieval." *Edad Media* 3 (2000): 39–60.

———. "Race and the Middle Ages: The Case of Spain and Its Jews." In *Rereading the Black Legend: The Discourses of Religious and Racial Difference in the Renaissance Empires,* ed. Margaret Greer, Walter Mignolo, and Maureen Quilligan. Chicago: University of Chicago Press, 2007. 71–87.

Nora, Pierre. *Les lieux de mémoire.* Paris: Gallimard, 1992.

Norton, Marcy. "Tasting Empire: Chocolate and the European Internalization of Mesoamerican Aesthetics." *American Historical Review* 111, 3 (2006): 660–91.

Palencia, Alfonso de. *Gesta Hispaniensia.* 2 vols. Ed. and Spanish trans. Brian Tate and Jeremy Lawrance. Madrid: Real Academia de la Historia, 1998.

Pastore, Christopher J. "Expanding Antiquity: Andrea Navagero and Villa Culture in the Cinquecento Veneto." Ph.D. dissertation, University of Pennsylvania, 2003.

Pérez de Hita, Ginés. *Guerras civiles de Granada.* Ed. Paula Blanchard-Demouge. 2 vols. Madrid: Bailly-Baillière, 1913.

———. *Historia de los bandos de Zegríes y Abencerrajes (Primera parte de las Guerras civiles de Granada).* Ed. Paula Blanchard-Demouge. Facsimile edition with a preliminary study by Pedro Correa Rodríguez. Granada: Universidad de Granada, 1999.

Phillips, William D., Jr. *Enrique IV and the Crisis of Fifteenth-Century Castile, 1425–1480.* Cambridge, Mass.: Medieval Academy of America, 1978.

Poché, Christian. *Dictionnaire des musiques et danses traditionelles de la Mediterranée.* Paris: Fayard, 2005.

Puente, Juan de la. *Conveniencia de las dos Monarquías Católicas, la de la Iglesia Romana y la del Imperio Español.* Madrid: Imprenta Real, 1612.

Pulgar, Fernando del. *Crónica de los Reyes Católicos.* Ed. Juan de Mata Carriazo. 2 vols. Madrid: Espasa-Calpe, 1943.

———. *Letras.* Ed. J. Domínguez Bordona, trans. David Boruchoff. Madrid: Espasa-Calpe, 1929.

Purdy, Daniel Leonhard, ed. *The Rise of Fashion: A Reader.* Minneapolis: University of Minnesota Press, 2004.

Querol Gavaldá, Miguel. *La música en las obras de Cervantes.* Barcelona: Comtalia, 1948.

Quevedo, Francisco de. *Poesía varia.* Ed. James O. Crosby. Madrid: Catedra, 1981.

"Relación de lo ocurrido en el viaje del Rey a Inglaterra, 1554." Biblioteca de El Escorial, ij-U-4.

Ricoeur, Paul. *Memory, History, Forgetting.* Trans. Kathleen Blamey and David Pellauer. Chicago: University of Chicago Press, 2004.

Robinson, Cynthia. "Mudéjar Revisited: A Prolegomena to the Reconstruction of Perception, Devotion and Experience at the Mudéjar Convent of Clarisas, Tordesillas, Spain (14th Century AD)." *Res* 43 (Spring 2003): 51–77.

Robinson, Cynthia and Leyla Rouhi, eds. *Under the Influence: Questioning the Comparative in Medieval Castile* Boston: Brill, 2005.

Rosenthal, Earl. *The Palace of Charles V in Granada.* Princeton, N.J.: Princeton University Press, 1985.

Rubiera Mata, María Jesús. "La familia morisca de los Muley-Fez, príncipes meriníes e infantes de Granada." *Sharq al-Andalus* 13 (1996): 159–67.

Rufo, Juan. *Las seiscientas apotegmas y otras obras en verso.* Ed. Alberto Blecua. Madrid: Espasa-Calpe, 1972.

Ruggles, D. Fairchild. *Islamic Gardens and Landscapes.* Philadelphia: University of Pennsylvania Press, 2008.

Ruiz Souza, Juan Carlos. "Castilla y Al-Andalus: Arquitecturas aljamiadas y otros grados de asimilación." *Anuario del Departamento de Historia y Teoría del Arte* (U.A.M.) 16 (2004): 17–43.

Said, Edward. "Prólogo a la nueva edición española." In Said, *Orientalismo.* Spanish trans. María Luisa Fuentes. Barcelona: Debolsillo, 2003. 9–10.

Sánchez de Sopranis, Hipólito. *Juegos de toros y cañas en Jerez de la Frontera.* Jerez: Centro de Estudios Históricos Jerezanos, 1960.

Sandóval, Prudencio de. *Historia de la vida y hechos del Emperador Carlos V.* 1604–6. Ed. Carlos Seco Serrano. Madrid: BAE, 1955.

Sanuto, Marino. *I diarii di Marino Sanuto (1496–1533).* Vol. 52. Ed. Rinaldo Fulin et al. Venice: F. Visentini, 1879. Translated as "Letter from Marco Antonio Marco to Marco Contarini, written at Bologna on 12 December 1529," Appendix 4 to *The Voyage of Sir Nicholas Carewe to the Emperor Charles V in the Year 1529,* ed. R. J. Knecht (Cambridge: Cambridge University Press, 1959).

Sanz Egaña, Cesáreo, ed. *Tres libros de la Jineta de los siglos XVI y XVII.* Madrid: Sociedad de Bibliófilos Españoles, 1951.

Shipley, George A. "La obra literaria como monumento histórico: el caso de *El Abencerraje.*" *Journal of Hispanic Philology* 2, 2 (Winter 1978): 118–19.

Simonde de Sismondi, J. C. L. *De la littérature du midi de l'Europe.* 4 vols. Paris: Treuttel et Würtz, 1813.

Smith, Colin. "*Convivencia* in the *Estoria de España* of Alfonso X." In *Hispanic Medieval Studies in Honor of Samuel G. Armistead,* ed. Michael Gerli. Madison: Hispanic Seminary of Medieval Studies, 1992. 291–301.

Smith, Paul Julian. *Representing the Other: "Race," Text, and Gender in Spanish and Spanish American Narrative.* Oxford: Clarendon, 1992.

Soria Mesa, Enrique. "De la conquista a la asimilación. La integración de la aristocracia nazarí en la oligarquía granadina. Siglos XV–XVII." *Areas* 14 (1992): 51–64.

———. "Una versión genealógica del ansia integradora de la élite morisca: el *Origen de la Casa de Granada.*" *Sharq al-Andalus* 12 (1995): 213–21.

Spenser, Edmund. *A View of the Present State of Ireland.* 1596. Ed. W. L. Renwick. Oxford: Clarendon, 1970.

Subirats, Eduardo, ed. *Américo Castro y la revisión de la memoria: el Islam en España.* Madrid: Libertarias, 2003.

Surtz, Ronald E. "Crimes of the Tongue: The Inquisitorial Trials of Cristóbal Duarte Ballester." In *Interrogating Iberian Frontiers*, ed. Barbara F. Weissberger with María Judith Feliciano, Leyla Rouhi and Cynthia Robinson. *Medieval Encounters* 12, 3 (2006): 519–32.

———. "Maurofilia y maurofobia en los procesos inquisitoriales de Cristóbal Duarte Ballester." In *Mélanges Luce López Baralt*, ed. Abdeljelil Temimi. 2 vols. Zaghouan: Fondation Temimi, 2001. 2: 711–21.

Sweet, James H. "The Iberian Roots of American Racist Thought." In *Constructing Race: Differentiating Peoples in the Early Modern World. William and Mary Quarterly* 54, 1 (January 1997): 143–66.

Tanner, Marie. *The Last Descendant of Aeneas: The Hapsburgs and the Mythic Image of the Emperor.* New Haven, Conn.: Yale University Press, 1993.

Taylor, Gary. *Buying Whiteness: Race, Culture, and Identity from Columbus to Hip-Hop.* New York: Palgrave, 2005.

Torrecilla, Jesús. *España exótica: la formación de la imagen española moderna.* Boulder, Colo.: Society of Spanish and Spanish-American Studies, 2004.

Tueller, James B. *Good and Faithful Christians: Moriscos and Catholicism in Early Modern Spain.* New Orleans: University Press of the South, 2002.

Valdés, Juan de. *Diálogo de la lengua.* Ed. Juan M. Lope Blanch. Madrid: Castalia, 1984.

Valencia, Pedro de. *Tratado acerca de los moriscos de España.* 1606. Ed. facsimile Joaquín Gil Sanjuan. Málaga: Algazara, 1997.

Vincent, Bernard. *1492: L'année admirable.* Paris: Aubier, 1991.

———. *Minorías y marginados en la España del siglo XVI.* Granada: Diputación de Granada, 1987.

———. "¿Qué aspecto físico tenían los moriscos?" *Actas del II Coloquio Historia de Andalucía: Andalucía Moderna.* Córdoba: Monte de Piedad y Caja de Ahorros de Córdoba, 1983. 2: 335–40.

Vital, Laurent. *Premier voyage de Charles-Quint en Espagne.* In *Collection des voyages des souverains des Pays-Bas.* Ed. M. Gachard. 4 vols. Bruxelles: F. Hayez, 1874–82. Vol. 3.

Weissberger, Barbara F., ed., with María Judith Feliciano, Leyla Rouhi and Cynthia Robinson. *Interrogating Iberian Frontiers. Medieval Encounters* 12, 3 (2006).

———. *Isabel Rules: Constructing Queenship, Wielding Power.* Minneapolis: University of Minnesota Press, 2004.

Whitenack, Judith A. "The *alma diferente* of Mateo Alemán's 'Ozmín y Daraja.'" *Romance Quarterly* 38, 1 (1991): 59–71.

Woolard, Kathryn A. "Bernardo de Aldrete and the Morisco Problem: A Study in Early Modern Spanish Language Ideology." *Comparative Studies in Society and History* 44, 3 (July 2002): 446–80.

Wunder, Amanda. "Classical, Christian, and Muslim Remains in the Construction of Imperial Seville (1520–1635)." *Journal of the History of Ideas* 64, 2 (2003): 195–212.

Yiacoup, Sizen. "Memory and Acculturation in the Late Medieval and Early Modern Frontier Ballad." *Journal of Romance Studies* 4, 3 (Winter 2004): 61–78.

Index

Acknowledgments

IN WRITING AN INTERDISCIPLINARY BOOK, one relies even more than usual on the generosity and support of scholars in a wide range of fields. *Exotic Nation* has benefited from the expertise of Jodi Bilinkoff, Cammy Brothers, Renata Holod, Fernando Martínez Nespral, Gridley McKim-Smith, Daniel Nemser, Nichole Prescott, Larry Silver, and Amanda Wunder, who helped guide me in my study of art, architecture, and material culture. Every chapter was improved by the combined eagle eye of my Works-in-Progress group: Kevin Platt, Paul Saint-Amour, Maurice Samuels, and Emily Steiner, to whom I am profoundly grateful. Meredith Ray kindly vetted my translations from the Italian. I also owe thanks to the many friends who read portions of the book and gave me their valuable suggestions: Roger Abrahams, Laura Bass, Marina Brownlee, Israel Burshatin, Román de la Campa, Karina Galperín, Karla Mallette, Yolanda Martínez-San Miguel, Teófilo Ruiz, Michael Solomon, and Ronald Surtz. Barbara Weissberger, who read the entire manuscript for Penn Press and made wonderful recommendations, has been a most generous reviewer. Meeting María Judith Feliciano and benefiting from her expertise on every page has been one of the great pleasures of this project. I owe her a particular debt, which my dedication can only begin to acknowledge. I dedicate the book also to Javier Irigoyen-García, as a small token of my appreciation. Our work together on this project, and on his, has made him a most treasured interlocutor. I have been fortunate in working with other fine research assistants: Brooke Stafford, Madera Allan, and Cyrus Mulready. Audiences at Penn, the University of London, Cornell, Stanford, Princeton, and SUNY Stonybrook helped refine the book's arguments.

Jerry Singerman, at Penn Press, has been an exemplary editor, and his assistant, Mariana Martínez, unfailingly patient. As always, I thank Todd Lynch for his unwavering support. His passion for architecture, it turns out, is contagious.

Earlier versions of portions of Chapter 2 first appeared as "In Memory of Moors: 'Maurophilia' and National Identity in Early Modern Spain,"

Journal of Early Modern Cultural Studies 2, 1 (2002) and as "1492 and the Cleaving of Hispanism," *Journal of Medieval and Early Modern Studies* 37, 3 (2007): 493–510; an early version of Chapter 5 appeared as "The Spanish Race" in *Rereading the Black Legend: The Discourses of Religious and Racial Difference in the Renaissance Empires*, ed. Margaret Greer, Maureen Quilligan, and Walter Mignolo (Chicago: University of Chicago Press, 2007). Reprinted by permission. I owe thanks to the various editors and readers for their suggestions. For kindly granting permissions for images, I am grateful to Charles Stopford Sackville, Esq.; the Casselman Archive at the University of Wisconsin; the Anne S. K. Brown Military Collection, Brown University Library, the Biblioteca "José María Lafragua" of the Benemérita Universidad Autónoma de Puebla, México, the Germanisches Nationalmuseum Nürnberg, and the Museo Municipal de Madrid. Special thanks also to Jane Cunningham of the Courtauld Institute of Art.

Exotic Nation was made possible by grants from the John Simon Guggenheim Memorial Foundation, the University Research Foundation at Penn, and the Penn Humanities Forum.

Lightning Source UK Ltd.
Milton Keynes UK
UKHW012152130721
387081UK00008B/291